IMAGES
of America

JONESBOROUGH

ON THE COVER. Mrs. Jess Patton Hayworth organized concerts, volunteered as a music teacher at the local public schools, taught private lessons, and also organized the Opus Music Club. Opus Club participants pictured on the cover, from left to right, are Caroline Metzger, Eula Kate Archer, Mitchell Broyles, Jess Patton Hayworth, and Maxine McClaine. (Courtesy of Lyle Haws.)

IMAGES
of America

JONESBOROUGH

Sonya A. Haskins

ARCADIA
PUBLISHING

ISBN 978-0-7385-1804-6

Published by Arcadia Publishing
Charleston, South Carolina

Printed in the United States of America

Library of Congress Catalog Card Number: 2005923388

For all general information contact Arcadia Publishing at:
Telephone 843-853-2070
Fax 843-853-0044
E-mail sales@arcadiapublishing.com
For customer service and orders:
Toll-Free 1-888-313-2665

Visit us on the Internet at www.arcadiapublishing.com

For Sarah, Micah, Christopher, Daniel, and Hannah, who are true blessings from our Father.

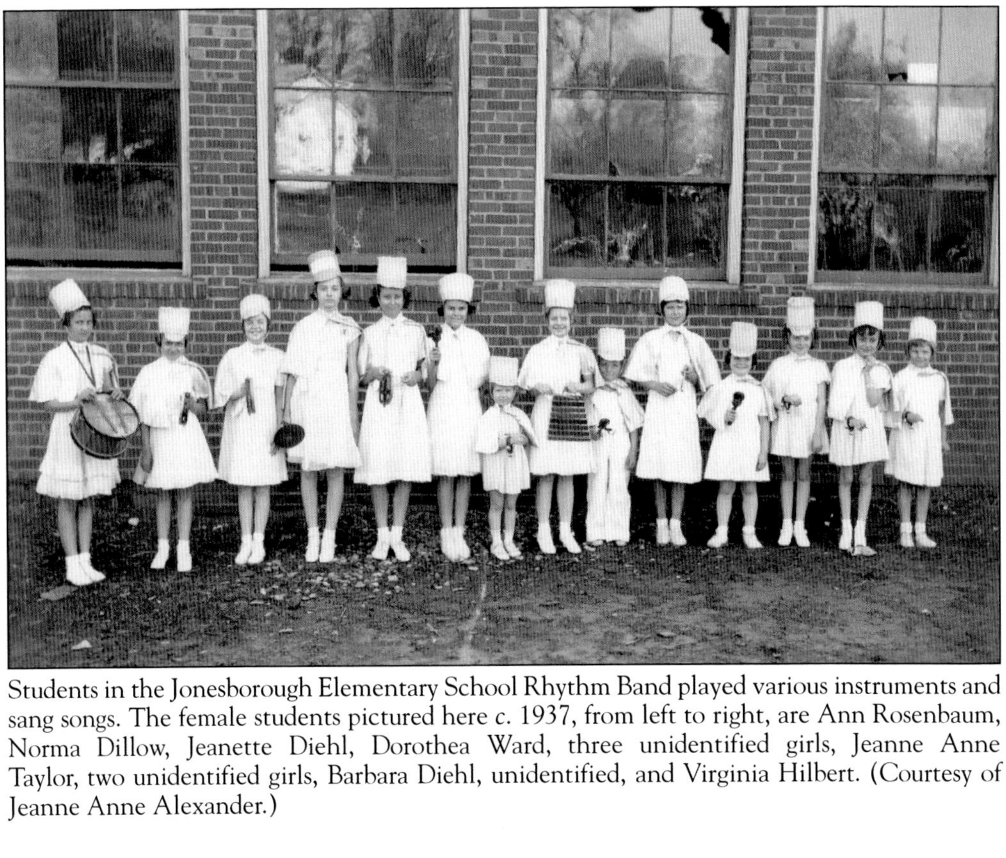

Students in the Jonesborough Elementary School Rhythm Band played various instruments and sang songs. The female students pictured here c. 1937, from left to right, are Ann Rosenbaum, Norma Dillow, Jeanette Diehl, Dorothea Ward, three unidentified girls, Jeanne Anne Taylor, two unidentified girls, Barbara Diehl, unidentified, and Virginia Hilbert. (Courtesy of Jeanne Anne Alexander.)

CONTENTS

ACKNOWLEDGMENTS

I would especially like to thank Betty Jane Hylton, Sue Henley, and Elaine Cantrell for the extensive work they've done to make certain our history isn't lost. I also extend my appreciation to the other individuals whose names are listed with the images. Thank you for allowing me to use your pictures and share your stories!

Acknowledgment also goes to Adam Latham, acquisitions editor at Arcadia Publishing, for being helpful and encouraging throughout the conception and birth of this book.

Thanks to my friends—Steven and Liesl Huhn, Heather Hull, Kim Jones, Sandy Howard, Lori Keck, Marla Freeman, Lanette Depew, Susan Seaman, and my homeschooling friends—for being encouraging.

Jimmy Neil Smith, Ned Irwin, Deborah Montanti, Guy Weems, Rebecca Stevens, William Jones, and Laura Williams also helped in various ways. I am grateful to each of them for their willingness to provide assistance on short notice. The staff at Washington College Academy and workers at the Washington County Courthouse were incredibly friendly and helpful. Thank you!

A special thanks goes to my husband, Chris, for cooking meals, cleaning house, and changing diapers while I was out scanning photographs. You will always be my best friend.

ABOUT THE AUTHOR

Sonya Haskins has a bachelor's degree in English from King College in Bristol, Tennessee. She has written hundreds of articles for newspapers and magazines, including *Writer's Digest*, *Guideposts for Teens*, *Decision*, *Physician's Practice Digest*, *College Bound*, *Educational Dealers*, and *Homeschooling Today*. Sonya is also the author of Images of America: *Johnson City*. She lives in Jonesborough, Tennessee, with her husband, Chris, and children, Sarah, Micah, Christopher, Daniel, and Hannah.

INTRODUCTION

In the late 1700s, American pioneers were eager for land and anxious to explore. They began to leave the areas already settled by white men and stretch into this area we now call Upper East Tennessee. The first permanent settlement was made in 1769 by Capt. William Bean on what is now called Boone's Creek. Around the same time, other settlers from Virginia and the mountains from North Carolina were building small log cabins in the area of Jonesborough.

Word had come from England that settlers were not supposed to colonize west of the Appalachian Mountains. Rebellious pioneers anxious to test their limits continued to stream over the mountains. In 1772, the settlers of what are now the Jonesborough, Johnson City, and Elizabethton areas met and established the Watauga Association.

The population increased rapidly as did the tension with the British authorities ruling North Carolina, who were dictating to the settlers what they could and couldn't do. One of the largest land purchases was the very controversial Transylvania Purchase, which was soon declared illegal by the Continental Congress.

In 1779, Maj. Jesse Walton introduced a bill to the North Carolina legislature to lay out a town in Washington County called Jonesborough. The legislature accepted the bill, and Jonesborough was established. Named in honor of Willie Jones, a North Carolina man who had supported the cause of the "overmountain men," Jonesborough became the first town west of the mountains. The site for the town was selected for the convenience of settlers who were living near the Watauga and Nolichuckey Rivers. Communication was impossible without travel, and travel was difficult, so a central location for the county seat was selected.

In the summer of 1780, tensions had risen to the point that Maj. Patrick Ferguson sent a threatening message to the overmountain men. If they didn't pledge loyalty to the king, he declared, troops would be sent to destroy their homes and hang the leaders. With that, mountain men from all over the region, including Jonesborough, met at Sycamore Shoals in Elizabethton for a trek across the mountains to defend their land. This march ended at Kings Mountain, South Carolina, where a vicious battle took place, marking an enormous victory for the patriots in the American Revolution.

With only Native American footpaths to journey upon, travel to the area from Virginia and especially North Carolina was difficult. However, the political road also would be tumultuous. By 1784, local citizens were dissatisfied with their representation in the North Carolina government. They were building their own schools, roads, and courthouses. In addition, there were frequent Native American attacks by the Cherokee and other frontier tribes that had to be combated without the help of the North Carolina militia. It seems that even if quick communication hadn't been an issue, the mountains would have been.

Since they had previously governed themselves under the Watauga Association, which had proven successful, the disgruntled citizens west of the mountains held at least a couple of meetings in Jonesborough in 1784. The government of North Carolina had recently ceded all of its overmountain territory to the United States government, which further fueled the fires of dissatisfaction with the state. The citizens living in the western country decided to secede from North Carolina and form their own government. Jonesborough was chosen as the first capital of the state of Franklin, named in honor of founding father Benjamin Franklin, but by 1789, it had collapsed. It wasn't until seven years later, in 1796, that a congressional assembly admitted Tennessee as the 16th state of the union.

In the late 1700s and early 1800s, Jonesborough was visited by some of the most outstanding settlers, explorers, and leaders in our nation's history. Andrew Jackson came to Jonesborough in 1788 to practice law. David Crockett was born only a few miles away, though the exact location is undetermined. Andrew Johnson gained political expertise at our courthouse. Soldiers from the North and the South traveled through the area that was divided in sentiment on the issue of slavery. James K. Polk visited Jonesborough on numerous occasions as he campaigned for political office. Physicians built their homes here as they traveled throughout the area treating the sick, and the town was a perfect place for lawyers to make their homes as the county courthouse is located here.

Since settlers began arriving in this area, there have been a few names, in addition to presidential ones, that stand out—Embree, Sherfy, Poteat, May, Rhea, Couch, Keen, and others—but there have also been numerous people who have contributed to the history of this town simply by being a part of it. In this book, the reader will meet many of the more celebrated people of Jonesborough's history as well as some who weren't quite as renowned, but who contributed nonetheless.

Jonesborough continued to grow throughout the 1800s as hotels, livery stables, depots, several general stores, taverns, schools, and churches were built. By 1929, it was already time for the Tennessee's oldest town to celebrate its 150th year anniversary, which the town did a year later.

A multi-million dollar restoration and preservation movement occurred in the late 1960s and 1970s, which helped make Jonesborough the popular tourist attraction it is today. Then, in 1973, Jimmy Neil Smith organized the first National Storytelling Festival, which is held annually and is highly praised as one of the Top 100 Events in North America. Another annual event is Historic Jonesborough Days, held each year around the Fourth of July to celebrate the history of Jonesborough with crafts, food, fireworks, a parade, and old-fashioned fellowship. Whether one is in Jonesborough to live or to visit for a short while, the experience is certain to be a delightful look at history.

One

BUILDINGS

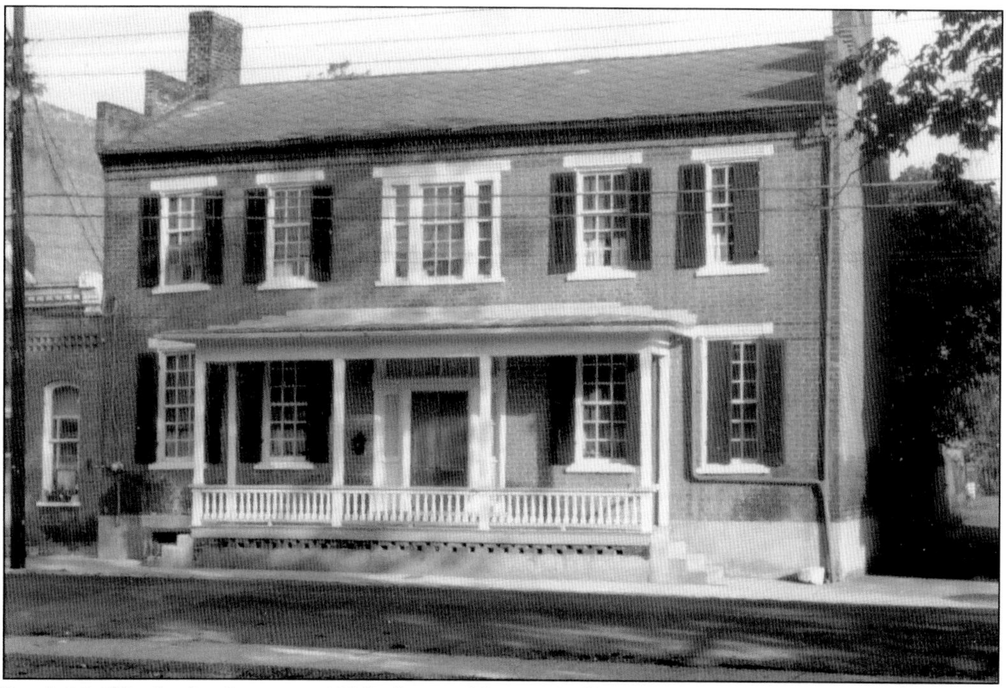

Jacob Naff built this house *c.* 1835, then sold it to William H. Crouch *c.* 1845. According to current owner Sue Henley, the home was also owned by John E. Williams, John H. Fain, and then E.J. Baxter. Baxter, who served as the president of the 1912 homecoming celebration, purchased the house in October 1929. The Henley family purchased it from Baxter's daughter in 1987. (Courtesy of Sue Henley.)

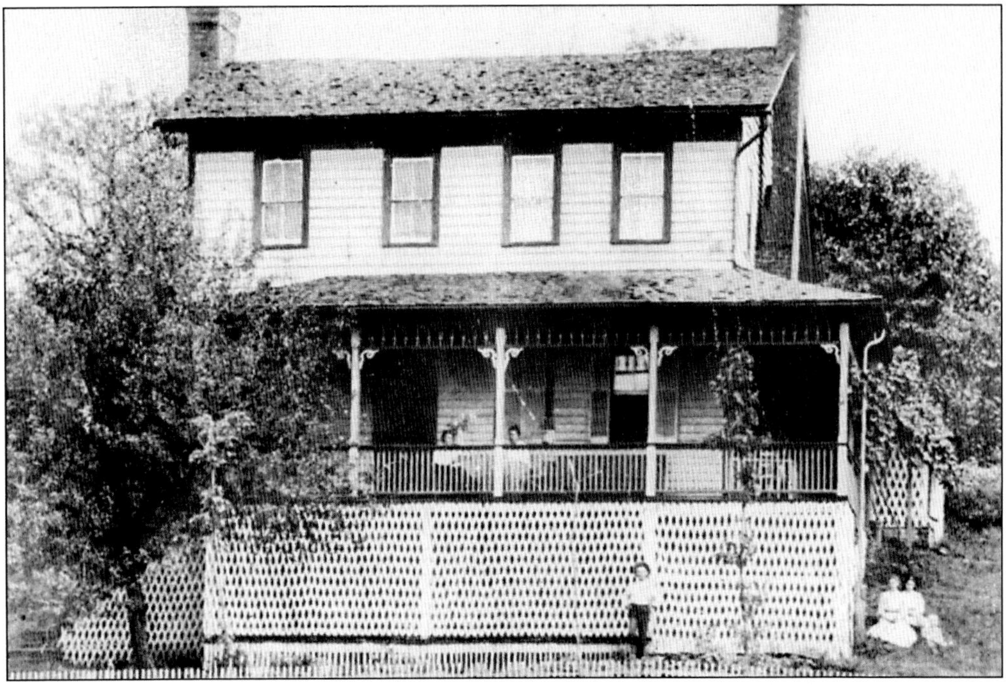

This home was originally owned by a Catherine Jacobs, who married Thomas Emmerson. Emmerson became Knoxville's first mayor, served as a judge in the Supreme Court of Errors and Appeals, and was editor and publisher of a Jonesborough paper called the *Washington County Republican and Farmer's Journal.* The Jacobs/Emmerson House was built c. 1830 and is located on East Woodrow Avenue. (Courtesy of Betty Jane Hylton.)

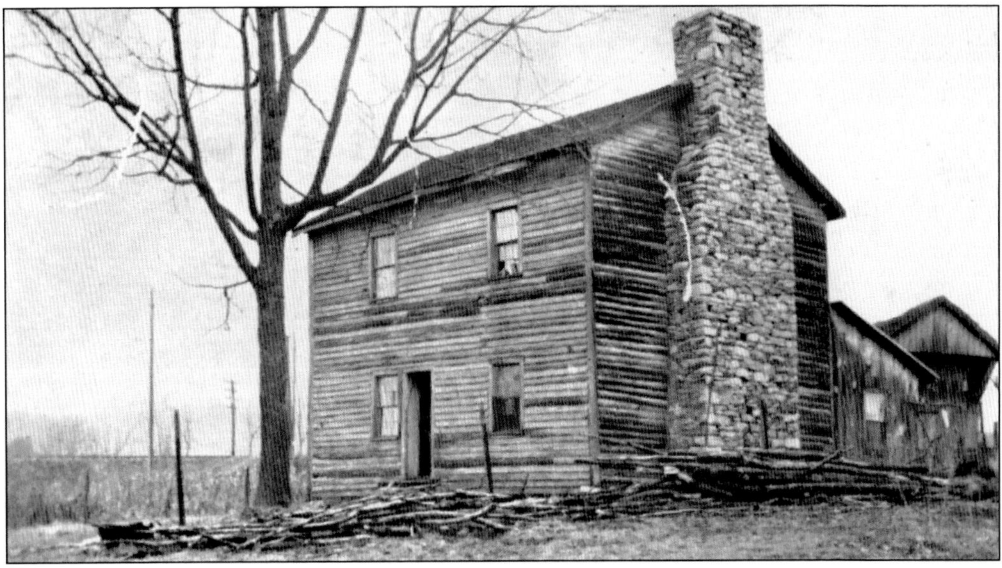

Although Andrew Jackson was born in South Carolina in 1767, as a young man he came to practice law in Jonesborough. Jackson later went on to serve as the first man from Tennessee elected to the House of Representatives, became a hero in the War of 1812, and served as president of the United States. Shown here is his home two miles west of Jonesborough. (Courtesy of Betty Jane Hylton.)

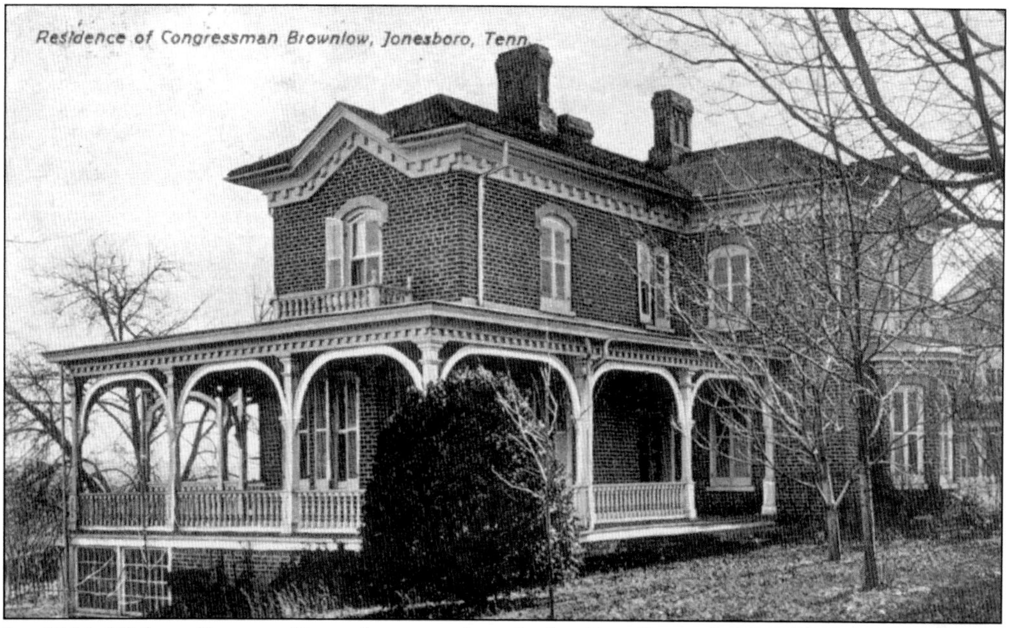

In 1876 Walter Preston Brownlow purchased the *Jonesborough Herald and Tribune*. He also served as postmaster at Jonesborough and was elected to the United States House of Representatives. Brownlow was instrumental in the establishment of the National Soldiers' Home in nearby Johnson City as he introduced the bill to build the facility locally. (Courtesy of Betty Jane Hylton.)

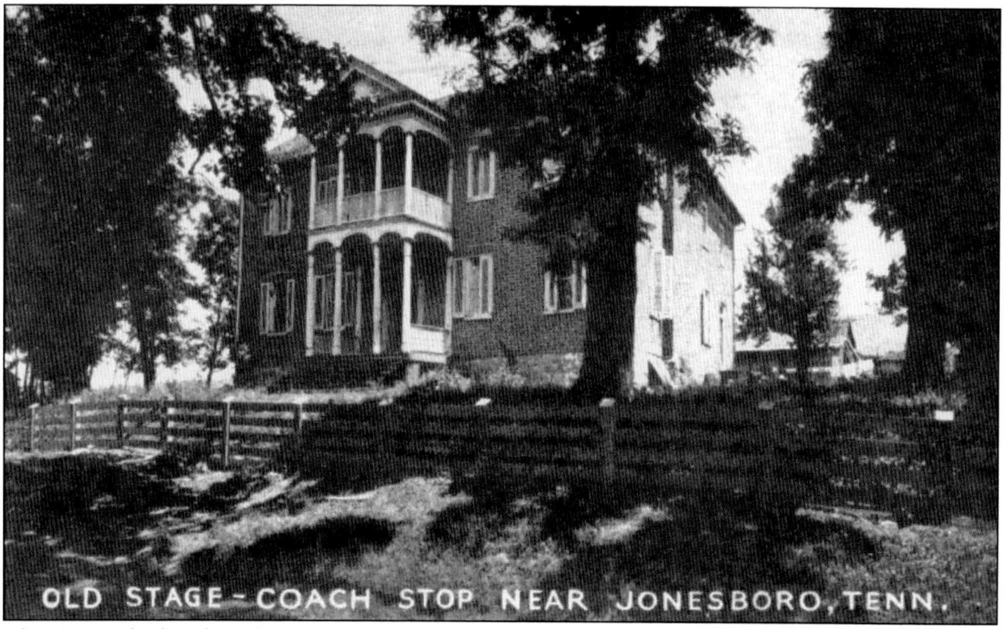

The DeVault family, whose descendents still live in the area, built this house in 1820 on what is now called the Old Stagecoach Road. Notable men such as Andrew Jackson and Andrew Johnson made speeches beneath the large oak in the front yard. The house, also known as the DeVault Tavern, is a wonderful example of late 19th-century architecture. (Courtesy of Betty Jane Hylton.)

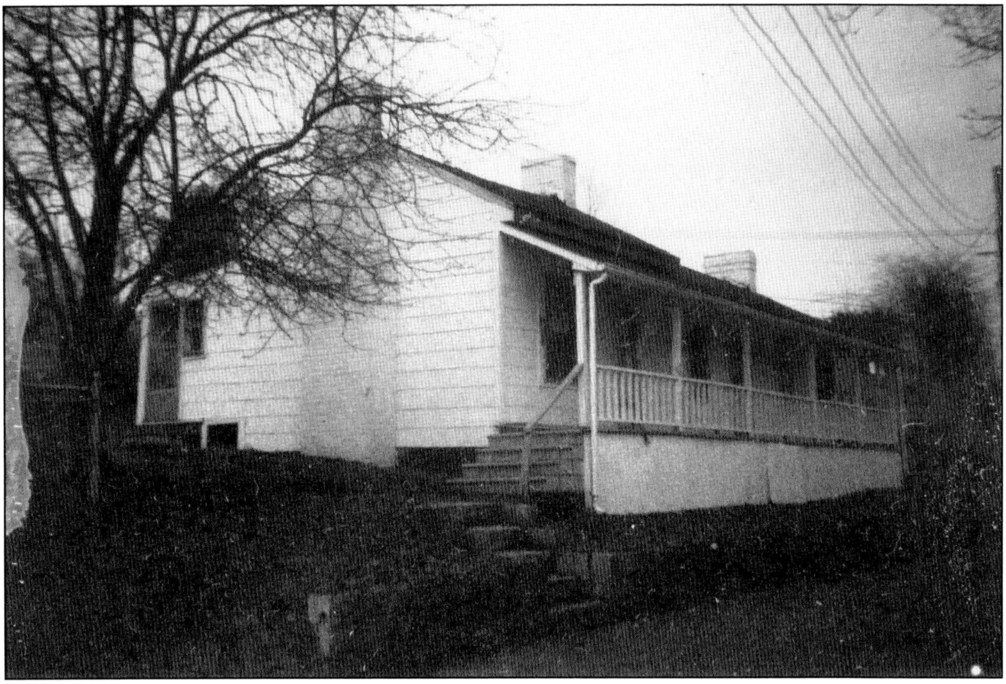

Rhea Wells, author and illustrator of children's books, willed this house to the town of Jonesborough to be used as a library. The house, built in 1849 and originally used as slave quarters, was sold to private owners, and the money was invested to build the current Jonesborough–Washington County Public Library. (Courtesy of the Schubert Club and the Jonesborough–Washington County Public Library.)

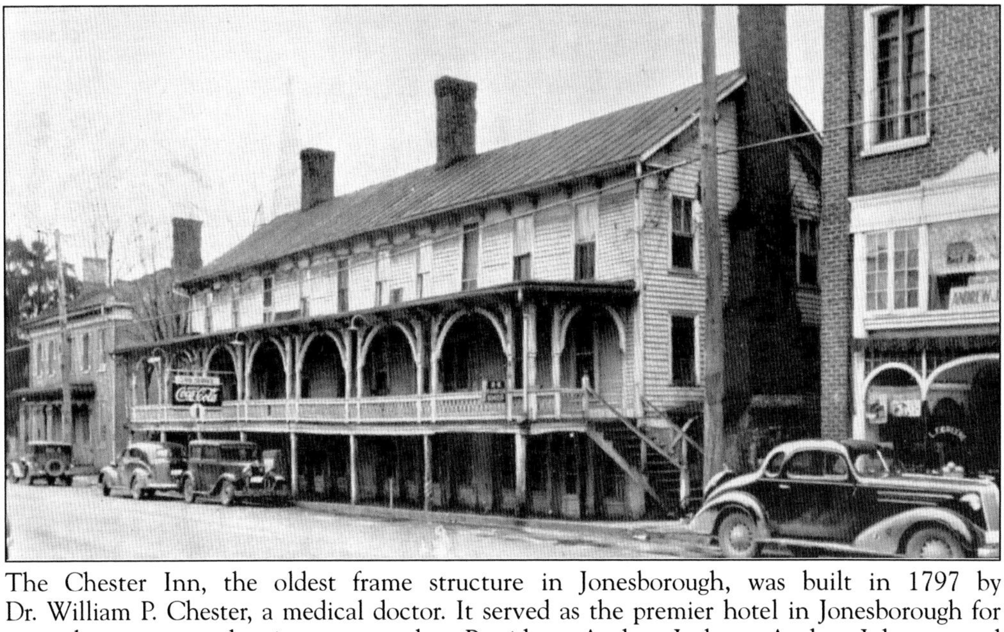

The Chester Inn, the oldest frame structure in Jonesborough, was built in 1797 by Dr. William P. Chester, a medical doctor. It served as the premier hotel in Jonesborough for more than a century, hosting guests such as Presidents Andrew Jackson, Andrew Johnson, and James K. Polk. Today, the Chester Inn serves as the home of the International Storytelling Center. (Courtesy of Paul Stone.)

Here is a fine example of stepped gables on the home of Martha Stephenson and her first husband, Milton Sutton. The house was built c. 1830. (Courtesy of Martha Stephenson.)

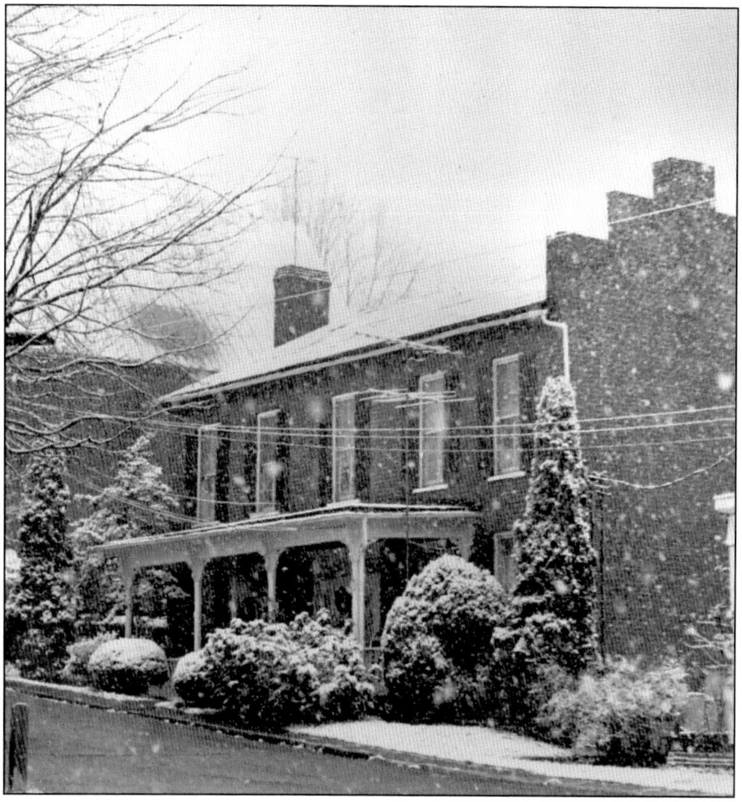

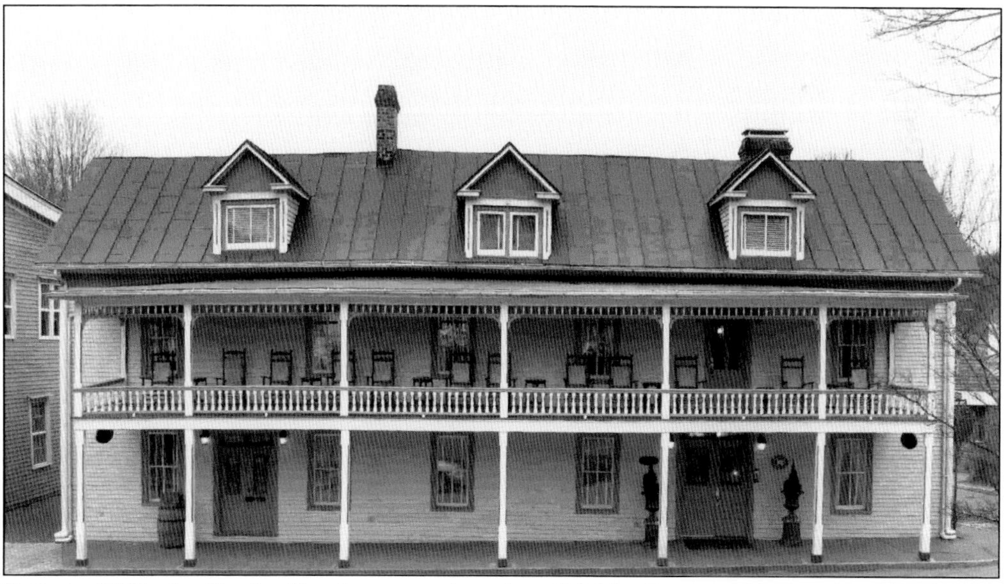

Built in 1797, the Eureka Hotel was purchased in 1900 by Peter and Harriett Miller for the purpose of offering hospitality to guests traveling through the area. Though the hotel was closed for some time, it reopened in 2000 to provide "the charm and romance of a turn-of-the-century inn." (Photograph by the author.)

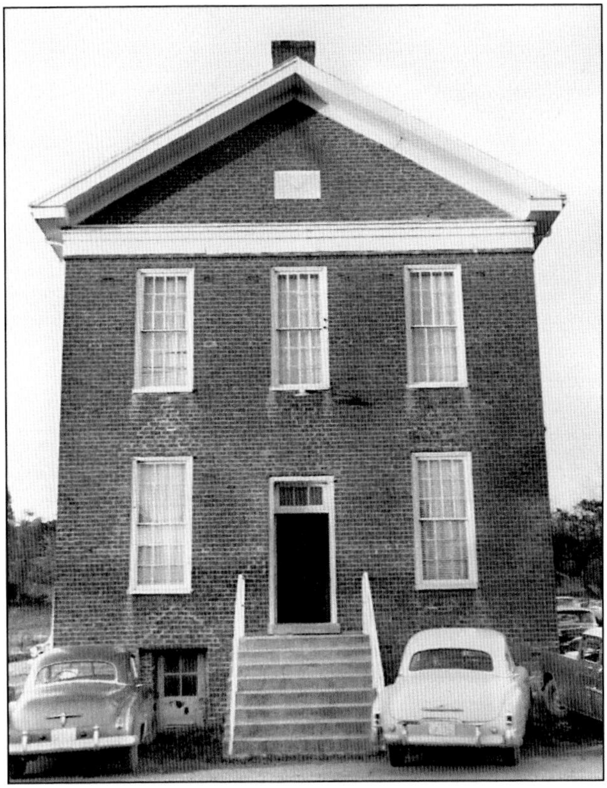

The Masonic Hall of Fall Branch, approximately 12 miles from downtown Jonesborough, was built in 1869. The downstairs was used as a post office for a while and also has hosted Eastern Star meetings and Masonic meetings. The main focus of the fraternal Masonic organization is helping one another and the community. The Masons are still very active in the area. (Courtesy of Norma Bacon Davick.)

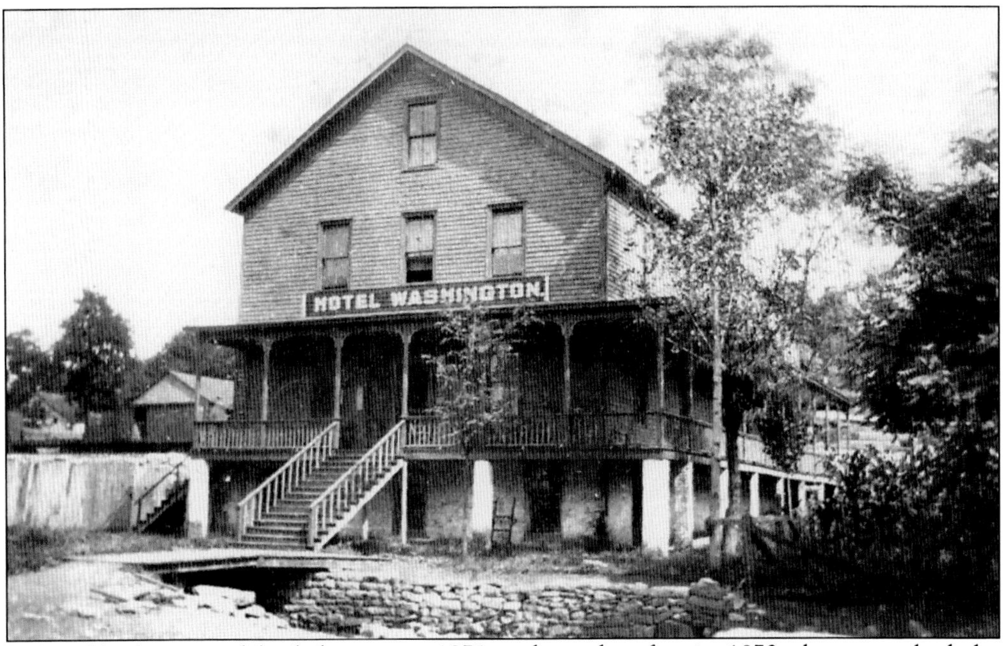

A horrible fire caused by lightning in 1871 and another fire in 1873 almost reached the Washington Hotel, to which it is more commonly referred, but the structure was saved by the laborious efforts of local citizens. David Peter Campbell owned the hotel and nearby livery stable. (Courtesy of the Jonesborough Public Library.)

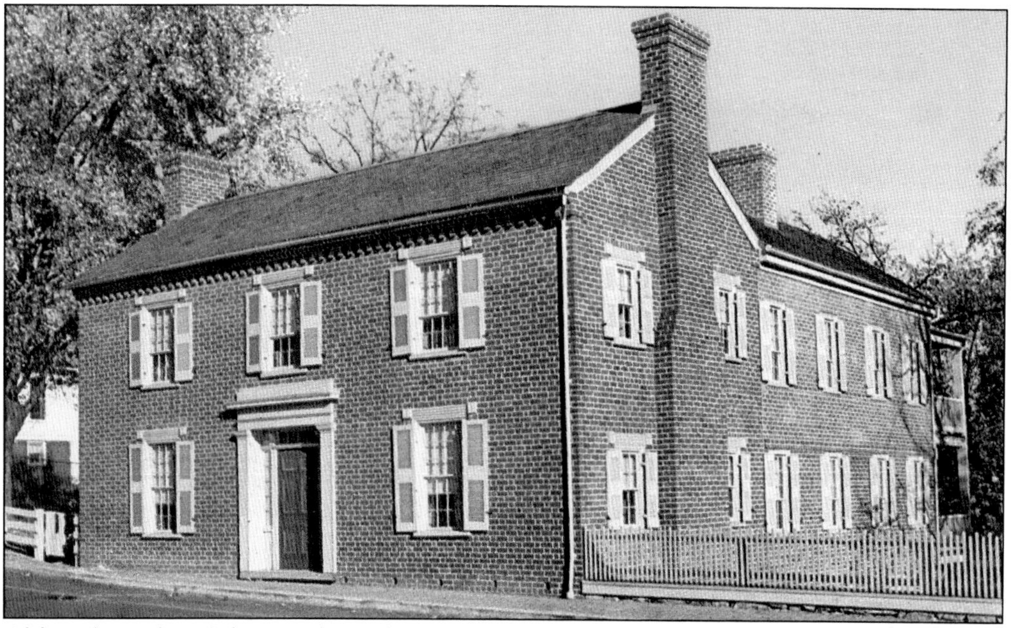

Although Andrew Johnson, the 17th president of the United States, lived in Greeneville, he frequently visited Jonesborough for political and social events. His home, shown here, is part of the National Monument in Greeneville. (From the author's collection.)

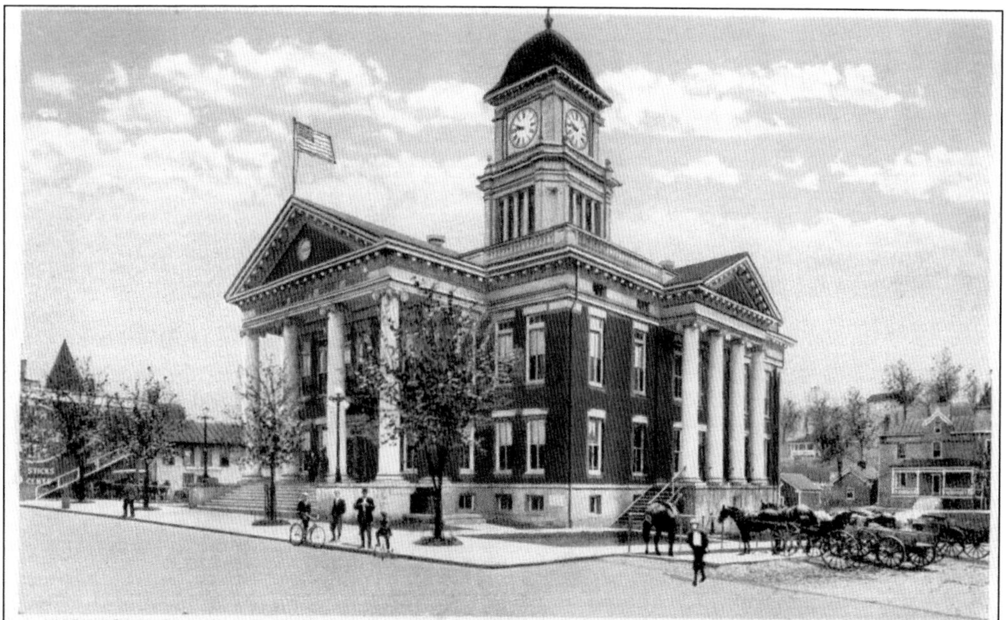

The old jail is visible to the far right of this photo of the Washington County Courthouse. The smaller building to the left of the jail is the kitchen, housed separately to prevent fires from destroying the jail. The cornerstone for the present courthouse, shown here, was laid on August 15, 1912. (Courtesy of Paul Stone.)

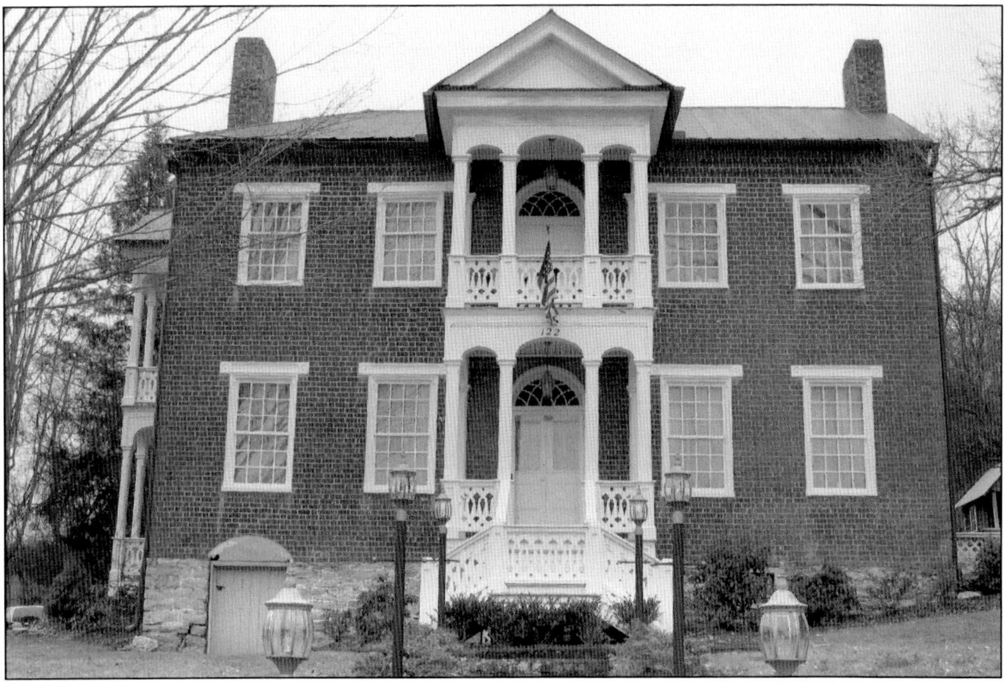

John Green built this house *c.* 1825. The home appears to have remained in the Green family until the early 1900s and is now occupied by the Florence family. Set on a stone foundation, the house has distinguishing federalist-style characteristics and all the original brickwork remains, but the house was partially destroyed in 1944 by fire. (Courtesy of Joe Florence.)

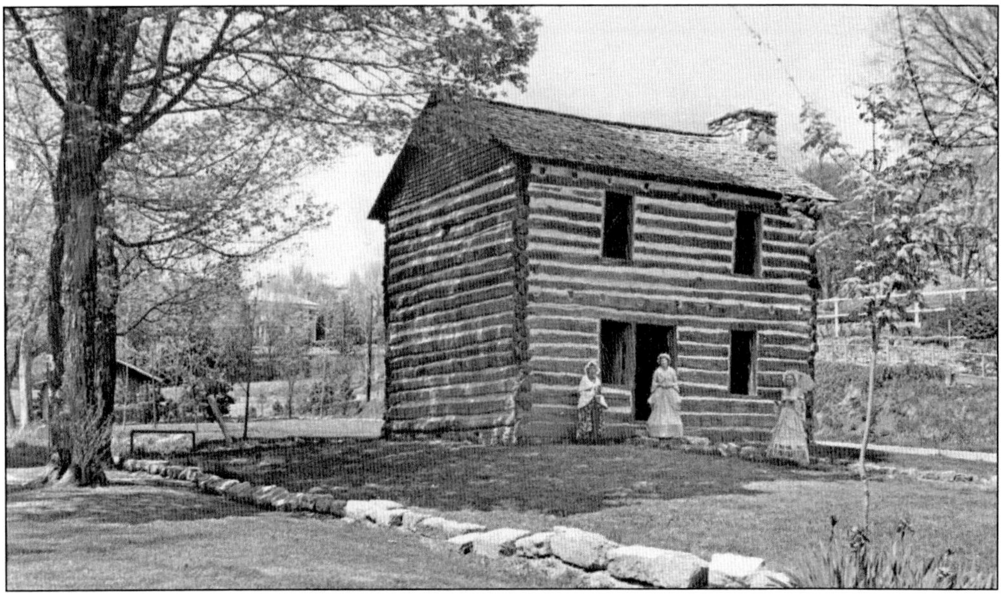

Christopher Taylor was a veteran of the French and Indian War and a major in the Revolutionary War. Andrew Jackson lived in Taylor's home on the second floor while he practiced law in Jonesborough. The Christopher Taylor House was built *c.* 1777 and was moved from the original site to the present location on Main Street in 1975. (Courtesy of Betty Jane Hylton.)

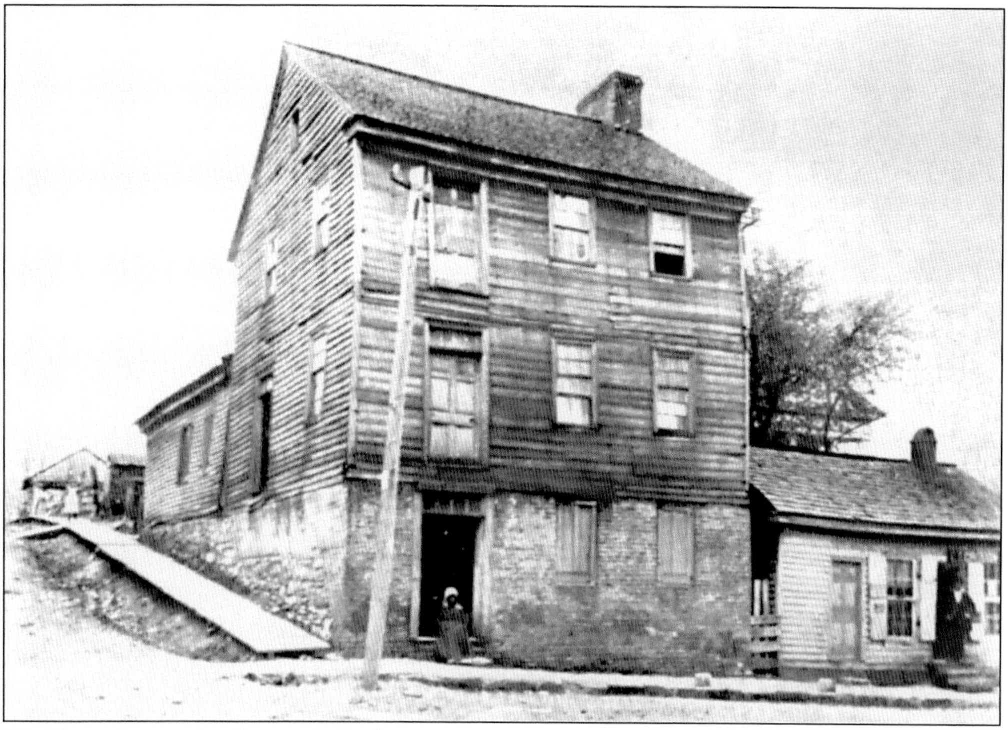

The Emancipator, the first periodical in the United States devoted exclusively to abolishing slavery, was produced in this building by editor Elihu Embree, a former slave-holder. Elihu joined the Quakers c. 1812 and began to work fervently for the cause of abolition. *The Emancipator* was published from 1819 to 1820 but ceased that year because of Elihu's untimely death. (Courtesy of Betty Jane Hylton.)

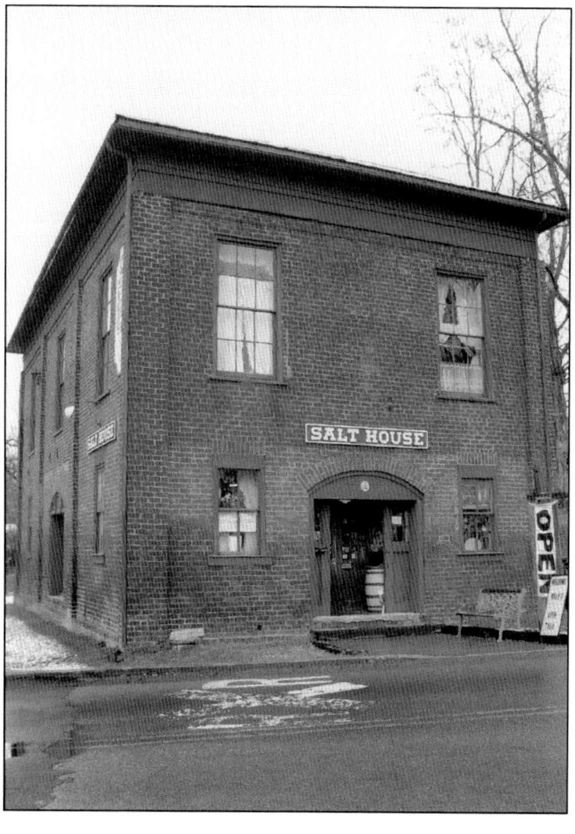

During the Civil War, the brick warehouse on the corner of Fox Street and Woodrow Avenue belonged to W.H. Crouch. Since salt essential for curing meat was in short supply, the county court authorized the purchase of salt, which was stored in the warehouse for distribution. Even though the building is no longer used for this purpose, it is still known as the Salt House. (Photograph by Chris Haskins.)

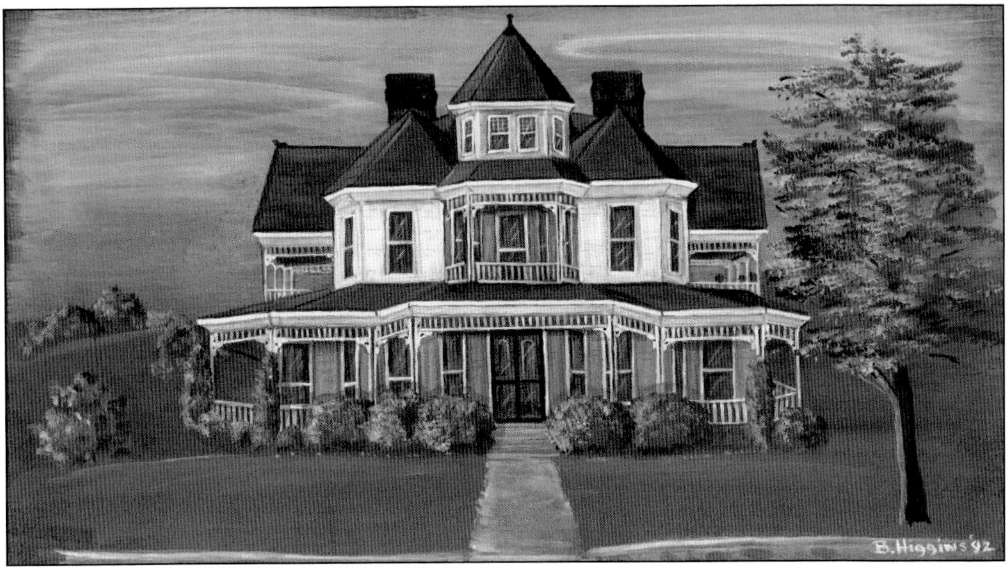

The Deakins home in Sulphur Springs was originally owned by Richard Martin Kitzmiller VanBuren Deakins and is still occupied by his descendents. Farmers Mutual Fire Insurance Company sold Deakins their first homeowners insurance policy on November 1, 1898; it is still in effect today as policy number one. This beautiful painting of the home was done by B. Higgins in 1992. (Courtesy of David Sherfey Deakins.)

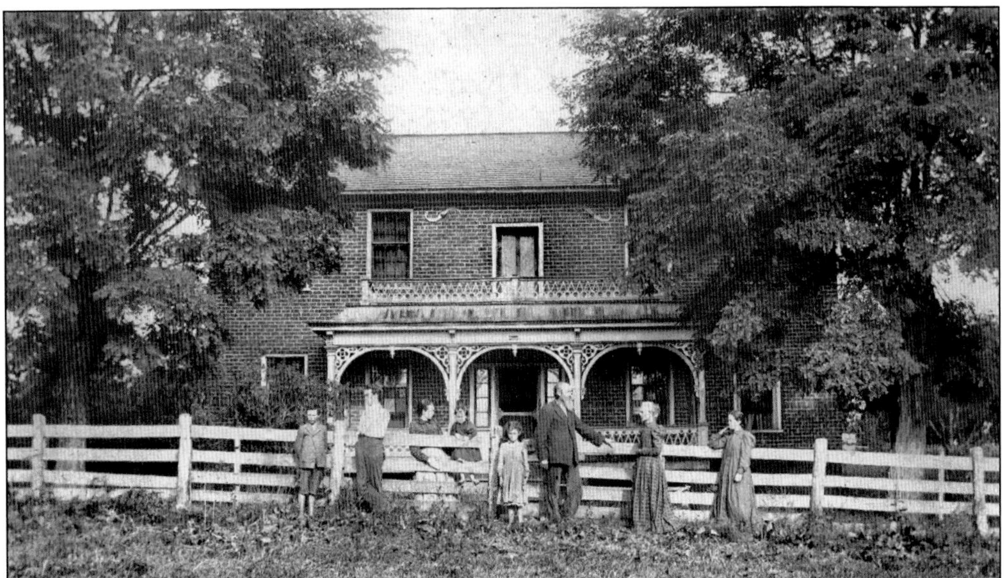

The Hopper home served as a boarding house for students of Fall Branch Seminary. As many as 50 students could be housed there at one time. This photo was taken *c.* 1900. (Courtesy of Jerry Deakins.)

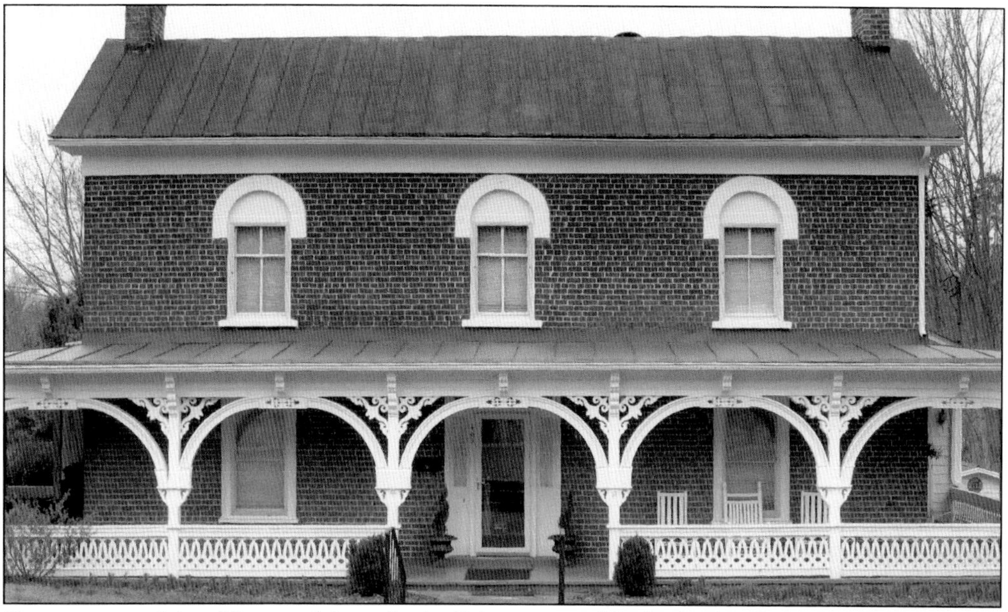

Congressman John Blair and Joseph A. Febuary possibly built this home as a spec house around 1852. Febuary was postmaster in Washington County from 1881 to 1885. Blair's, Febuary's, and Peter Miller's names are all on an early fire plan, so it is possible that the trio built the house to be sold. Tom and Joyce Pardue have lived in the house since 2002. (Photograph by the author.)

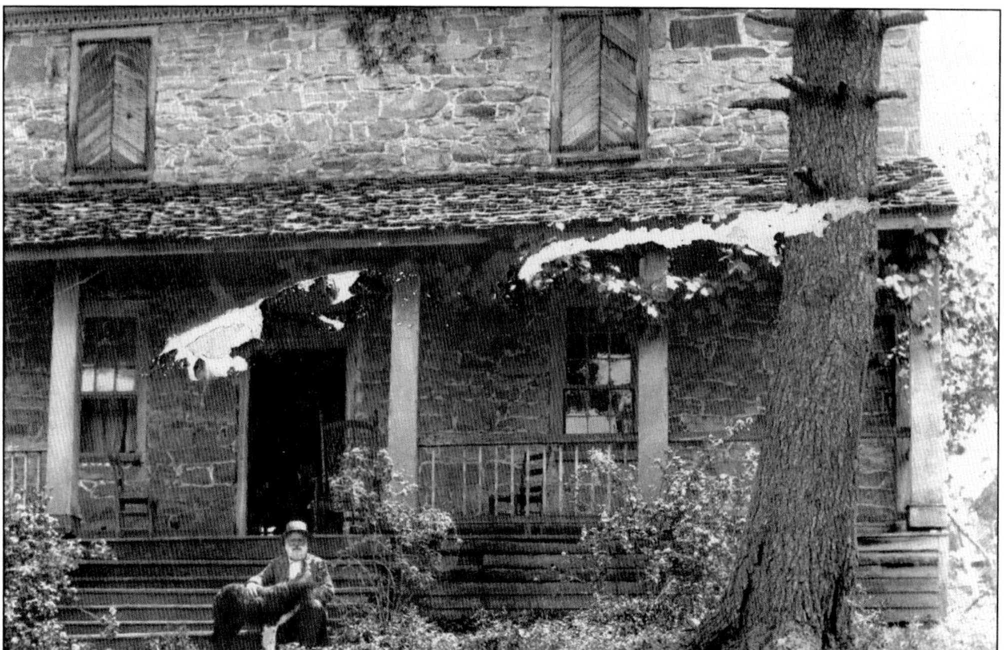

This stone house was built for George Gillespie by Seth Smith, a Quaker stone mason from Pennsylvania, c. 1770. Smith constructed the walls of limestone taken from local quarries. The house is located in Limestone, near Greene County. (Courtesy of Washington County Clerk's Office.)

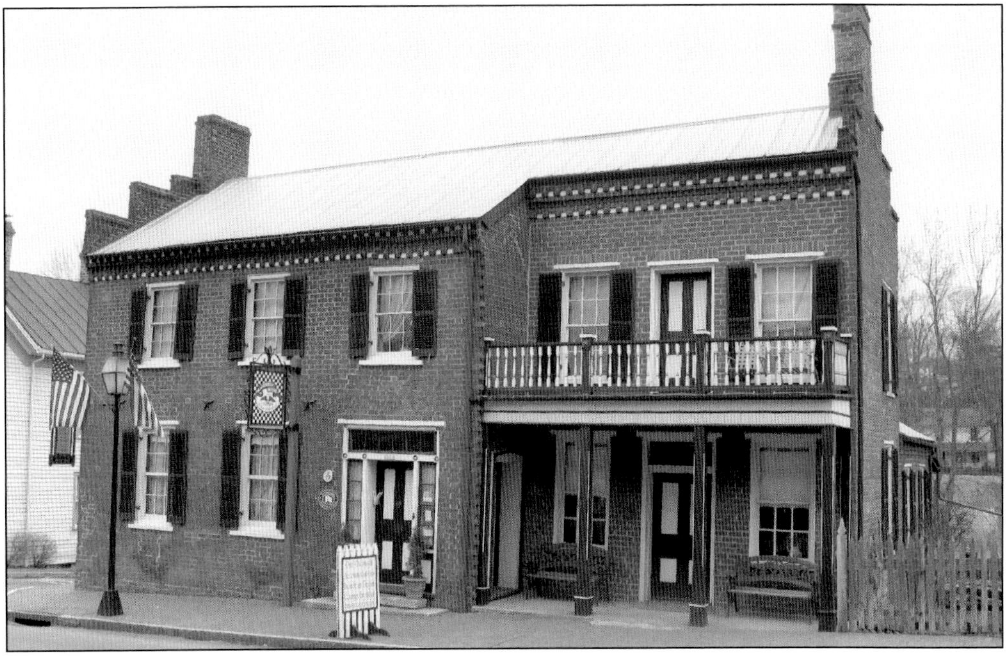

John Blair, who was an attorney and congressman, built this house at 201 West Main Street in 1832. Dr. Gibson purchased the house in the 1860s. Since Gibson enlarged the house from its original size, it is possible that he used the extra space for his medical practice. The Blair-Moore house, owned by Jack and Tami Moore, now serves as a bed and breakfast. (Photograph by the author.)

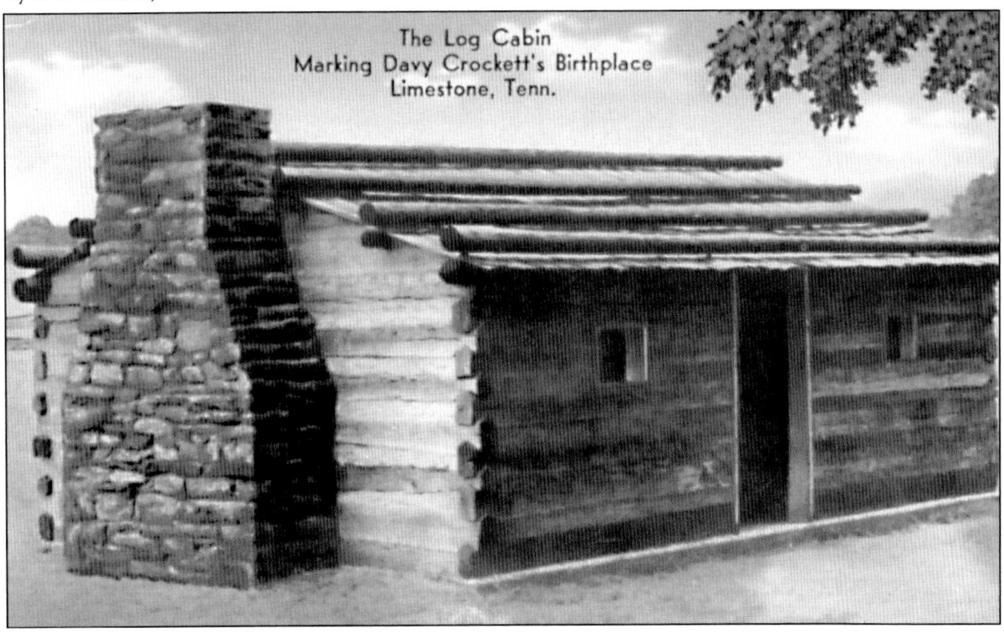

One of the most well-known pioneers in the history of our nation was born near Jonesborough, close to the small community of Limestone, on August 17, 1786. David Crockett was not only a trapper, scout, and explorer, but he was also a member of the state legislature. Crockett died at the Alamo in 1836. (From the author's collection.)

Two

STREET SCENES

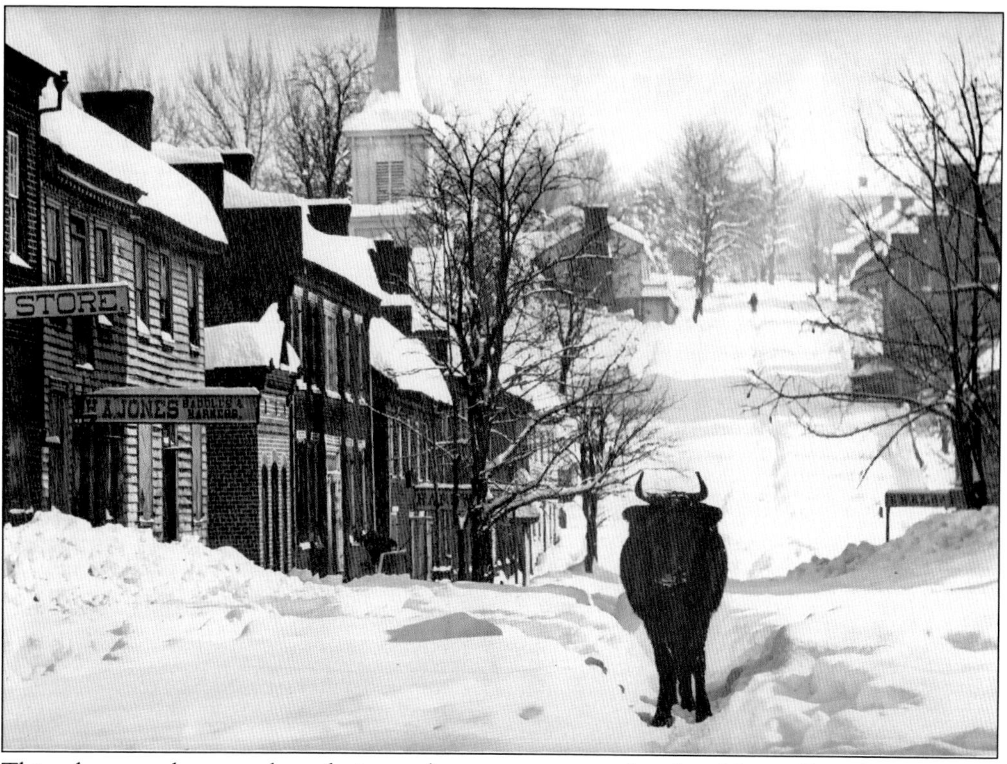

This photograph was taken during a huge snowstorm that hit Upper East Tennessee in December 1886. The actual photograph is considerably larger, but here one can see signs on the left for a bookstore and H.A. Jones Saddles & Harness, as well as the steeple of the First Baptist Church. (Courtesy of Washington County Clerk's Office; information courtesy of Mark C. Hicks Jr.)

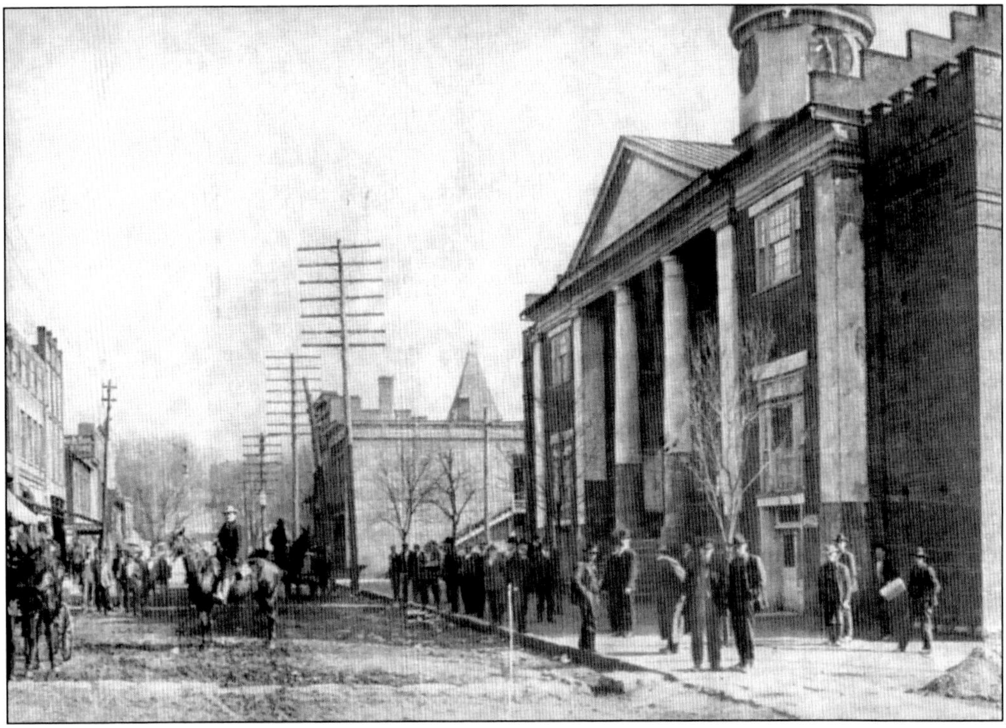

This photo is of Main Street in front of the Washington County Courthouse c. 1900. Notice the men on horses and the trees in front of the courthouse that are no longer present. (Courtesy of George Robert Campbell.)

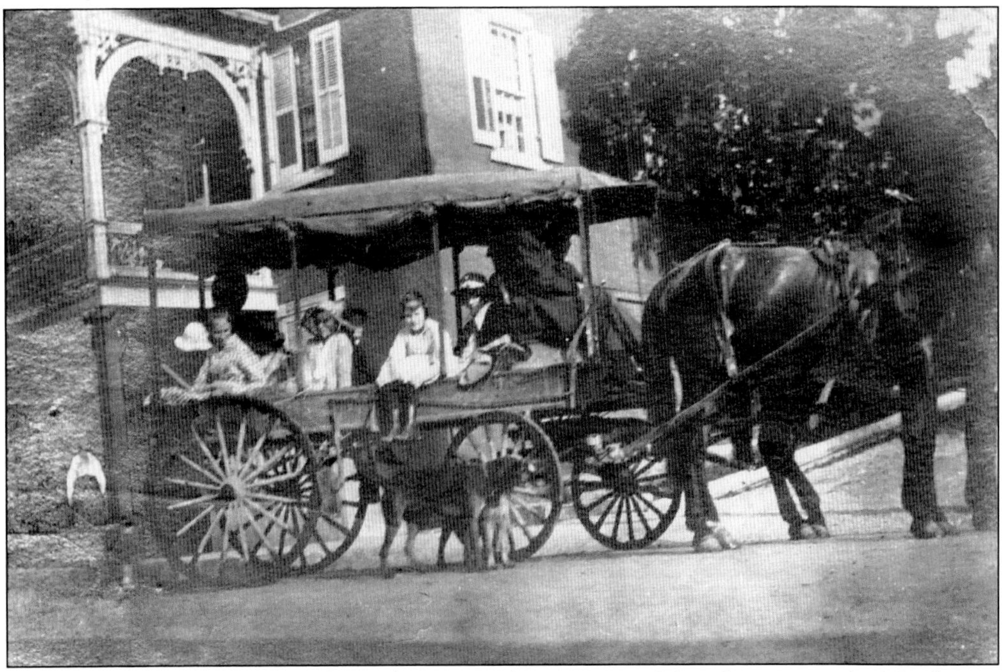

This photograph was taken in the early 1900s or late 1800s on Main Street near the May house. (Courtesy of Martha Stephenson.)

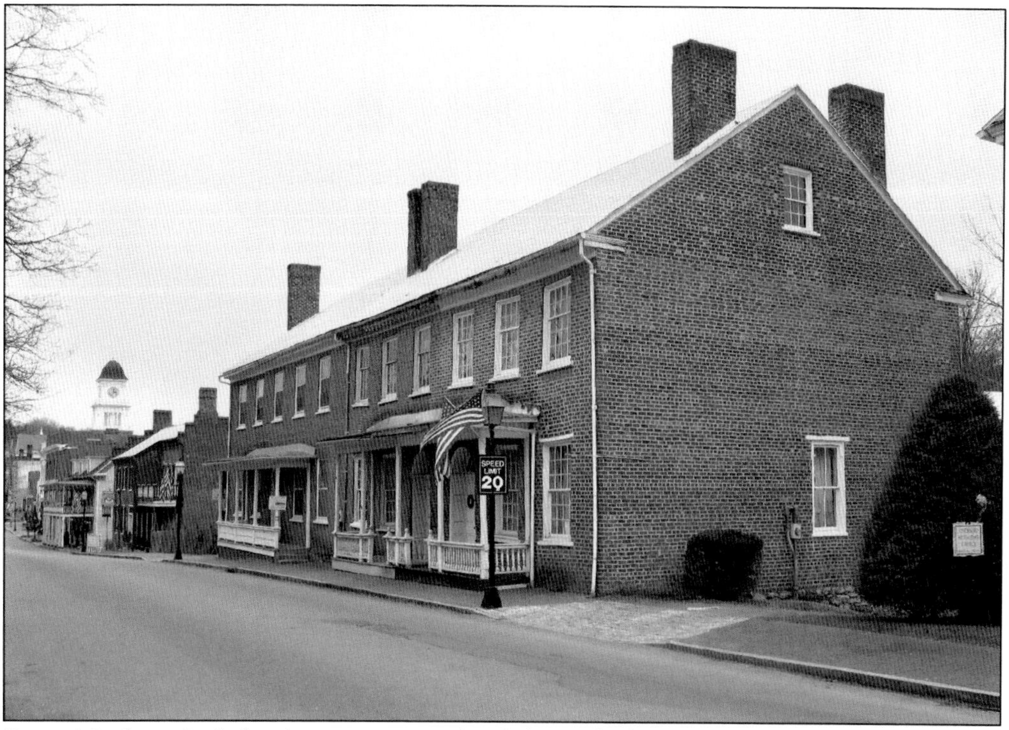

Samuel Jackson had this long, two-story brick home built in the 1820s. Whether Jackson originally intended for the three separate apartments in the building to be used for his three widowed daughters or for rental purposes is not positively known. Either way, at least one and probably all of the sisters lived in the building long known as Sisters' Row. (Photograph by the author.)

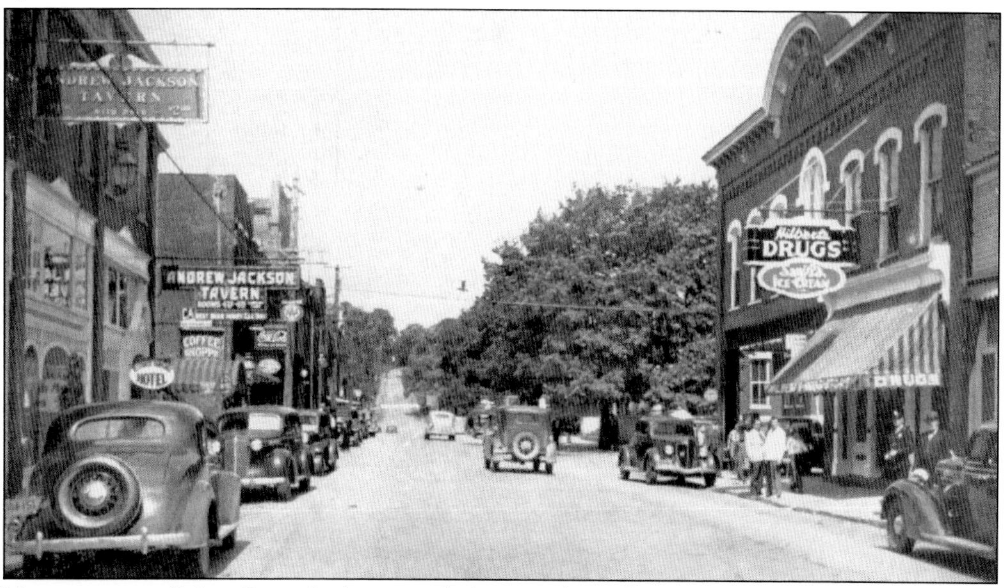

Here is a view of Main Street looking east before a multi-million dollar restoration took place in the 1960s. This restoration project allowed Jonesborough to become the first town in Tennessee to be placed on the National Register of Historic Places.

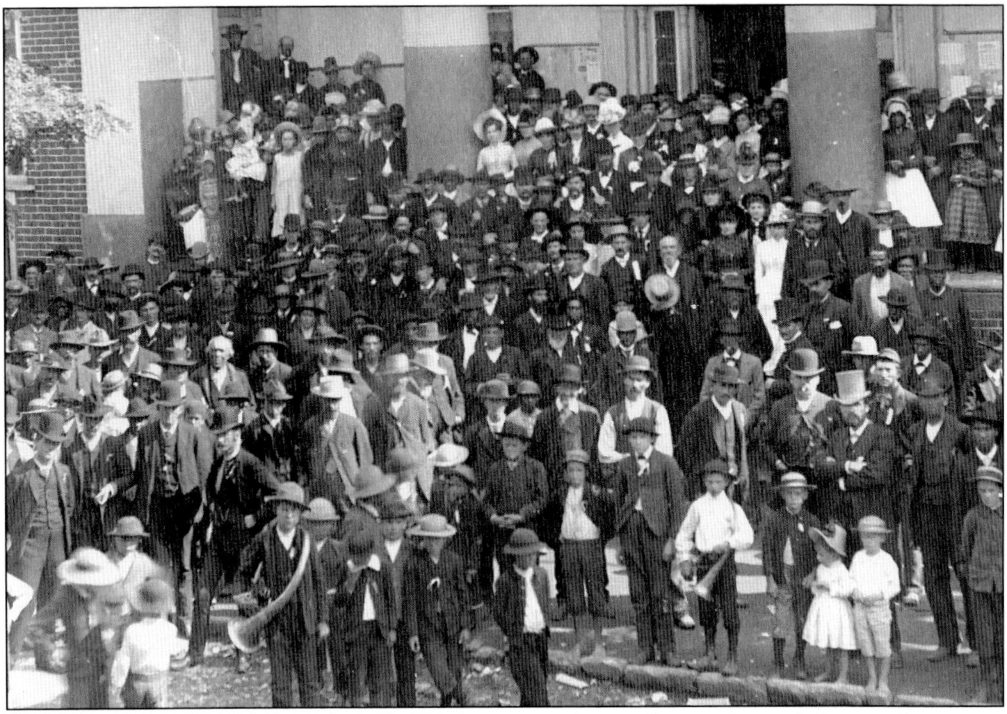

Men, women, and children gathered around the courthouse during the prohibition election in 1887. (Courtesy of Washington County Clerk's Office.)

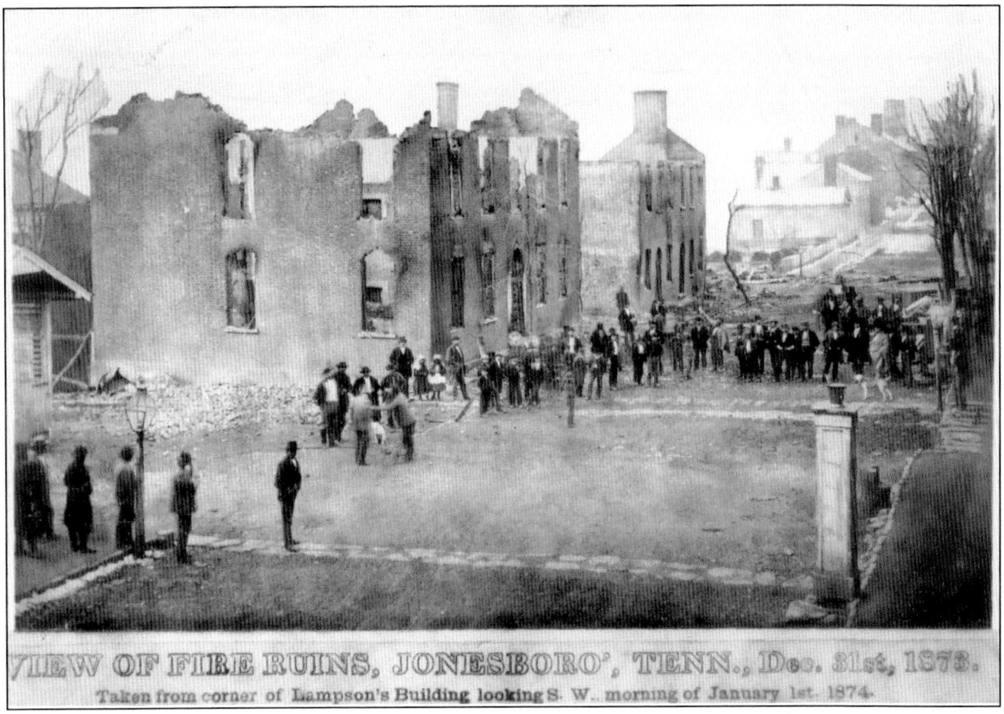

A devastating fire occurred in downtown Jonesborough in late 1873, destroying numerous buildings, offices, and residences. (Courtesy of Sue Henley.)

Three

FRIENDS, NEIGHBORS, AND FAMILIES

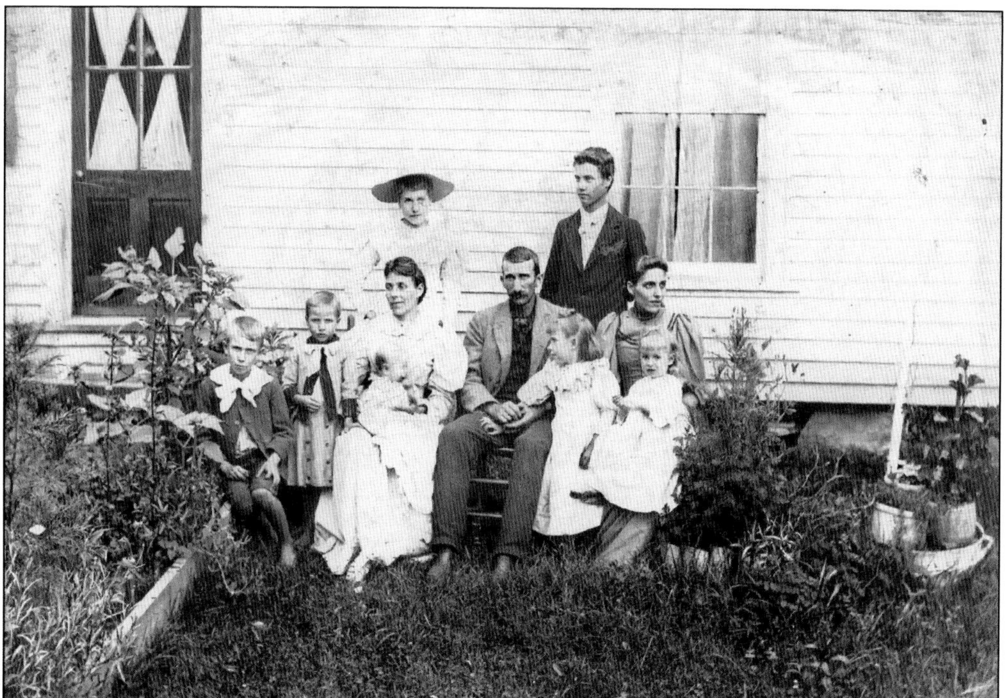

Members of the Campbell family pictured here, from left to right, are (front row) Albert Campbell, unidentified, Mayme Campbell on lap of Allie Campbell, David Peter Campbell, Blanch Campbell, and Pearl Campbell being held by Georgia Anna Campbell; (back row) Lottie McPherson and George McPherson. (Courtesy of George R. Campbell.)

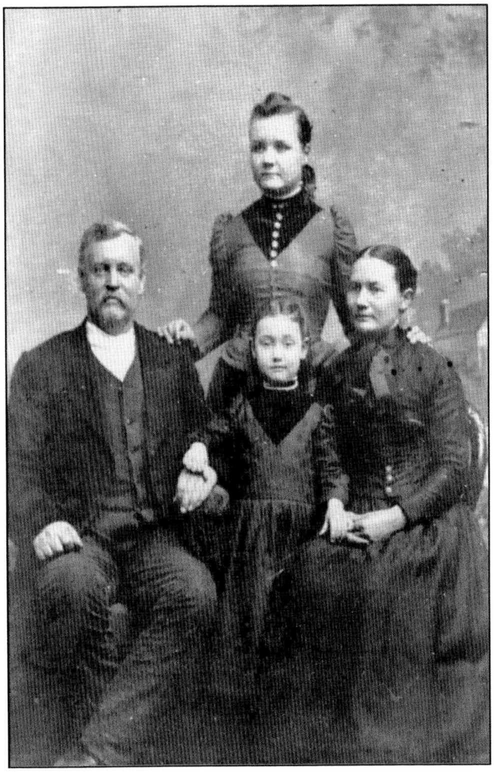

Members of the Dulaney family shown here, from left to right, are John Wesley Dulaney, Nora Dulaney Miller (standing), Frances Walters Dulaney, and Daisy Dulaney. Frances was born in 1874 and Daisy in 1885. Daisy was never married, though she was reportedly engaged at one time and decided she couldn't leave her home. (Courtesy of Ruth May Robinson.)

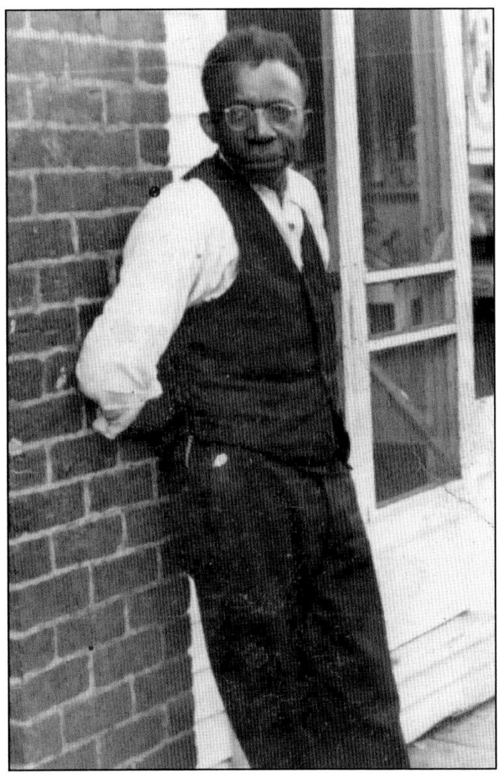

James Walter Greenlee Sr. was known to the community as "Doc." After working at a barber shop, Greenlee worked at Appalachian Hospital, where he gained his nickname and when he began doing private nursing, similar to home health nurses today. Greenlee also served as superintendent for the Jonesborough Water Department. He lived from December 25, 1885, until December 24, 1945. (Courtesy of Alfred and Gwendolyn Greenlee.)

Selma Cloyd Landreth and John Boring Landreth lived on what is now Forrest View Drive. John worked in the post office at the Mountain Home while Selma cared for their two children. John died in 1947 at the age of 69 and Selma died in 1972 at the age of 87. (Courtesy of Barbara G. Smith.)

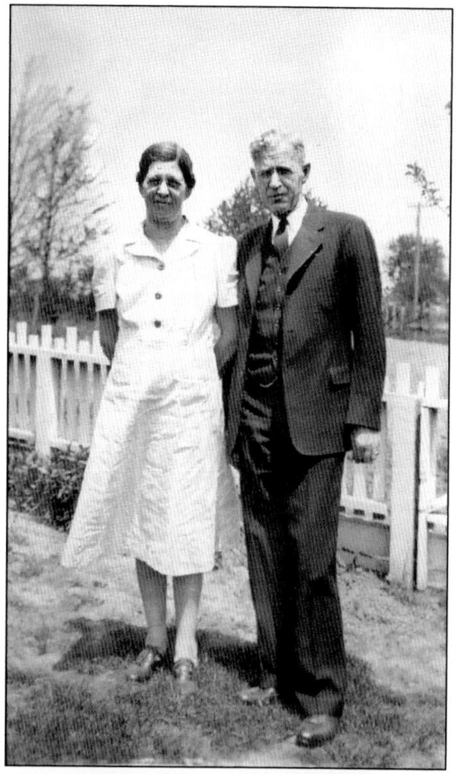

Clyde E. Miller lost his left hand and leg in a horse-and-wagon accident on his farm off Highway 11E. He continued to farm and work in his garden with a wooden leg and one hand. (Courtesy of Clarence and Linda Bailey.)

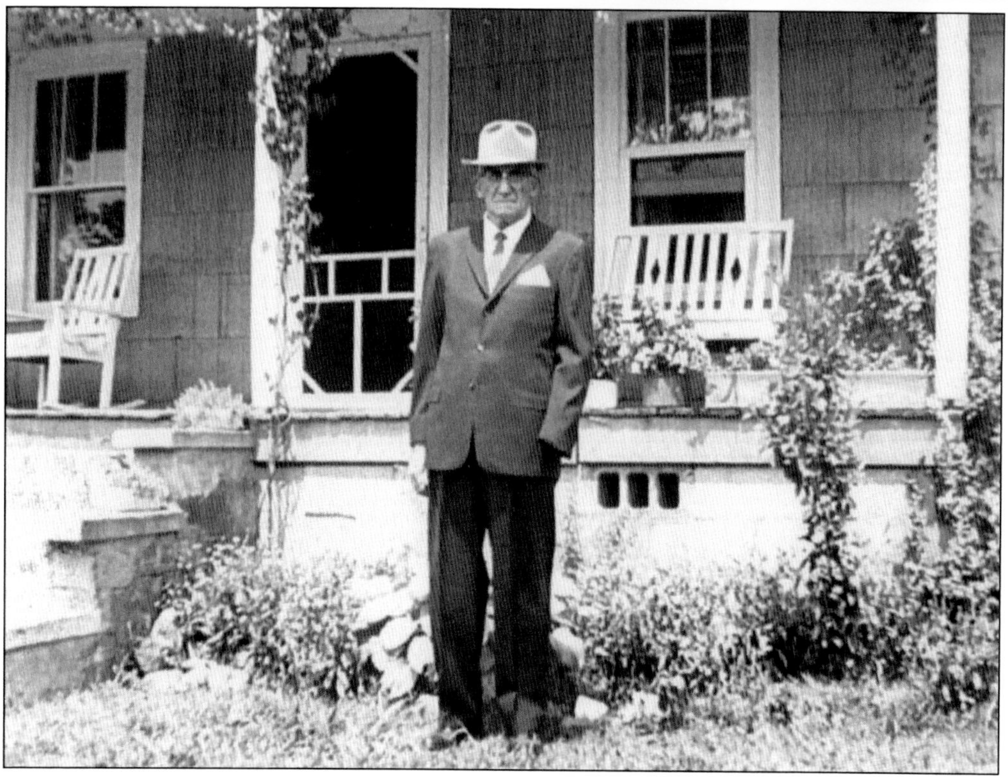

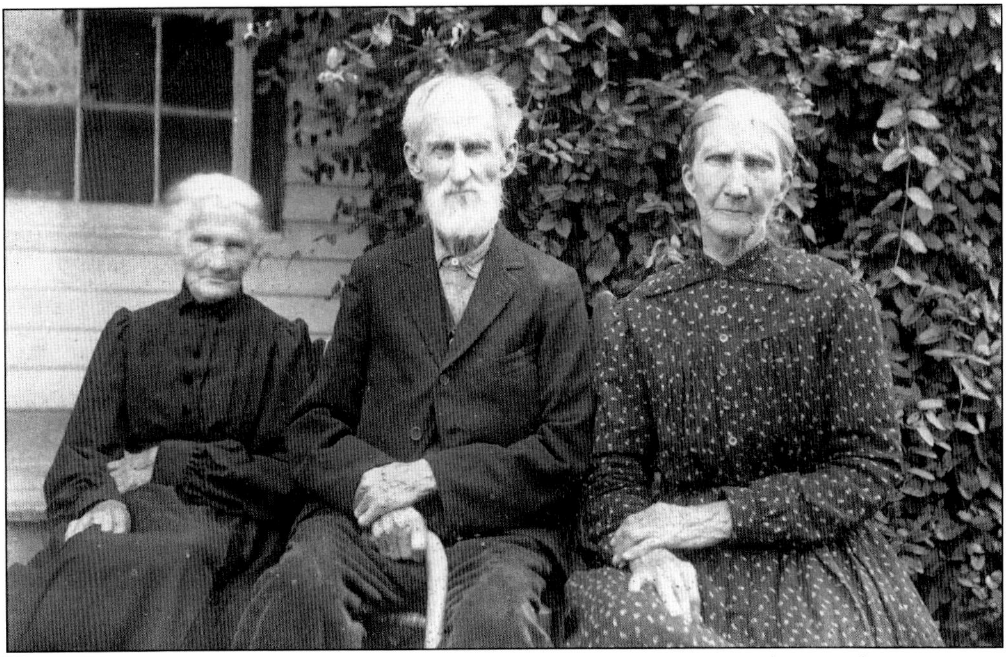

Pictured here *c.* 1910 are Sarah Scott Fine, Absalom Lowery Scott, and Maranda Scott Fine. The three are siblings whose parents were David Scott and Nancy Lowery. The Scott family originally came to Washington County from Scotland in the late 1700s. (Courtesy of Barbara S. Hilton.)

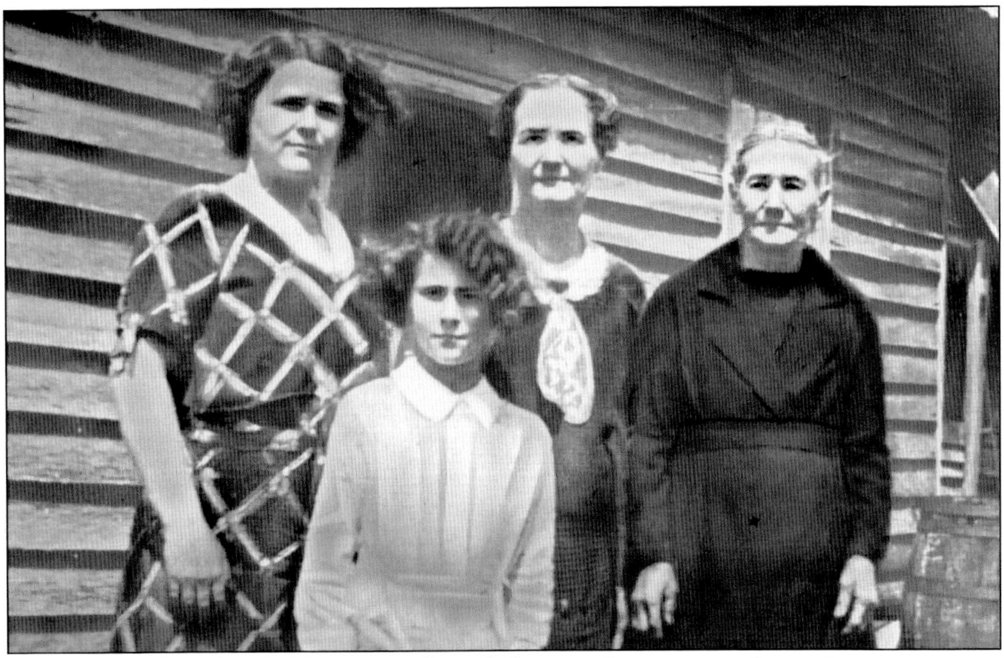

The similarity of facial features in these ladies is clear—pictured are four generations gathered in front of the Dulaney homestead, located past Buzzard's Roost between Eden Church and downtown Jonesborough. From left to right are Pearl Miller May, Ruth May, Nora Dulaney Miller, and Frances Walters Dulaney. (Courtesy of Ruth M. Robinson.)

At the time of the 1860 census, Caroline Wilds was seven years old. She is pictured here a few years earlier with her mother, Catherine. At the time of the census, others listed in the household were father David, age 35; sisters Mary, age 9, and Laura, age 7 months; and brother John, age 3. David's stated profession was "merchant." Laura's was "domestic." (Courtesy of Caroline M. May.)

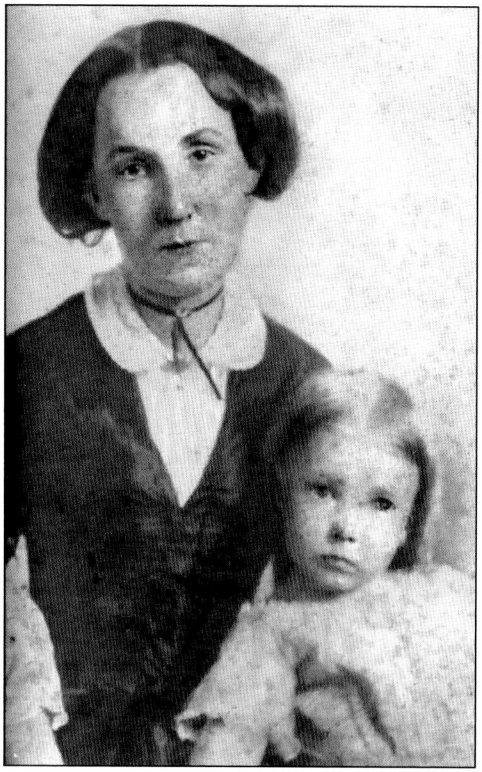

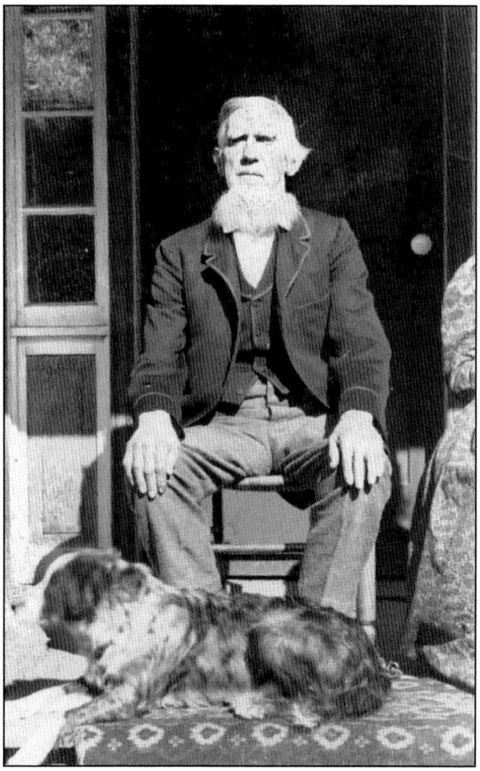

Jacob Fine is shown here with his dog in the late 1800s. Jacob lived from March 14, 1827, until November 25, 1897. He married Sarah Scott, shown on page 30, on October 10, 1850. (Courtesy of Barbara S. Hilton.)

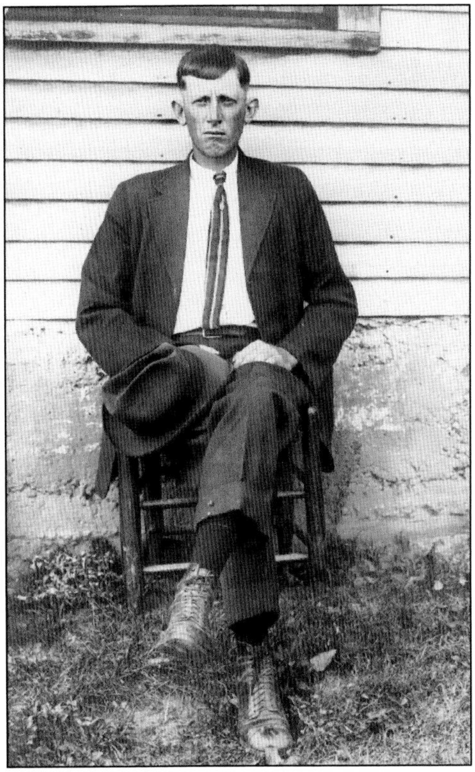

Moses Miller died on January 11, 1925, at the age of 32. The average life span in 1900 was only 45 years, but today, it is closer to 80 years. This is largely due to the development of antibiotics, the purification of drinking water, and the fact that we have vaccinations available for infectious diseases. (Courtesy of Barbara S. Hilton.)

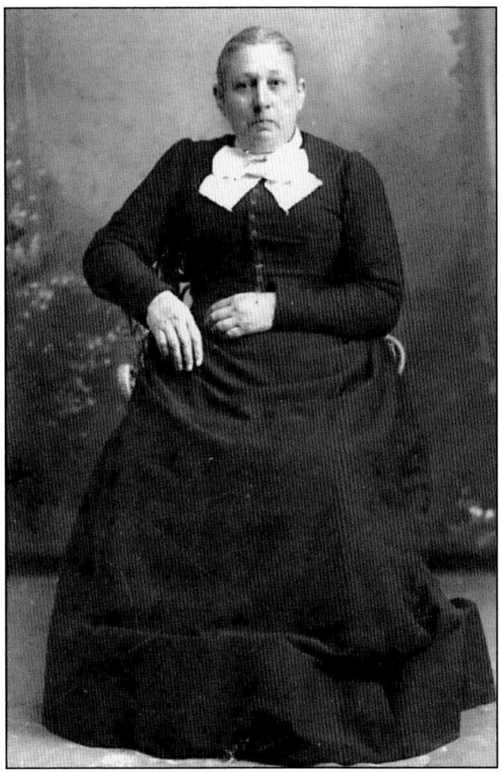

Sarah Priscilla May grew up off Greenwood Drive, which extends from Johnson City into the Lamar community of Jonesborough. Sarah was born on Independence Day in 1847 and married farmer Absalom Huffine on December 5, 1867, when she was 20 years old. Her father was Jacob May. Sarah died on May 24, 1910. (Courtesy of Barbara S. Hilton.)

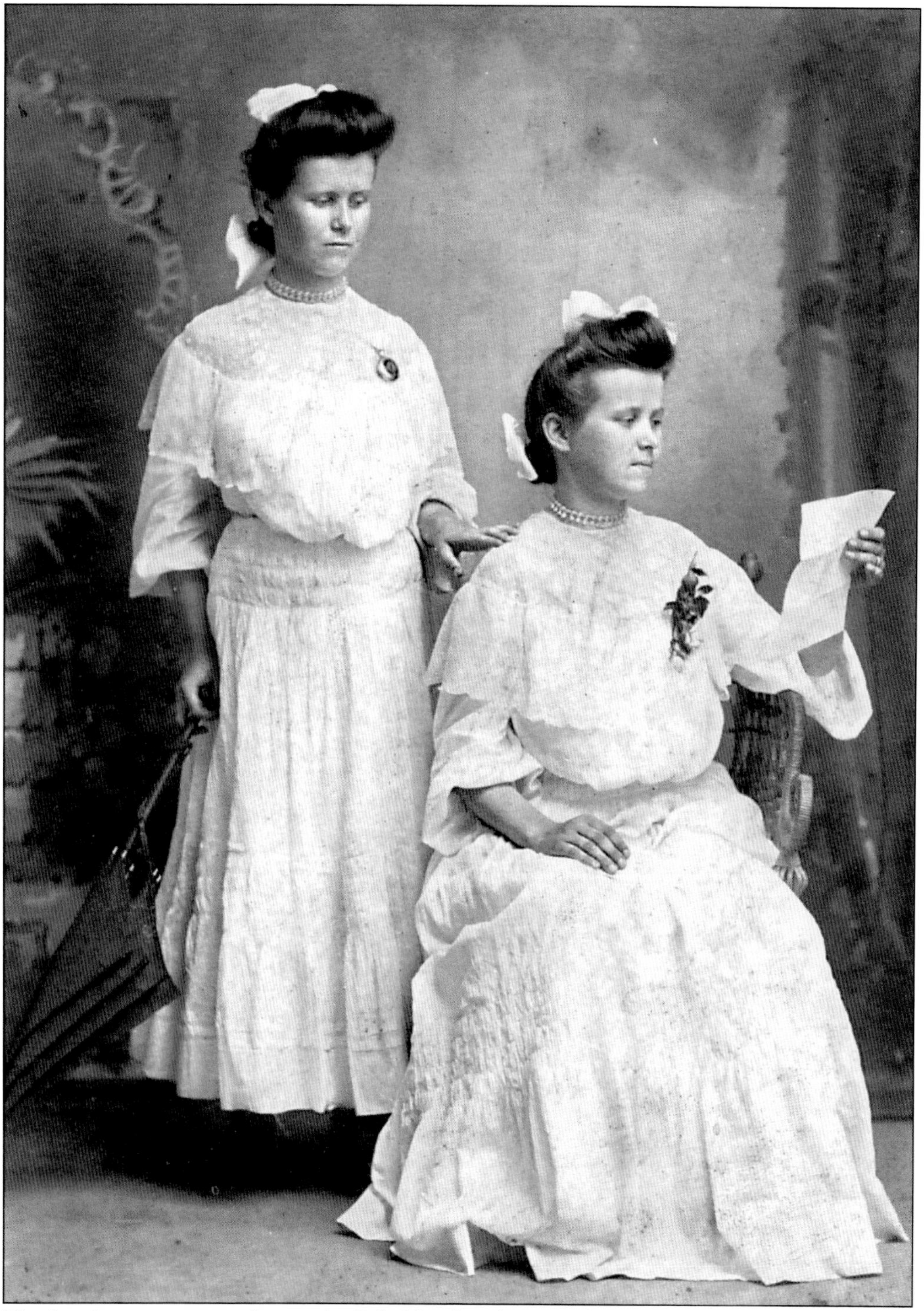

This lovely portrait was taken at the D.L. Hensley photography studio in Jonesborough *c.* 1905. Though Amy and Harriet lived closer to the Telford area, they came to Jonesborough to shop, seek entertainment, and have their photographs taken. As adults, Amy married James Taylor and Harriet married Charles McCracken. (Courtesy of Betty Jane Hylton.)

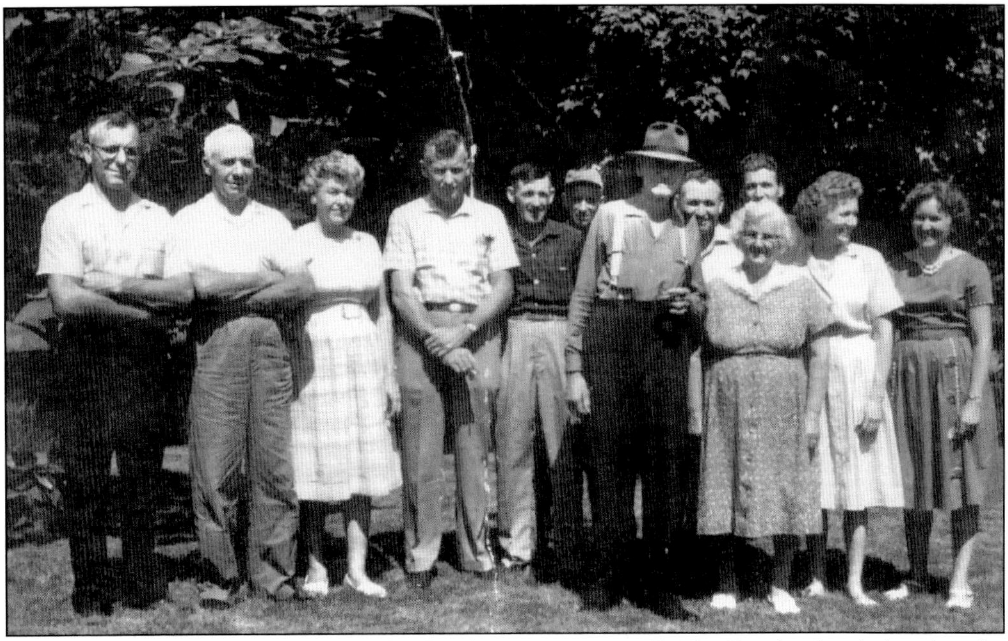

This photograph was taken at a Broyles family reunion, *c.* 1955. The Broyles family lived in the Bowmantown community. Pictured here, from left to right, are Ellis, Paul, Muriel, Jake, Glen, Dana Wayne, Jerome, Tom, Lola, Roy, Betty, and Gladys. Jerome and Lola had 12 children. Ten are pictured here as one child had been stillborn and another died in a barn accident. (Courtesy of Clarence and Linda Bailey.)

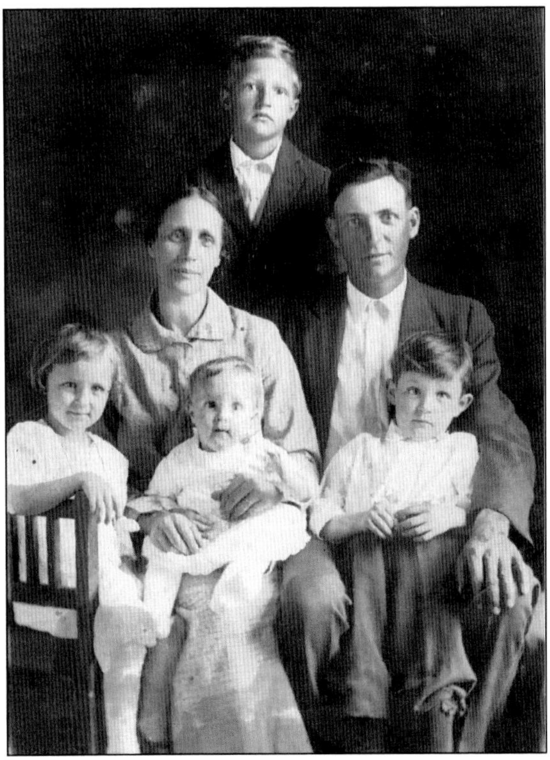

This wonderful family photo features "Grandmother Broyles, Auther, Lenord, Herbert, Bonnie, and Lawrence," but we aren't certain which individuals are which, except for "Grandmother Broyles," for whom no first name was written; she is the lady in the picture. (Courtesy of Clarence and Linda Bailey.)

This c. 1890 tintype photograph of Rufus May and W.S. Hickey was taken at L.W. Keen photography studio in Jonesborough. W.S. Hickey owned a wholesale house where the Salt House is currently located. (Courtesy of Caroline M. May.)

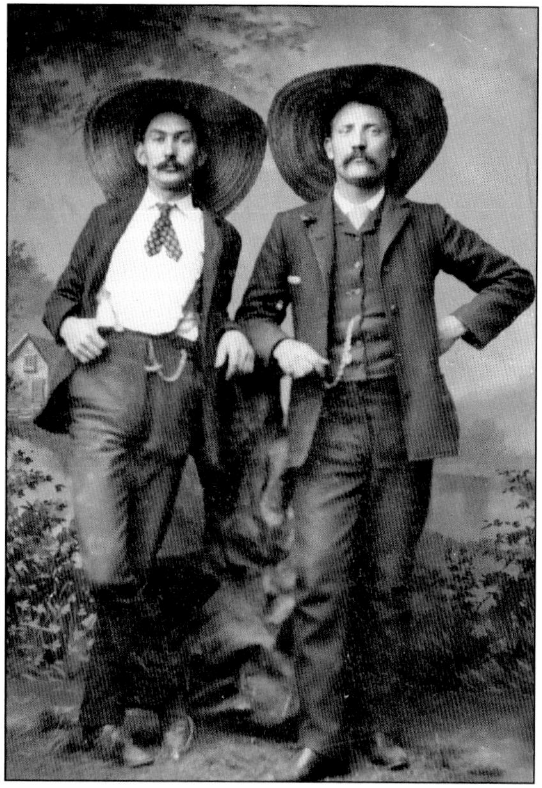

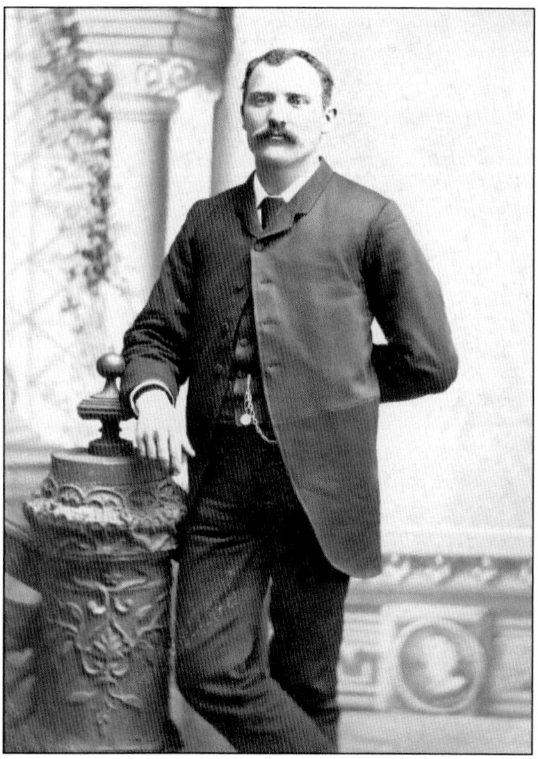

Rufus May was born November 1, 1821. He owned a general store on Main Street. According to the 1920 census, Rufus was the head of his household, where he lived with wife Dora, age 59; son Robert, age 15; and a boarder, Maude Rube, who was 16 years old. (Courtesy of Caroline M. May.)

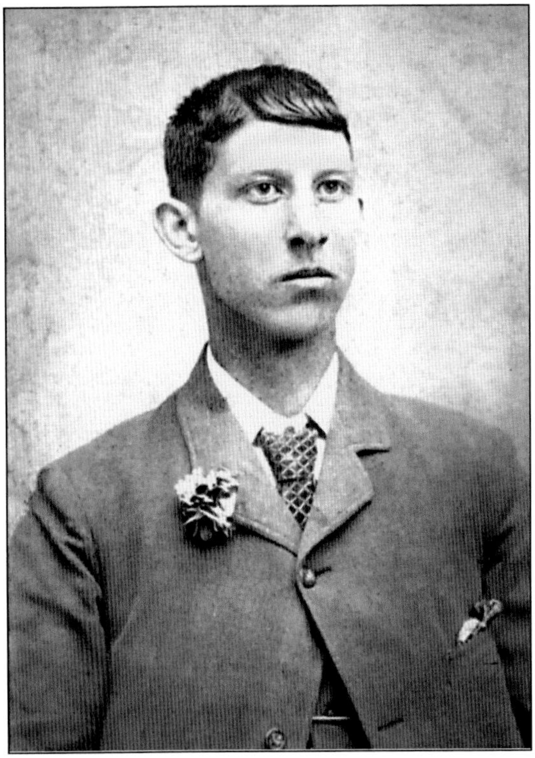

John D. Sherfey was born in 1865 and had this photo taken *c.* 1885. (Courtesy of Helen Deakins McCrary.)

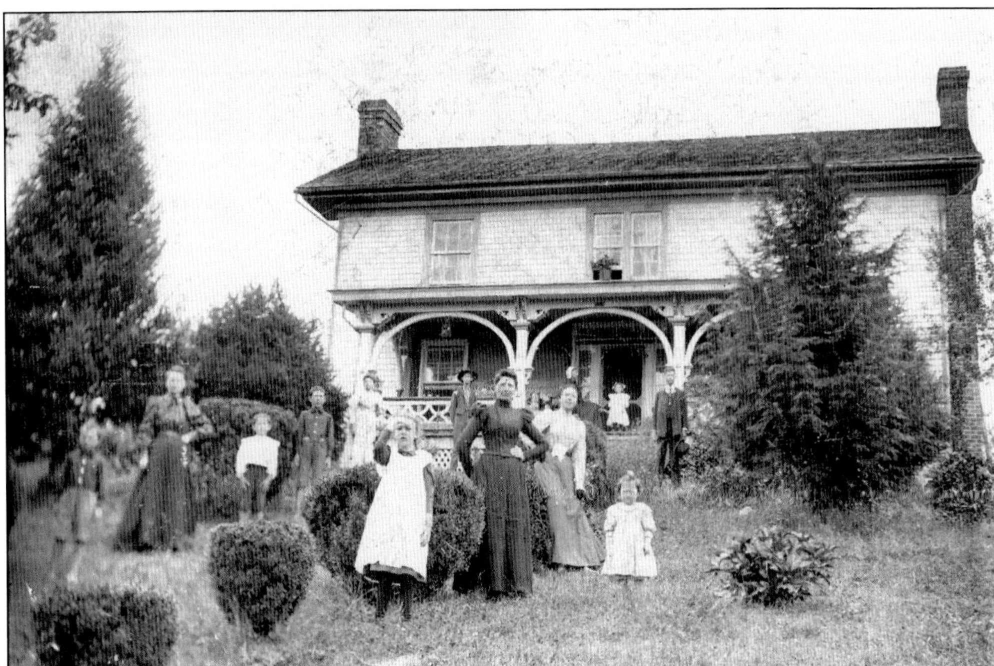

The John D. Sherfey homestead in Sulphur Springs, about seven miles from downtown Jonesborough, boasts numerous bushes and trees. Sherfey lived from 1865 until 1934 and was of German descent. His descendants still live in the area. (Courtesy of Helen Deakins McCrary.)

William H. Correll, who lived from 1851 until 1913, built houses and barns in the Jonesborough area. Correll also dealt in lumber. He lived on Boone Street in downtown Jonesborough with his wife, Sarah (below), and their children. (Courtesy of Karen Wise Bennett.)

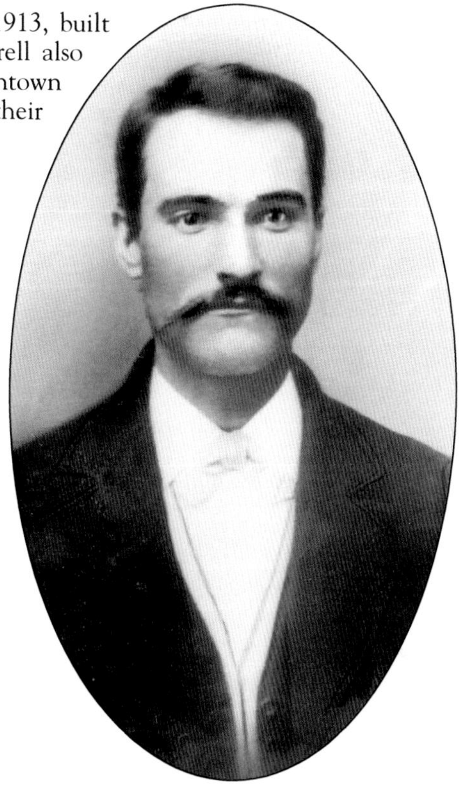

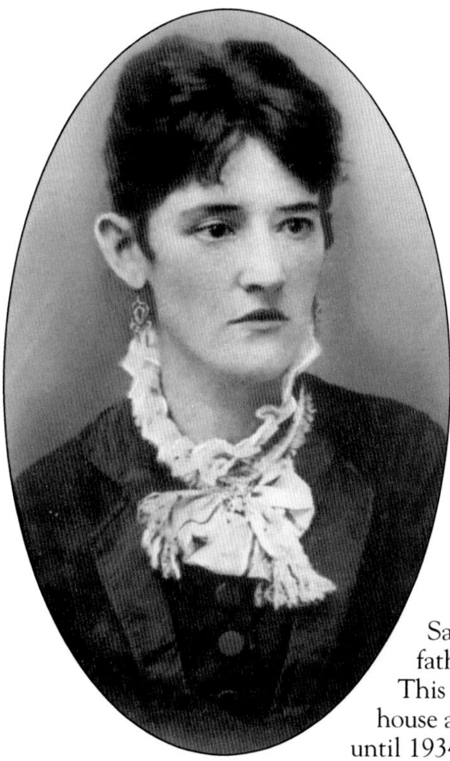

Sarah Naff Correll grew up on Main Street where her father had a tailor shop in the basement of their home. This house eventually became known as the Naff-Henley house and can be seen on page nine. Sarah lived from 1856 until 1934. (Courtesy of Karen Wise Bennett.)

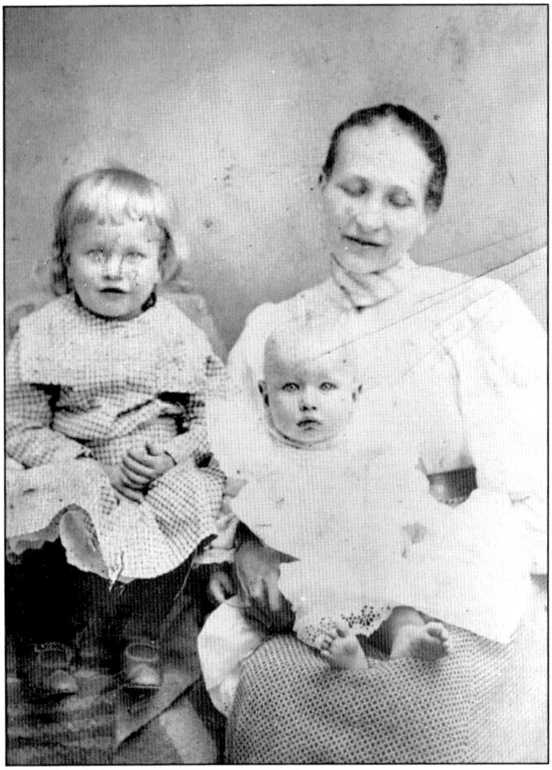

Bessie Lena Shaw Correll, shown here with her children, Eugene and Howard, is believed to be a Melungeon. Although no one is exactly sure of the true origin of the people known as Melungeons, it is speculated that they are of Portuguese, African, Moor, Native American, Spanish, and Mediterranean descent. This list is only a selection of the possible ancestries of the Melungeons. (Courtesy of Karen Wise Bennett.)

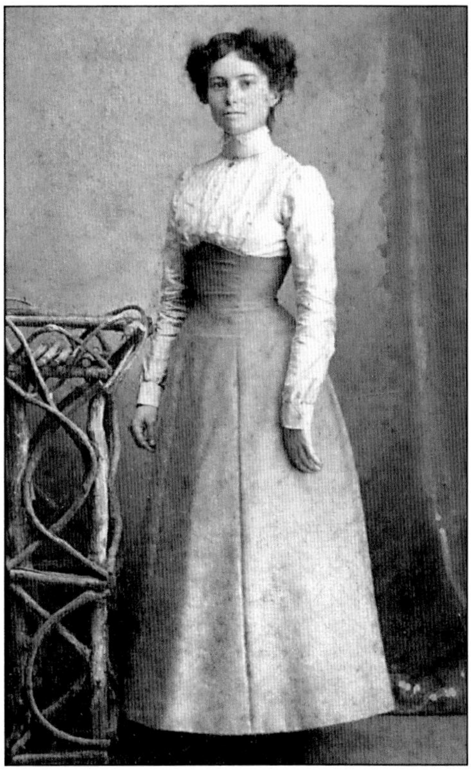

Lula Deakins Bacon was born in Sulphur Springs on September 26, 1883. Lula moved to Farragut later in life and died on July 7, 1921. (Courtesy of Helen Deakins McCrary.)

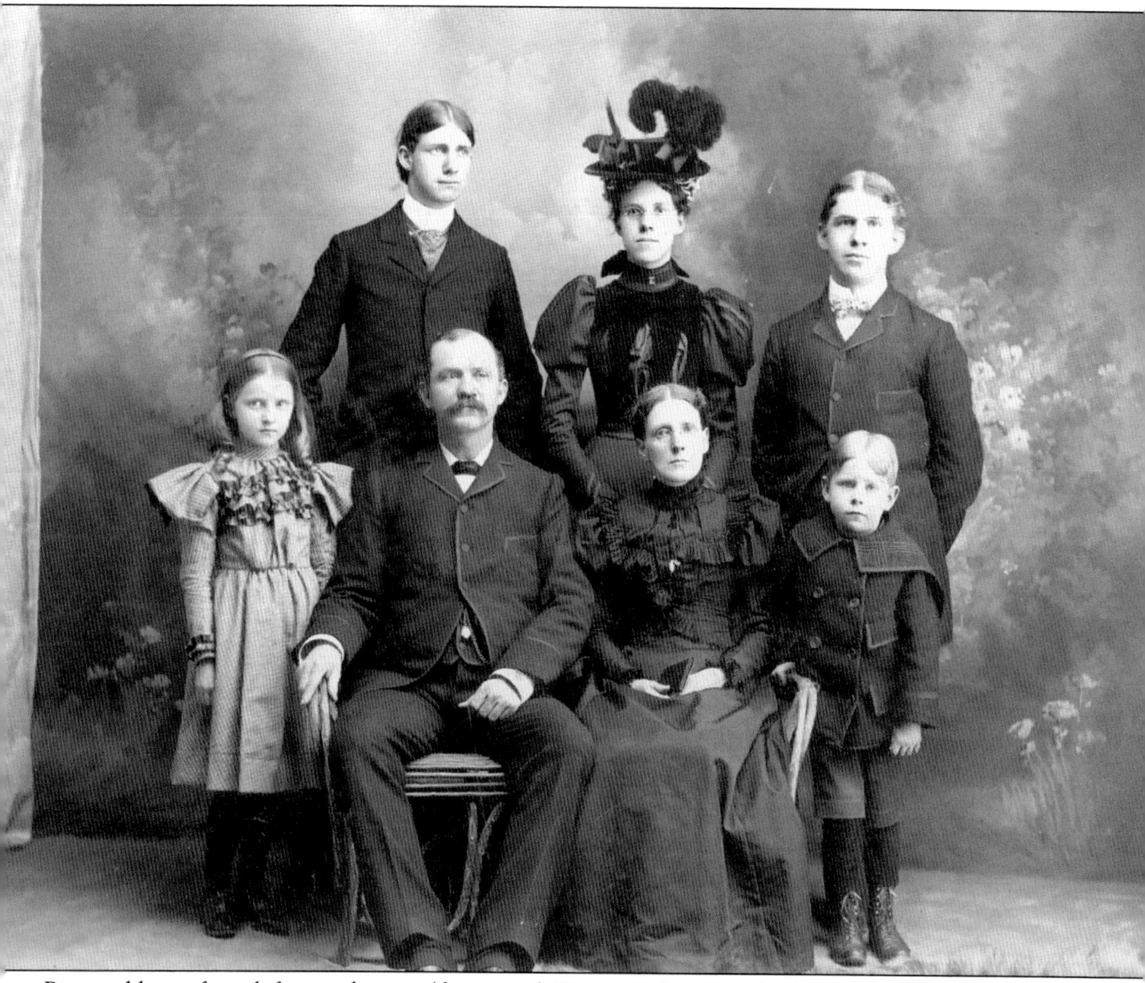

Pictured here, from left to right, are (front row) Carrie Culver Smith, George Leonides Smith, Caroline Rebecca Wilds Smith, and Leon Chester Smith; (back row) Rev. Henry Wilds Smith, Lula Smith, and William Dosser Smith. According to information on the 1900 census, Henry, William, Carrie, and Leon were children of George and Caroline. In 1900, although Henry was 24 and William was 20, they were listed as still living at home. Another interesting census note was that all the children were born in Tennessee except for Carrie, who was born in Missouri. (Courtesy of Caroline M. May.)

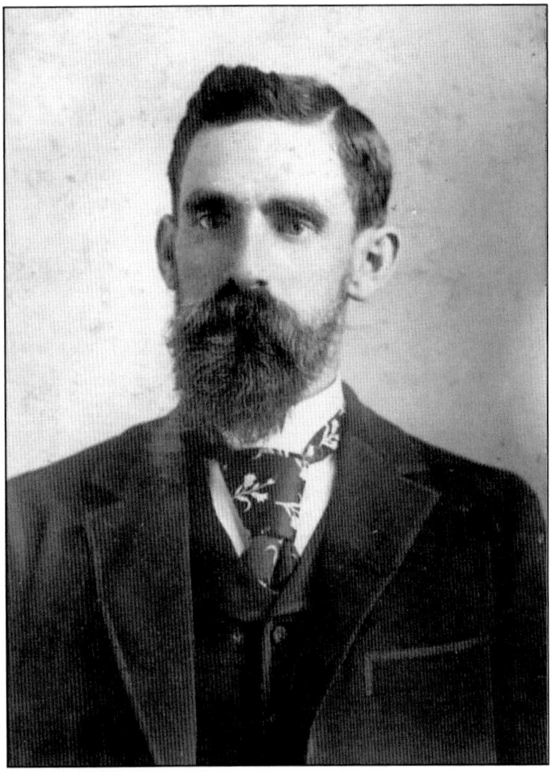

This is a photograph of Daniel Fine c. 1870. Fine married Lucy Farley and set up a homestead in Jonesborough. He died on June 26, 1933. (Courtesy of Barbara S. Hilton.)

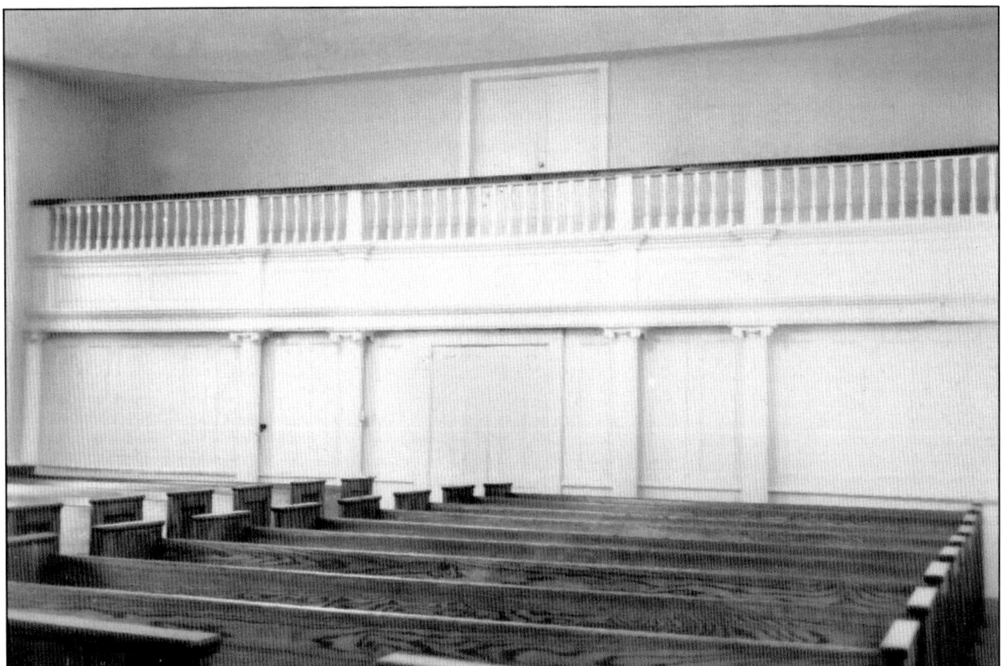

Popular postcards have called the balcony area of the Jonesborough United Methodist Church the "slave gallery" for years. In fact, the area was set aside for people of color who were slaves or free. (Courtesy of the Jonesborough United Methodist Church.)

Bruce and Dave Howren lived in the Embreeville community. This photograph was taken c. 1900. (Courtesy of Chip White.)

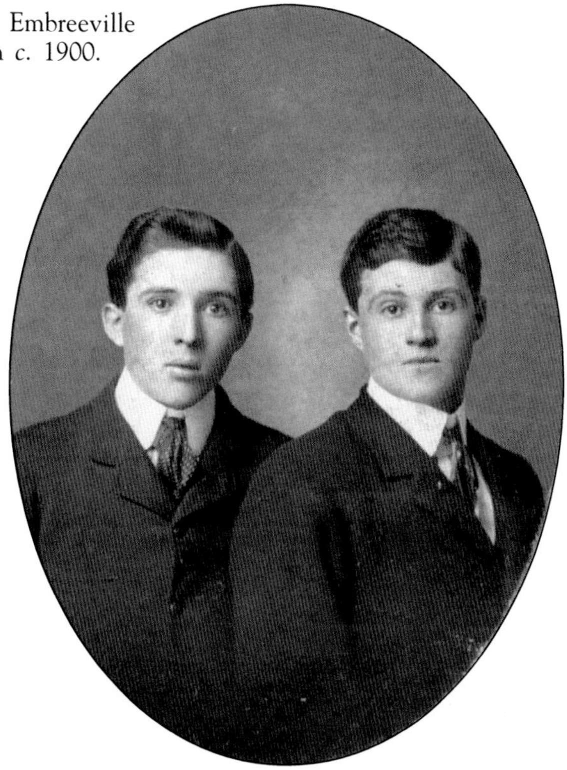

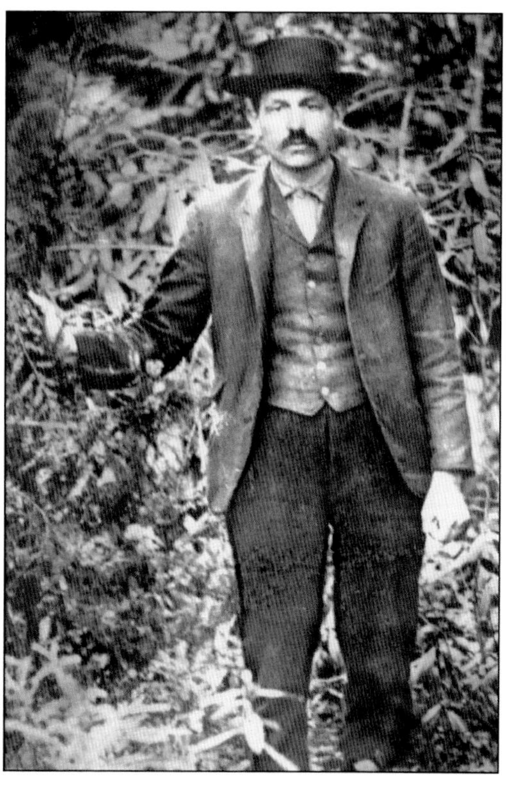

Benjamin Mitchell was originally from Limestone but came to Jonesborough in the late 1800s. He married Mona Laws, and they reared seven children. (Courtesy of Dennis and Jean Mitchell.)

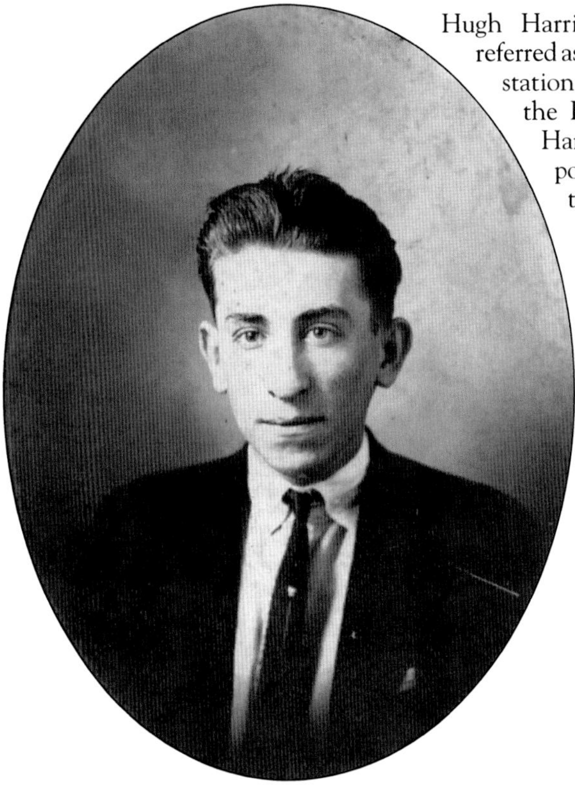

Hugh Harriman Campbell, to whom everyone referred as "Spooley," owned the Hermitage service station. When he was a boy, his father owned the Hotel Washington and a livery stable. Harriman would sometimes drive a team of ponies and transport visitors to and from the Embreeville Iron Mines. He lived from May 4, 1902, until April 8, 1970. (Courtesy of George R. Campbell.)

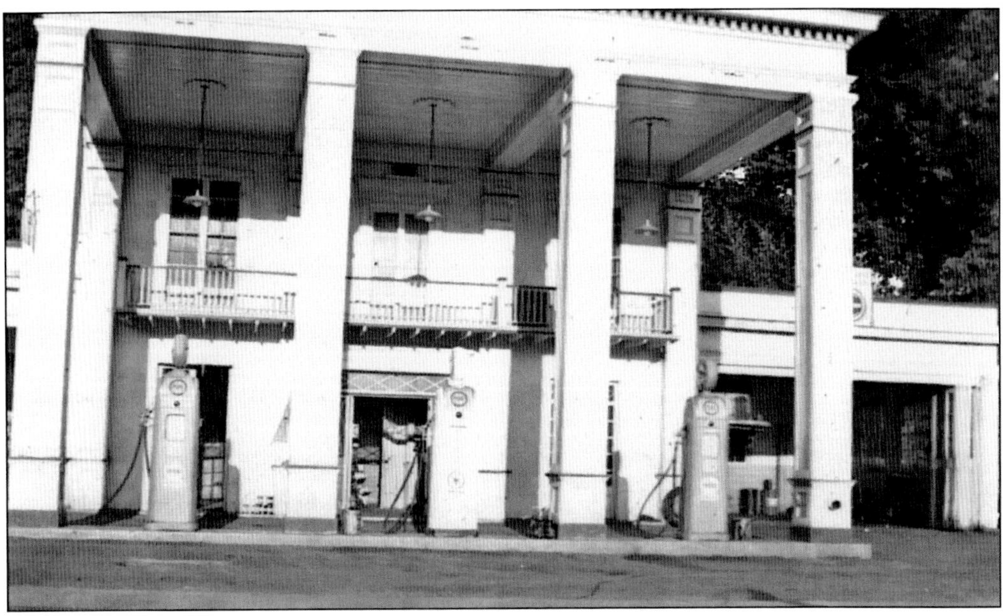

The Hermitage service station, where they sold Pure oil, was owned by Hugh Harriman Campbell in the early 1900s. After closing the service station, Harriman served as the superintendent of the Jonesborough Water Department. The building was sold in 1949, torn down c. 1950, and was located on Boone Street where Weem's Florist is now. (Courtesy of George R. Campbell.)

Sue Clark was the wife of Dr. Joseph Clark. Dr. Clark was listed on the 1880 census as a 23-year-old physician who was born in Tennessee. The couple lived in Jonesborough. This photograph of Sue, by the Cargille Studio in Johnson City, was probably taken *c.* 1885. (Courtesy of Martha Stephenson.)

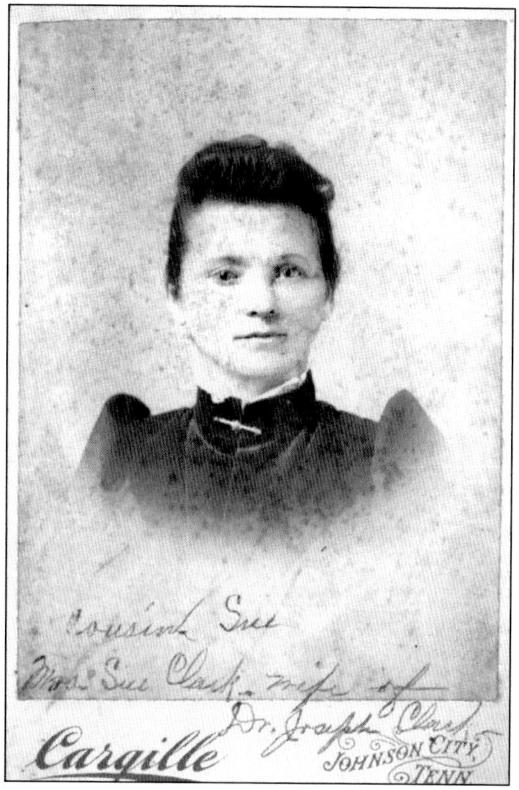

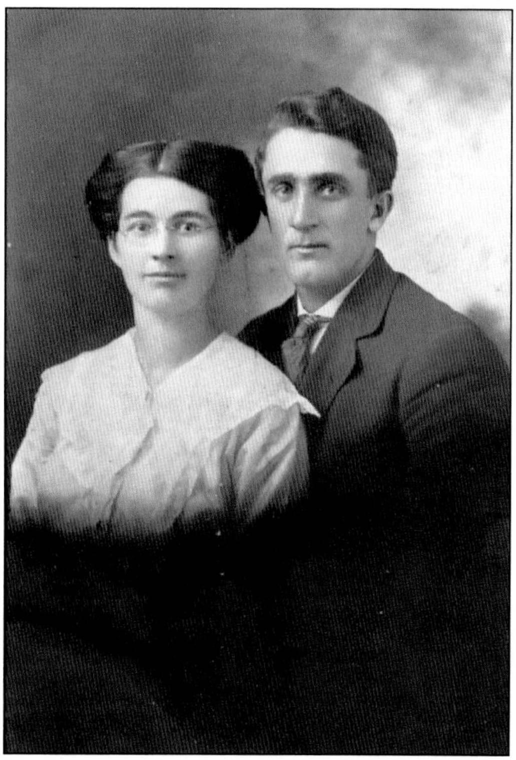

Laura Tennessee Cox and Frank W. Haws were married on August 9, 1900. The couple had five children, one of whom died in infancy. Frank was a farmer and later operated a general store. When Frank was elected as trustee of Washington County, the family moved to Jonesborough and purchased a home on Main Street *c.* 1925. Frank died in 1937 following surgery for ulcers. (Courtesy of Lyle Haws.)

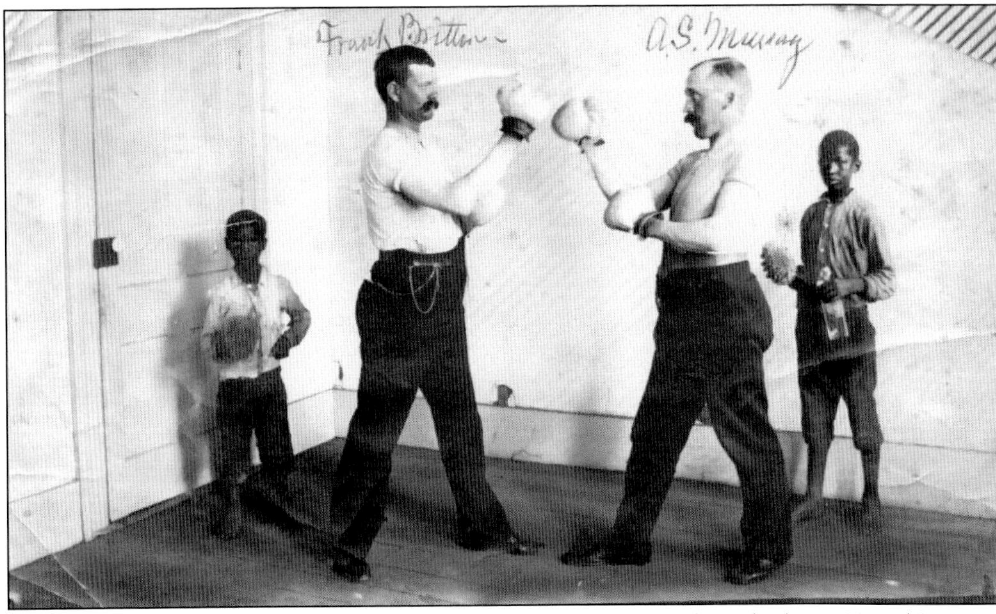

Frank Britton and A.S. Murray engaged in a friendly boxing match in the late 1800s. (Courtesy of Martha Stephenson.)

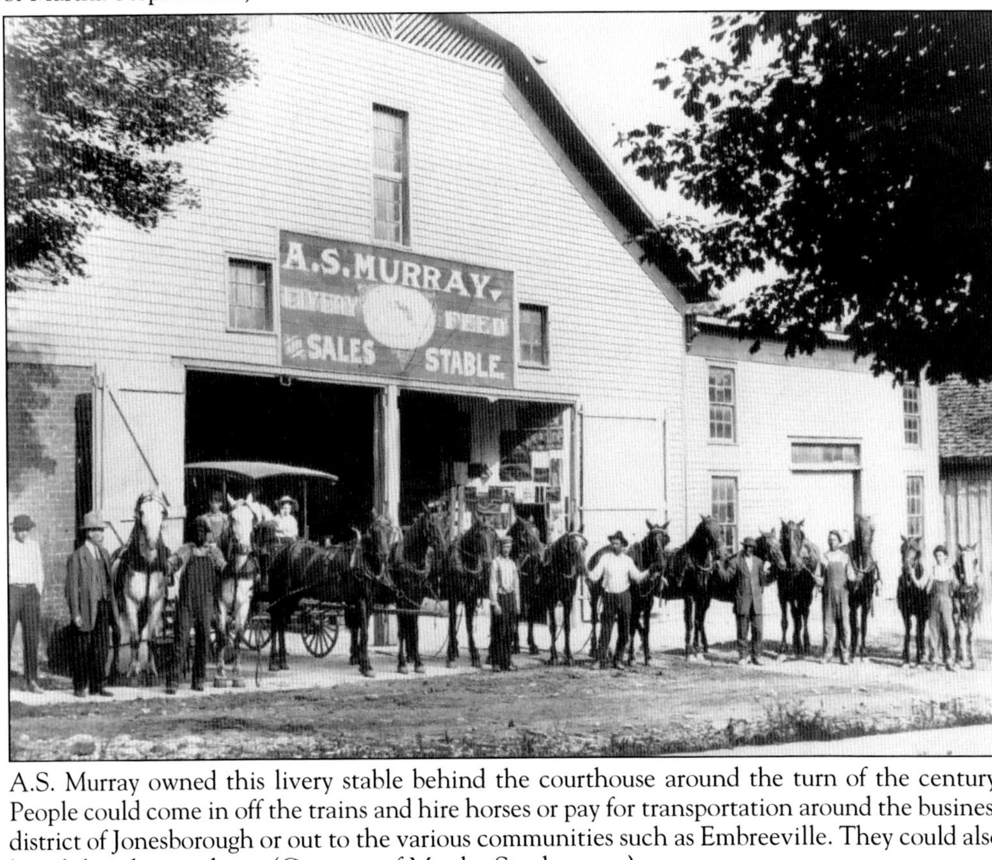

A.S. Murray owned this livery stable behind the courthouse around the turn of the century. People could come in off the trains and hire horses or pay for transportation around the business district of Jonesborough or out to the various communities such as Embreeville. They could also board their horses there. (Courtesy of Martha Stephenson.)

Unfortunately, not much was written about A.S. Murray in the history books, but this is a photograph of him that was probably taken in the late 1800s. (Courtesy of Martha Stephenson.)

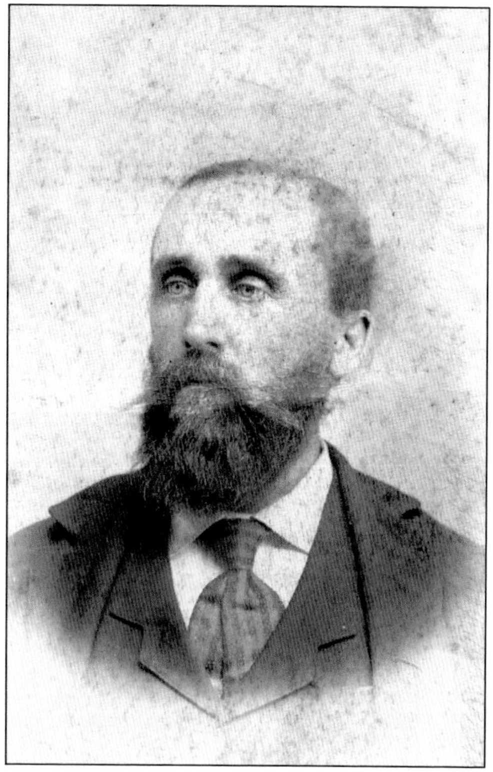

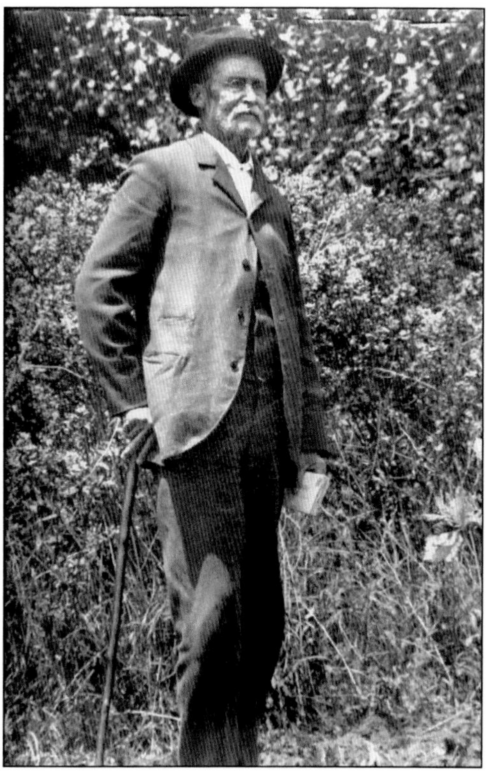

This well-preserved photograph was found in the basement of the Washington County Courthouse. It is speculated that the man in the image might have been associated with the Embreeville Iron Company since this photograph was among several of theirs. The clerk's office has requested money to preserve the numerous historic documents located at the courthouse and hopes to receive those funds at some point. (Courtesy of the Washington County Clerk's Office.)

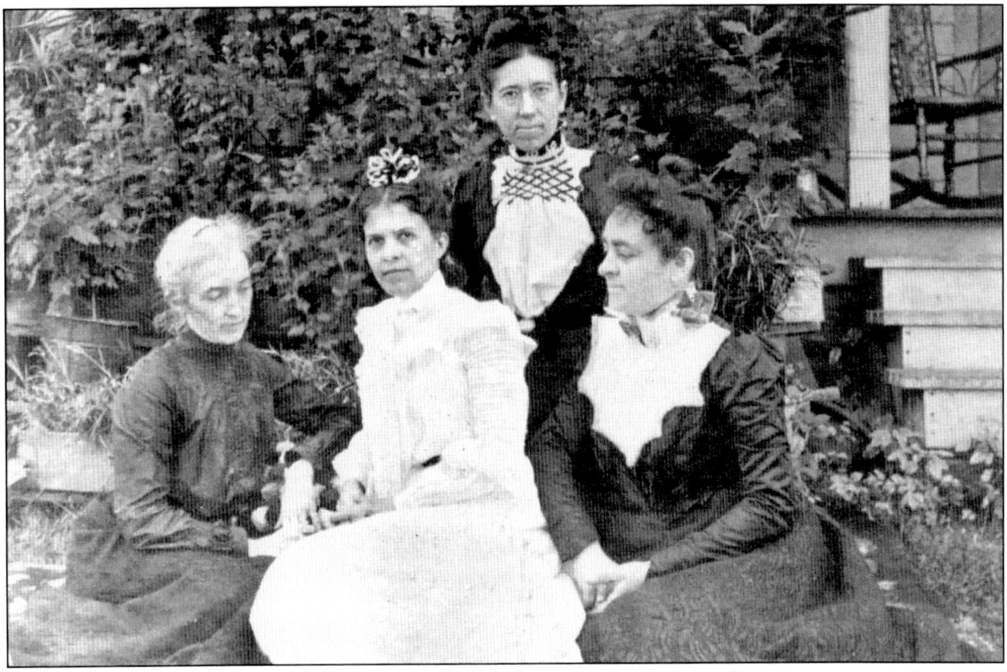

Based on the lush foliage, these unidentified ladies appear to have been enjoying a beautiful summer day outdoors. (Courtesy of Sue Henley.)

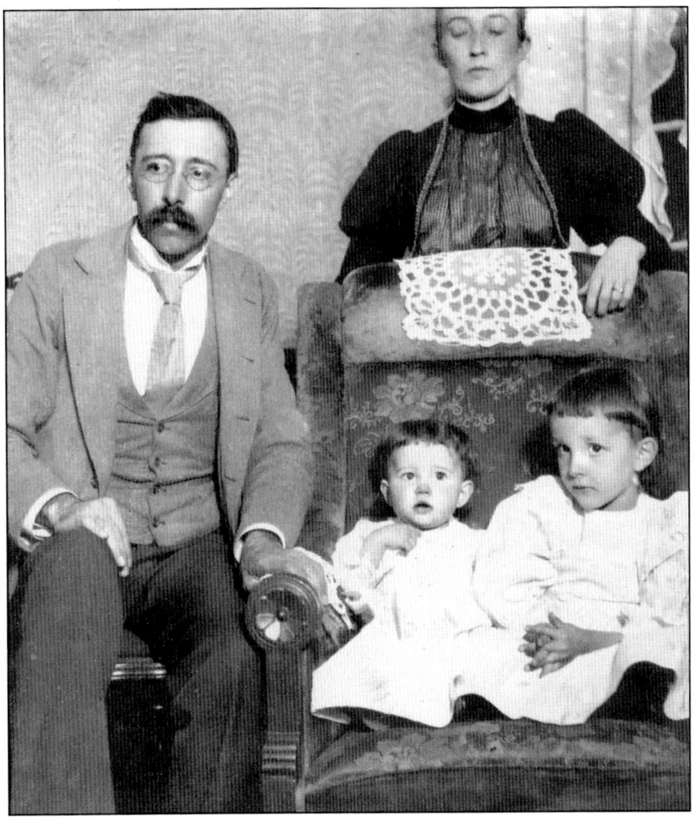

E.J. and Nell Baxter had this photograph taken with their children, Eleanor (left) and Martha, c. 1895 at their home at 127 East Main Street. The house can be seen on page nine. E.J. Baxter had a law office in Jonesborough. (Courtesy of Sue Henley.)

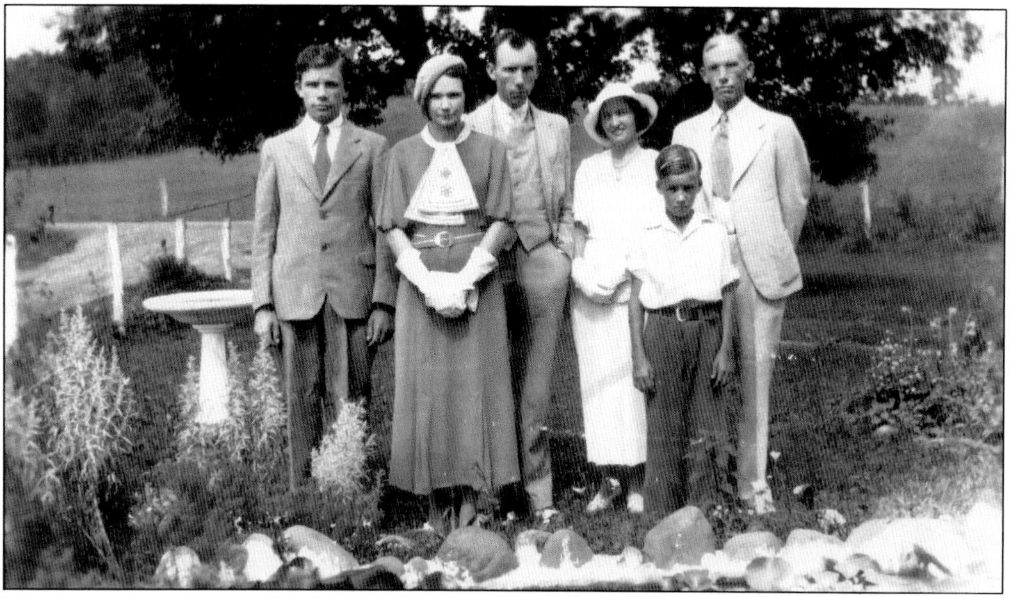

Members of the Poteat family have lived in Jonesborough for generations. June Poteat still runs a farm near Mountain View Estates, which used to be part of the farmland. Poteat family members pictured here *c.* 1930, from left to right, are Jim, Ann, John, Jessie, F.B. Jr., and F.B. Sr. (Courtesy of June and Ruby Poteat.)

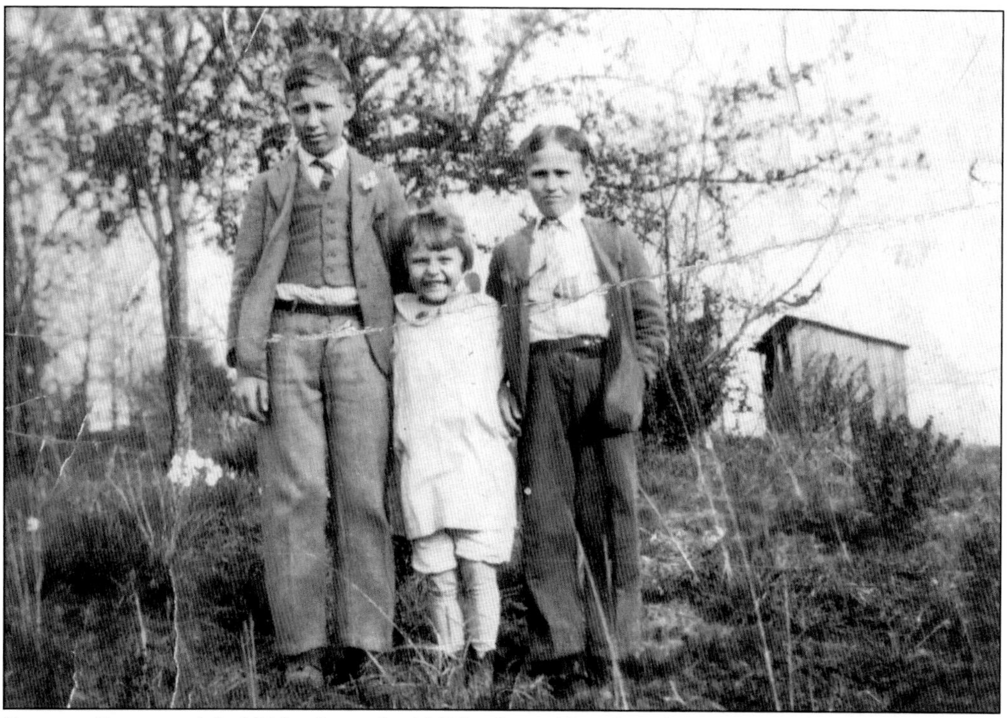

Eugene (January 16, 1915—June 3, 1995), Sara (October 29, 1920—July 26, 1999), and Howard Correll (September 28, 1917—present) are believed to be of partial Melungeon descent. A picture of their mother is on page 36. (Courtesy of Karen Wise Bennett.)

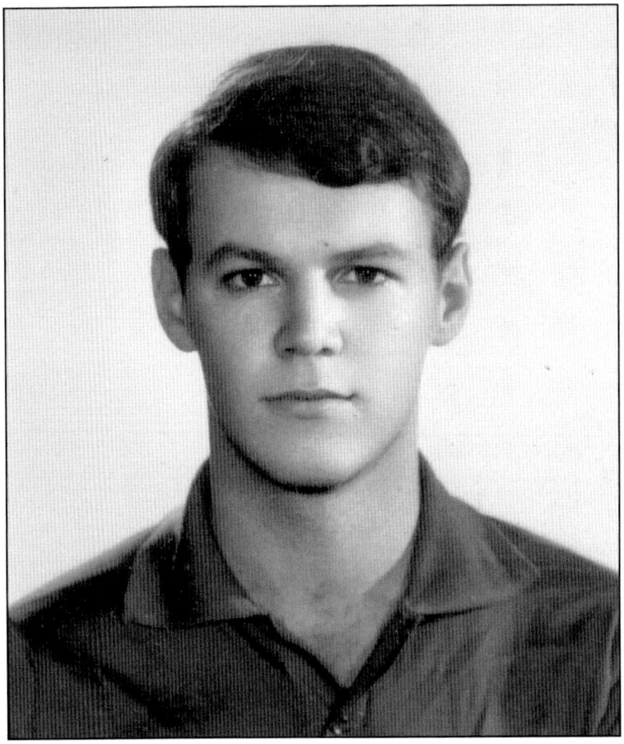

James May was born May 23, 1950, graduated from Jonesborough High School, and joined the United States Air Force. On a mission to support United States Marines, May was killed in Iraq on January 31, 1991, on an AC130 gunship. He left behind wife, Christina; children James Scott and April Anne; and stepson, Lee Anthony Pfalzgraf. (Photo courtesy of Jane May; information courtesy of Christina May.)

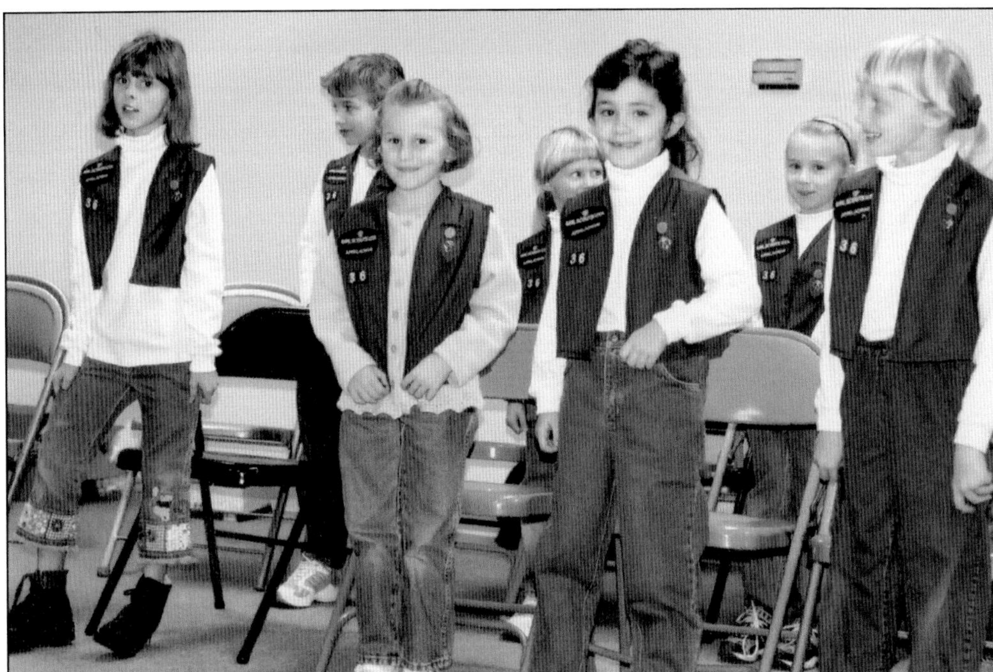

Juliette "Daisy" Gordon Low started the Girl Scout organization in 1912. Today, girls still assemble in the hopes of becoming better citizens. Members of a local Girl Scout troop in 2003, from left to right, are Lydia Hasch, Kristal Rheiner, Sarah Haskins, Hannah Voudrie, Alison Ledford, Megan Bailey, and Danielle Voudrie. (Photograph by the author.)

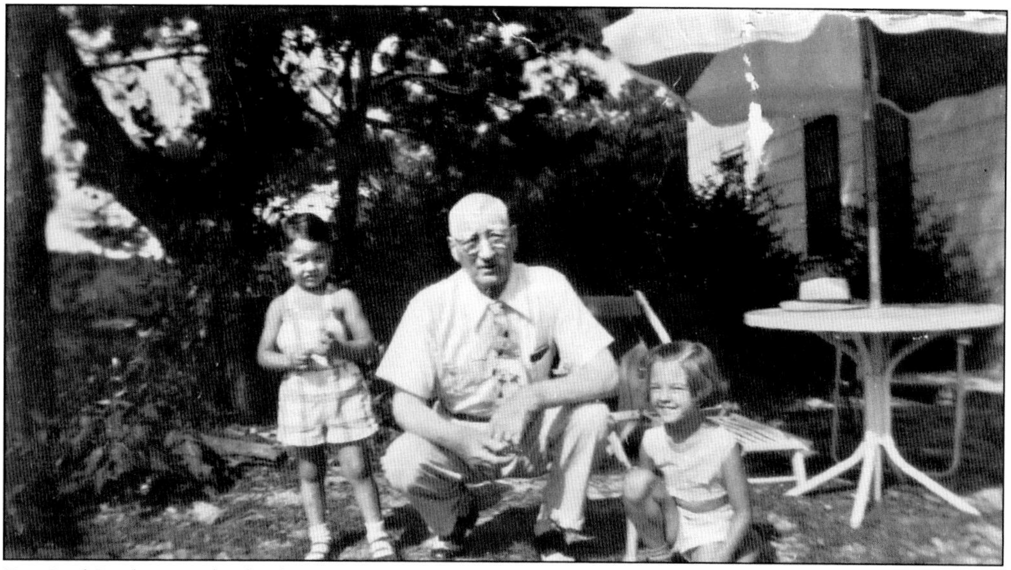

Dr. Carl Brabson, who had a practice in Jonesborough for a number of years, enjoys a sunny day with his nieces. (Courtesy of Jane May.)

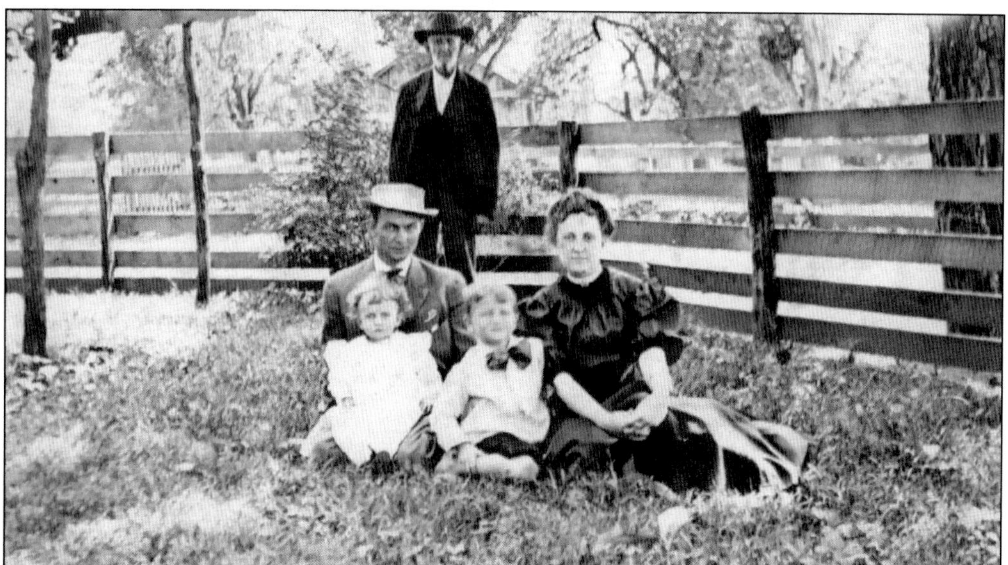

Pictured here, from left to right, are (front row) children Frank and William Mitchell; (back row) Sam and Minnie Mitchell; (standing) "Grandpa" Deakins. (Courtesy of Caroline M. May.)

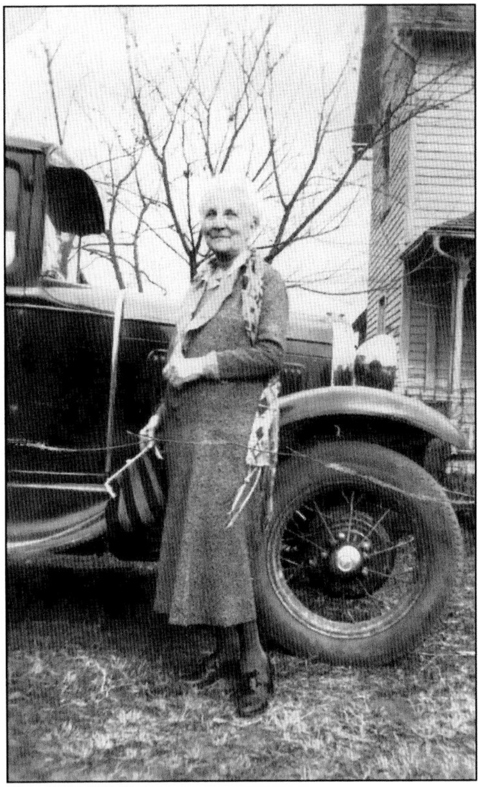

Mrs. Wymen, wife of the iron mines superintendent, is shown here at the Clubhouse in Embreeville. Clubhouses in the outlying communities of Jonesborough were essential to early residents for communication and socialization. (Courtesy of Chip White.)

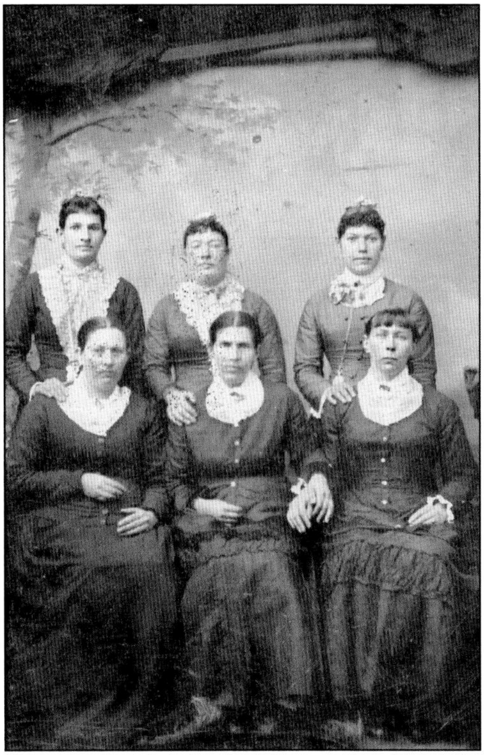

These are the daughters of Jacob and Mary McNabb May. Pictured from left to right are (front row) Sarah Pricilla May Huffine, Margaret May Slagle, and Lydia May Lloyd; (back row) Venie May Galloway, Hattie May Hartsell, and Rettie May Kyker. (Courtesy of Barbara S. Hilton.)

Sam Burton Correll was a carpenter by trade who served as chief of police and worked on the railroad for a period. Though it is not apparent in this photograph, Sam was a very tall man, approximately six feet, six inches. He died in 1929. (Courtesy of Karen Wise Bennett.)

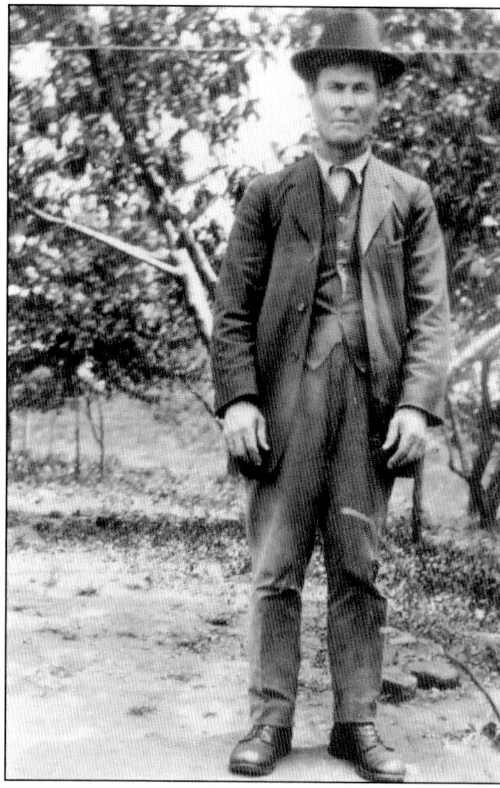

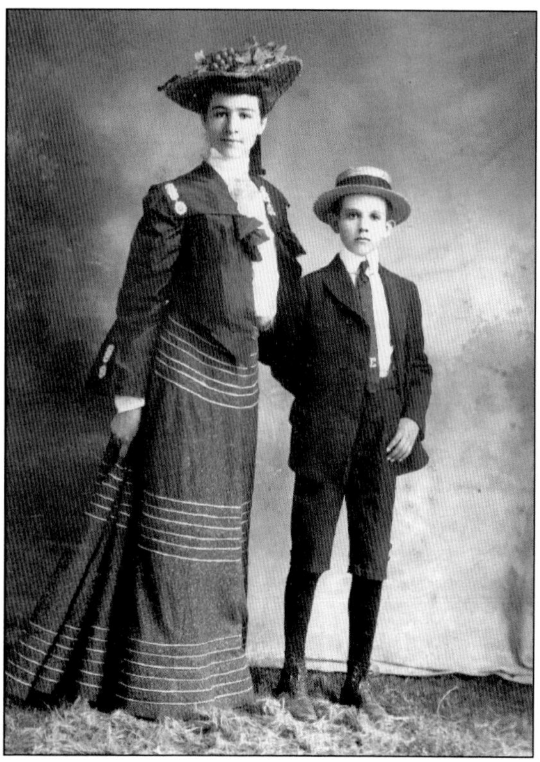

Maude Bright is shown here with her brother, Grince Ober Bright, c. 1900. Maude Bright married Dr. Joseph Roy McCrary on December 22, 1909, in Greeneville. They had four children and lived in the Wells-McCrary house in Fall Branch. The house, which was built in 1792, was taken by the federal government in 1971 to make way for Interstate 81. (Courtesy of Helen Deakins McCrary.)

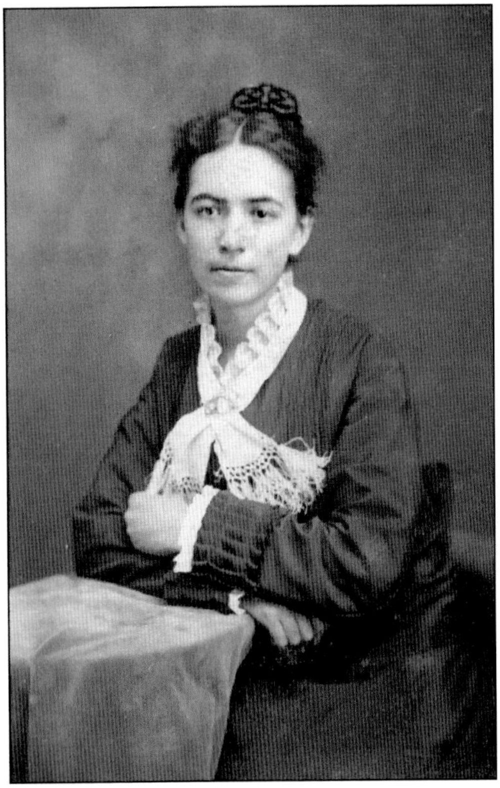

Elizabeth J. Bauchman Deakins lived from September 4, 1856, until July 6, 1937. She lived in Sulphur Springs with husband Richard and children Argil and Lula. (Courtesy of David Sherfey Deakins.)

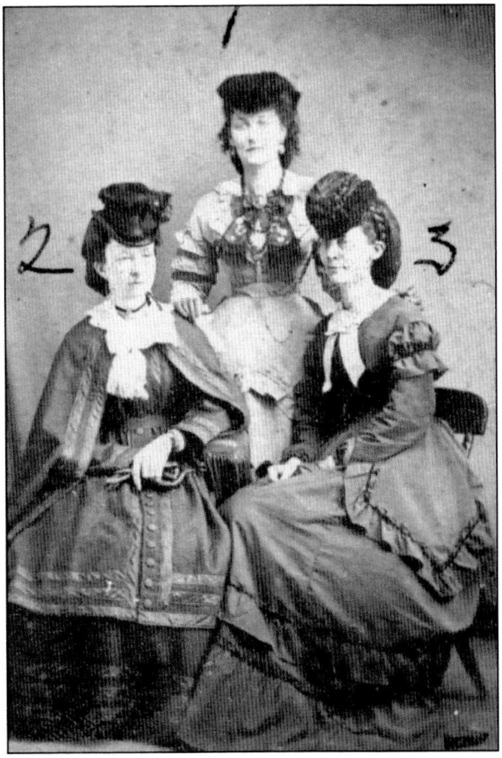

These women display late 19th-century clothing with full-length skirts, a cape, and stylish hats; the woman on the left is holding gloves. Although it isn't clear exactly who these ladies are, the names given, from left to right, appear to be Lamie Houston, unidentified, and Lillie Wood. They may have been relatives of the Baxter family. (Courtesy of Sue Henley.)

Nell Lampson married E.J. Baxter on June 8, 1893. The *Herald and Tribune* described the wedding at the Second Presbyterian Church as "quite a brilliant affair. . . . The church decoration was unique, elegant and attractive." After the wedding, a reception was given at the home of a Mrs. Fain on Main Street. Later, the couple left for Chicago and "other places west and north." (Courtesy of Sue Henley.)

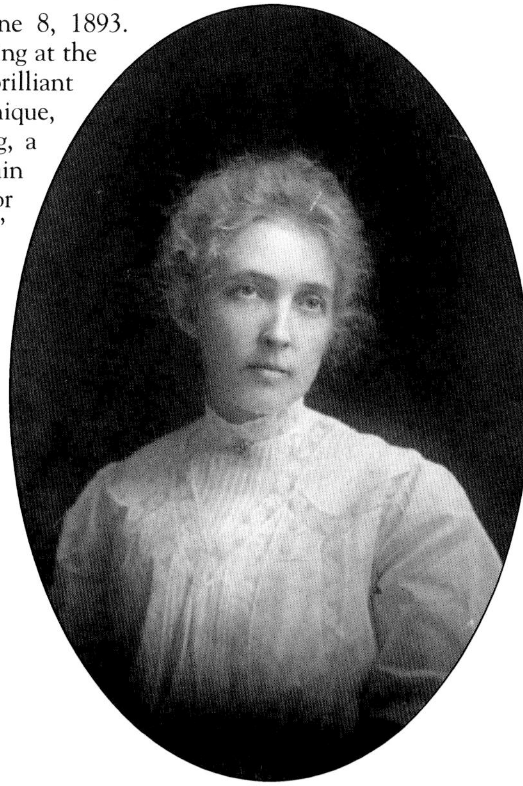

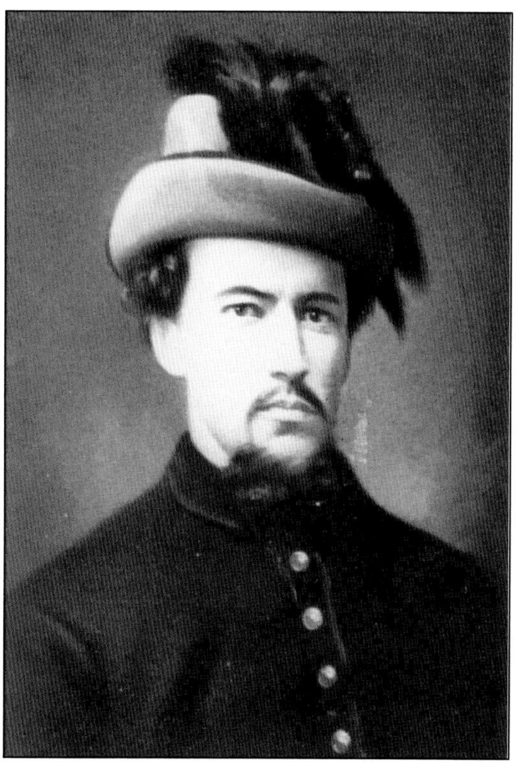

John Whitefield Doak only lived from 1838 until 1865. The exact relationship to the distinguished Samuel Doak, founder of Martin Academy (later called Washington College Academy), is unknown, but he was probably a great-grandson. Samuel Doak also established Presbyterian churches in local counties and was co-founder of Tusculum Academy, now Tusculum College. (Courtesy of Washington College Academy.)

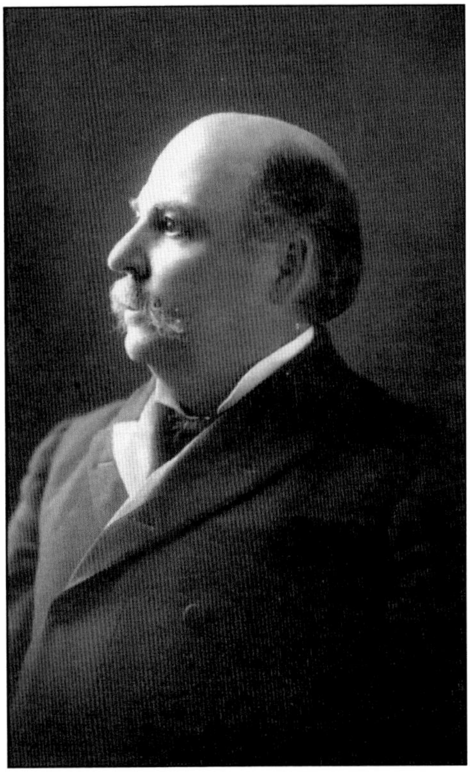

Alfred Alexander Taylor served as a member of the Tennessee House of Representatives and governor during his political career. He was the son of Nathaniel Green Taylor and brother of Robert Love Taylor, who defeated Alfred in the 1886 election for governor. Alfred practiced law in Johnson City and, like his brother, visited the Washington County seat of Jonesborough frequently. (Courtesy of Caroline M. May.)

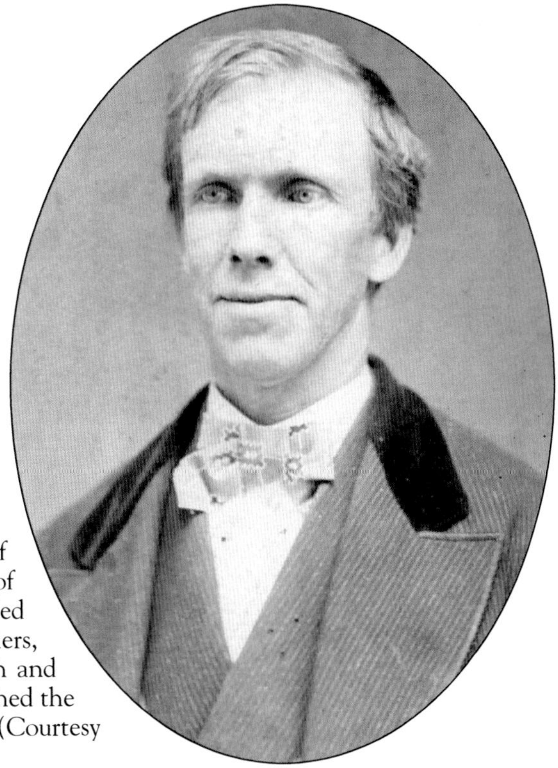

L.W. Keen took this photograph of Dr. M.S. Mahoney around the time of the Civil War. Since this area was traveled by both Union and Confederate soldiers, Mahoney treated soldiers from the North and South. In August 1869, Mahoney established the *Herald and Tribune* with Dr. C. Wheeler. (Courtesy of Caroline M. May.)

Nat Miller lived in the Embreeville community in the late 1800s. (Courtesy of John G. and Etta Love.)

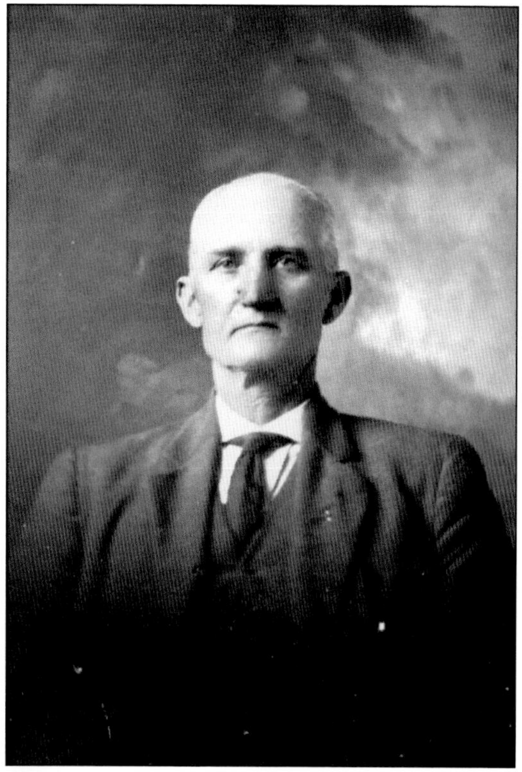

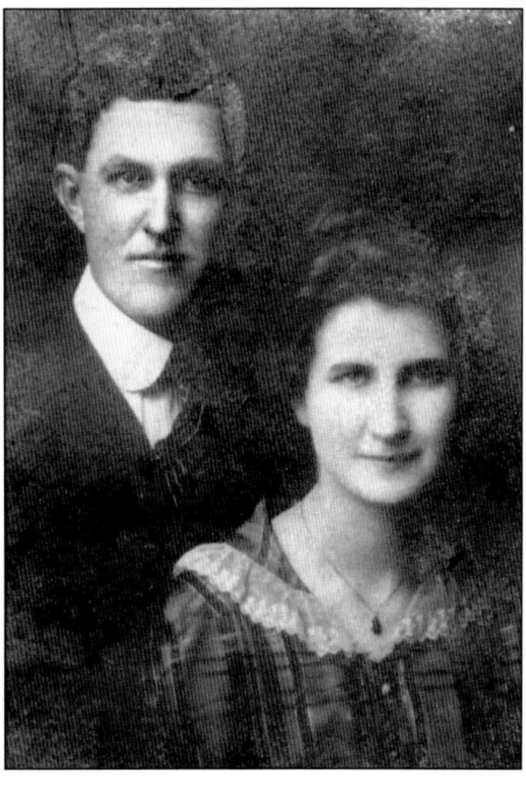

Walter Lee Love and Amelia Miller Love both grew up near the Nolichuckey River, married, and had four sons. After they were married, the Loves moved to Erwin and established the first dairy farm there. Amelia also taught music at local schools and privately. Walter lived from 1891 until 1980, and Amelia lived from 1896 until 1985. (Courtesy of John G. and Etta Love.)

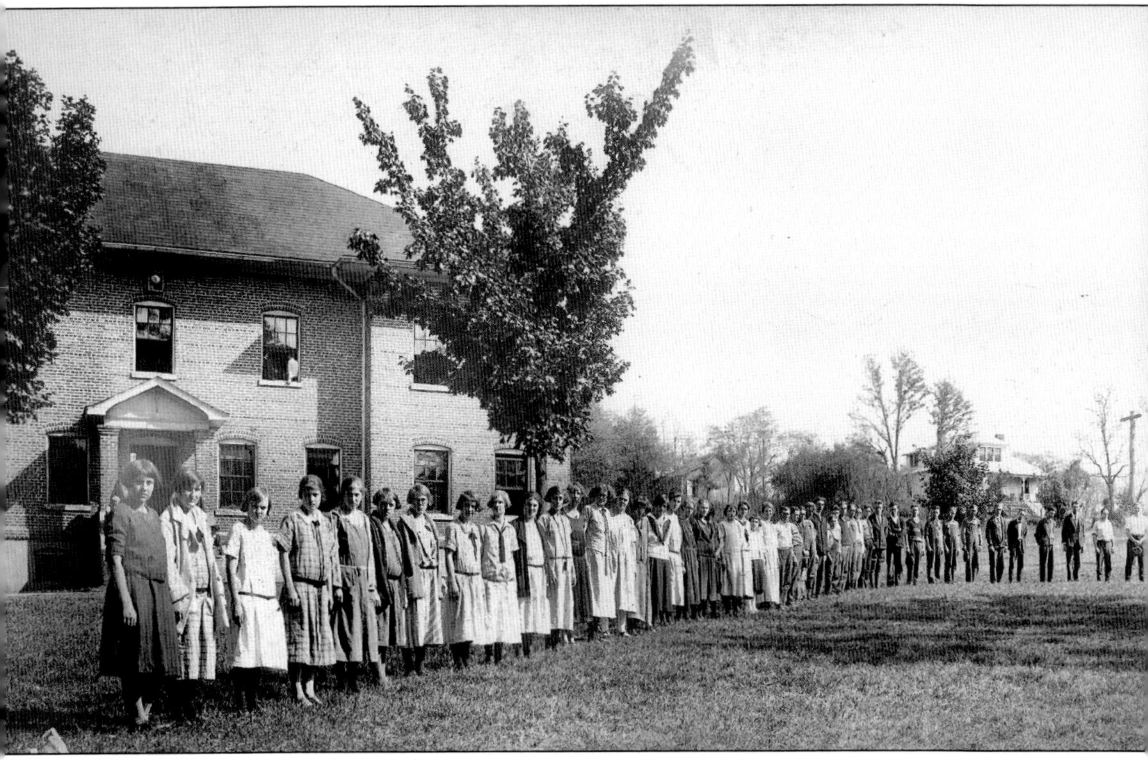

This is the "self-help family" from Washington College Academy in the 1920s. These students came from seven different states—Alabama, South Carolina, Tennessee, Virginia, West Virginia, Kentucky, and North Carolina. The students were "gathered from the Southern mountains. Five are orphans, several others have lost one parent. They can pay very little for their education, some cannot pay anything. Their ambition is so great that they are eager to work for their education." In exchange for their work, the students received room, board, and tuition for the school year of nine months. (Courtesy of Washington College Academy.)

Four

PEOPLE AT WORK

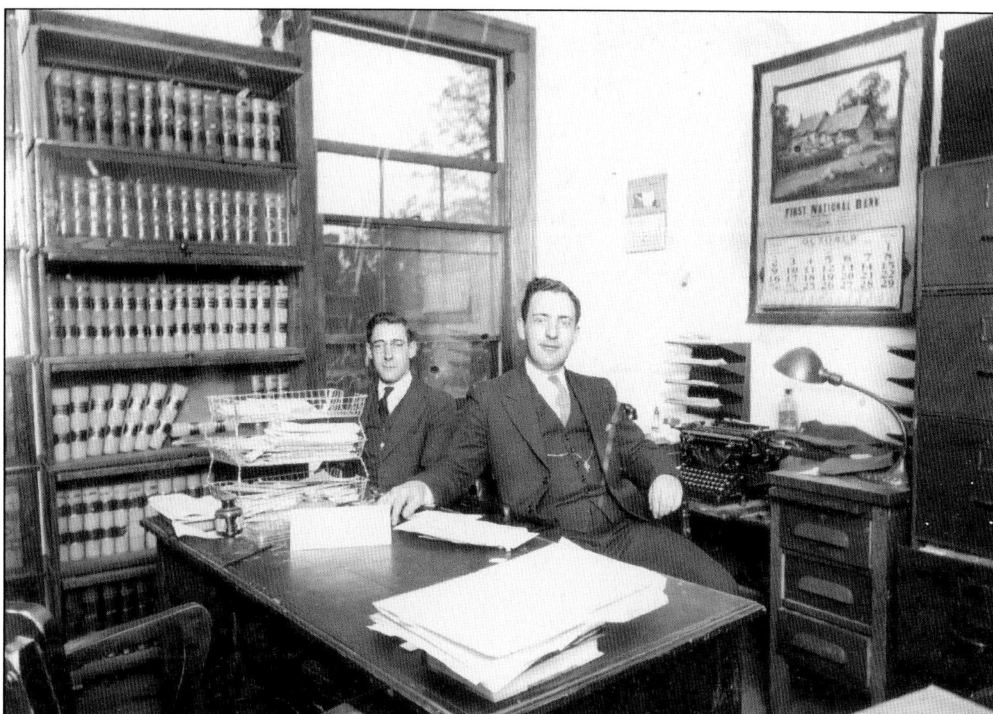

George Boyd and Robert May are shown here in October 1932 in May's first law office, which was located on Main Street. Robert May participated in the organization of the Washington County Historical Society in 1965. (Courtesy of Caroline M. May.)

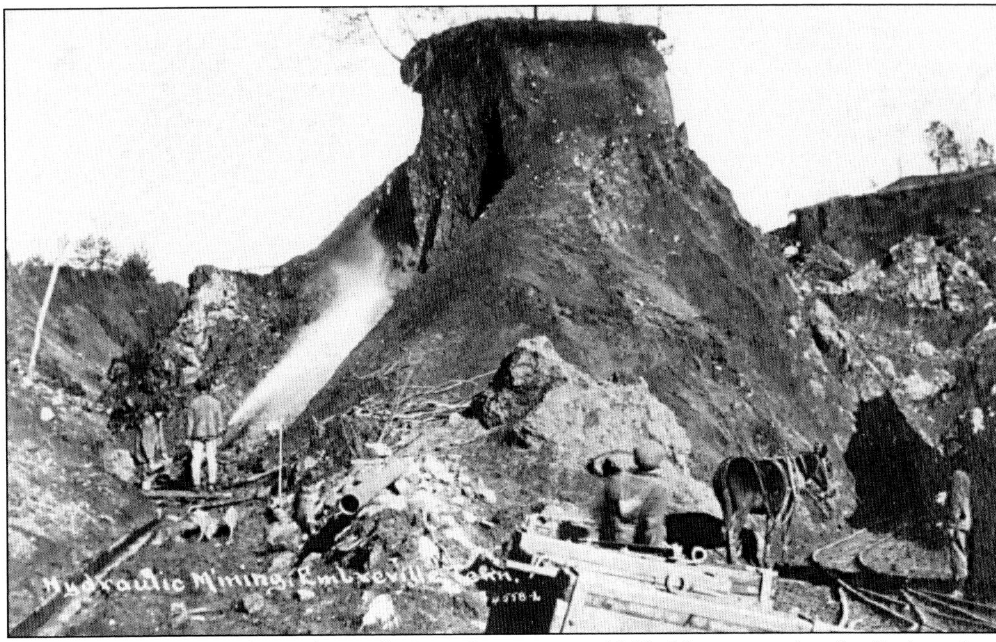

C.P. Perrin took over the Embreeville Iron Company in 1903. He renamed it the Embree Iron Company and introduced the method of hydraulic mining shown here. Iron was initially mined at Embreeville, but as the quality was poor as iron ore goes, containing only about 40 percent iron and zinc, in 1913, the mining of zinc began. Manganese mining began in 1932 and ended in 1960. (Courtesy of Chip White.)

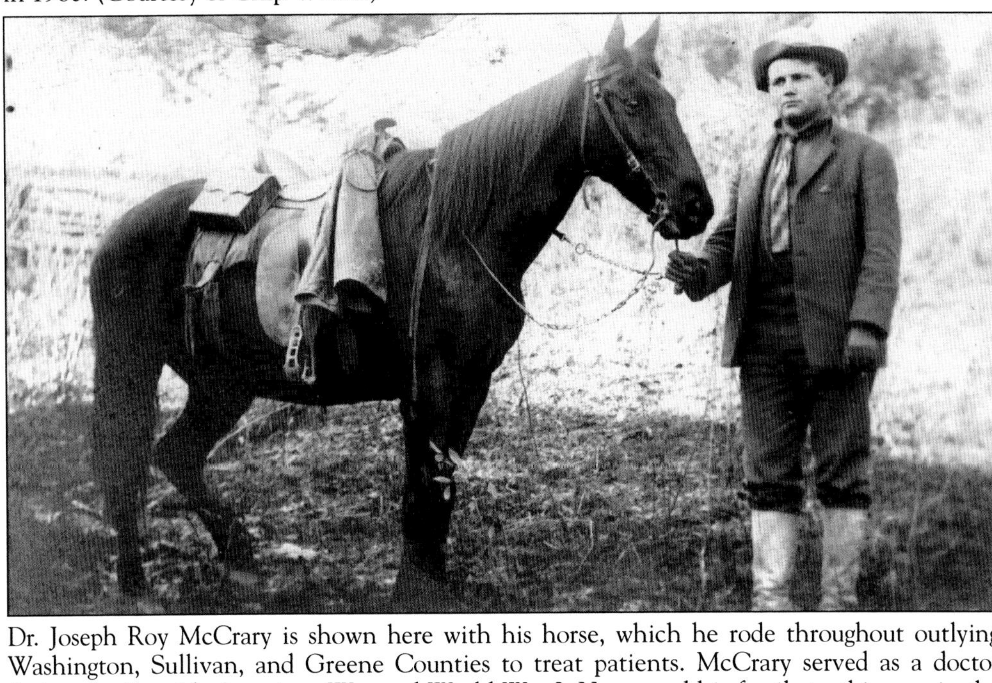

Dr. Joseph Roy McCrary is shown here with his horse, which he rode throughout outlying Washington, Sullivan, and Greene Counties to treat patients. McCrary served as a doctor during the Spanish-American War and World War I. He moved his family to this area in the early 1900s and lived in the Wells house in Fall Branch with his wife, Maude, and four children. (Courtesy of Helen Deakins McCrary.)

Eva Taylor is shown here with daughter, Jeanne Anne. Eva's brother, George Dillow, ran the Dillow Funeral Home. He had purchased the funeral home from the Keene family. When Eva was widowed with a small child, she went into business with her brother and created the Dillow-Taylor Funeral Home, which has been in business since 1929. (Courtesy of Jeanne Anne Alexander.)

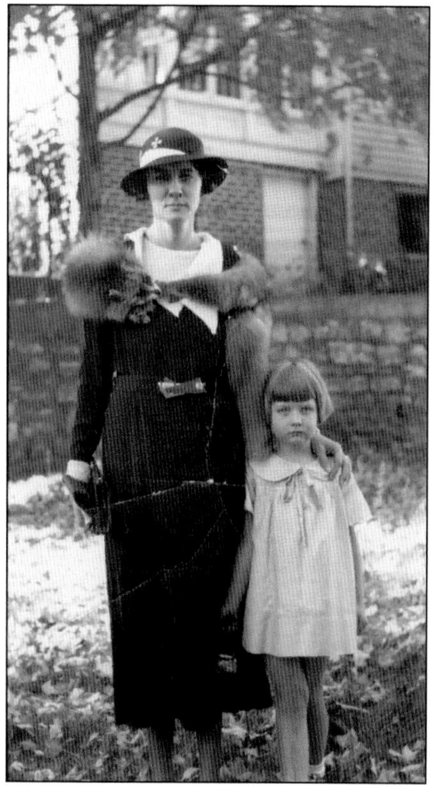

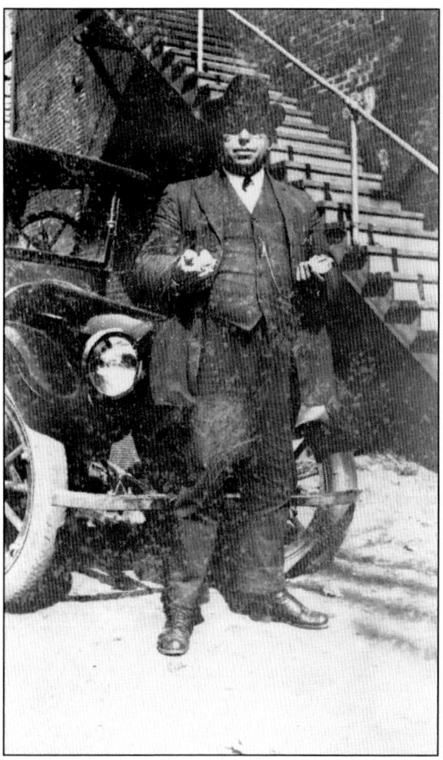

Drs. Samuel B. Cunningham, W.H. McCollum, Spencer E. Gibson, W.T.M. Outlaw, and John E. Cossum were only a few of the early doctors who traveled by horseback to visit their patients in the 1800s. Dr. G.C. Horne, shown here, and Drs. Blaine Mitchell and Jerry Atkinson came after the turn of the century and served the community until the mid-1960s. (Courtesy of George Robert Campbell.)

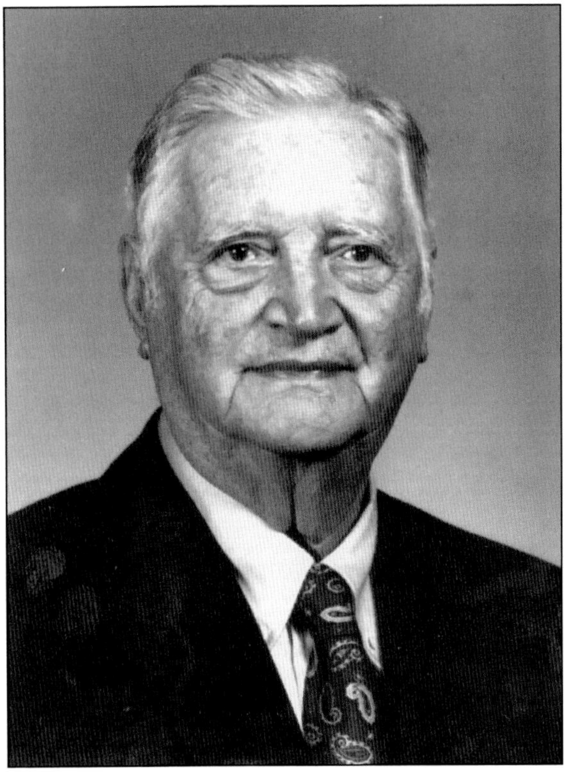

Lyle Haws was mayor of Jonesborough from 1966 through 1972. Tennessee legislature had just passed a law in 1965 enabling towns to begin preservation efforts. Haws appointed a historic commission, helped form the Jonesborough Civic Trust, and assisted in the application to name Jonesborough on the National Register of Historic Places. (Courtesy of Lyle Haws.)

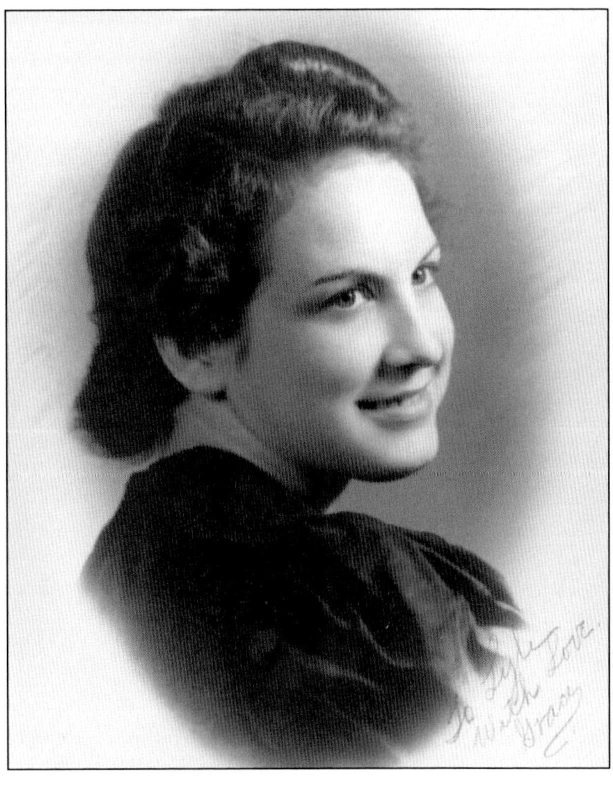

Grace Alice Shipley Haws was the daughter of Philip Andrew and Amie Olivean Stout. This photograph was taken when Grace was young, but the personalized sentimental note to her future husband is worth saving. Like husband Lyle, Grace also served as mayor of Jonesborough, from 1976 to 1978 and assisted in forming the first Jonesborough Days event. Grace Haws passed away on April 12, 1993. (Courtesy of Lyle Haws.)

In the late 1940s when Jackie Bair was 16, he began playing drums for Warren Brown & His Country Gentlemen, a band that advertised itself as "playing and singing the latest in both popular and hillbilly music." Bair also played with the Bob Woods Band. Much of the entertainment took place at the American Legion/Woodland Lake building. (Courtesy of Jackie and Pat Bair.)

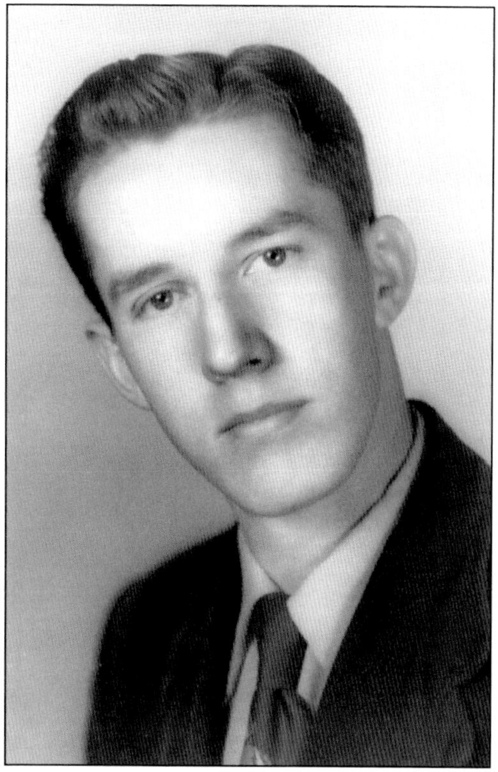

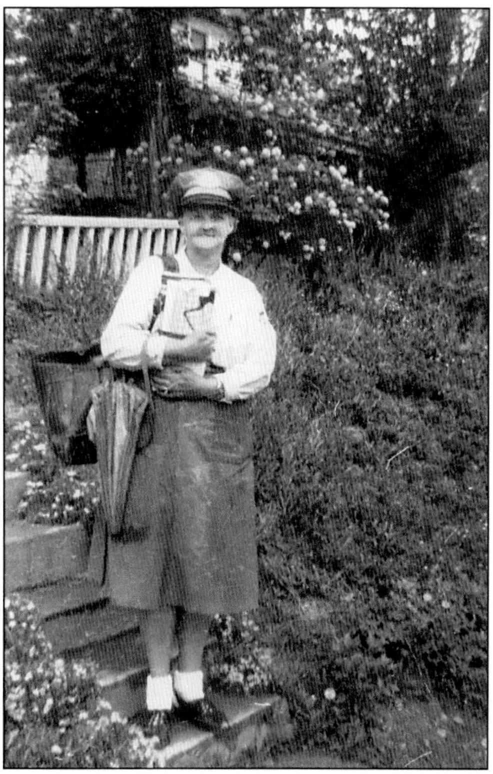

An unidentified postal lady carries mail throughout Jonesborough, a large portion of which was Route 1. Although this photograph is from the 20th century, a post office had been established in Jonesborough by 1796. Initially, mail delivery was about once per week, and mail was picked up at the home or store of the postmaster. (Courtesy of Chuck and Nancy Mason.)

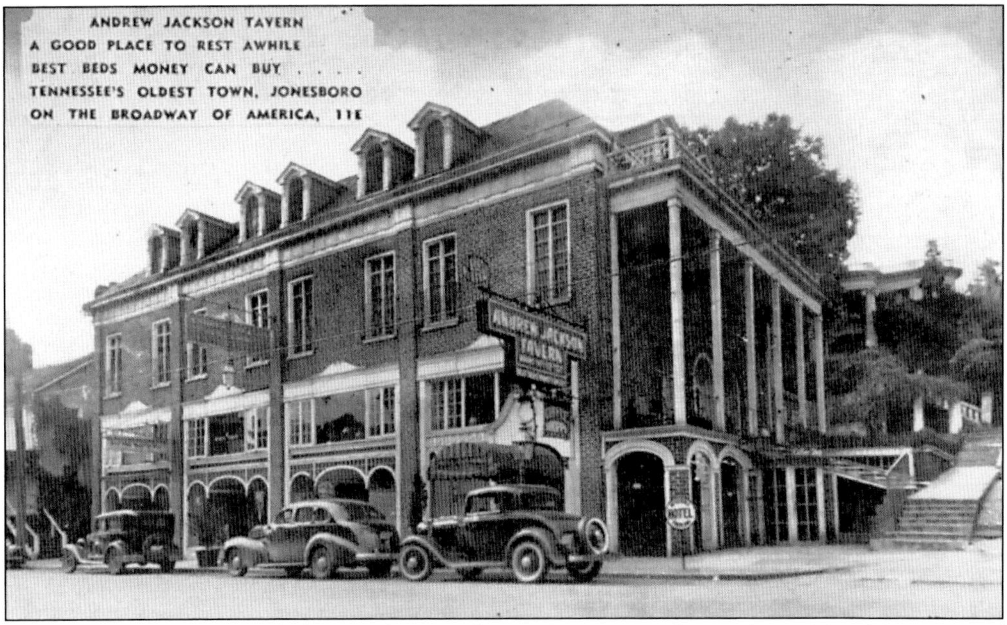

This is a photograph of the Andrew Jackson Tavern in the early 1900s. (Courtesy of Betty Jane Hylton.)

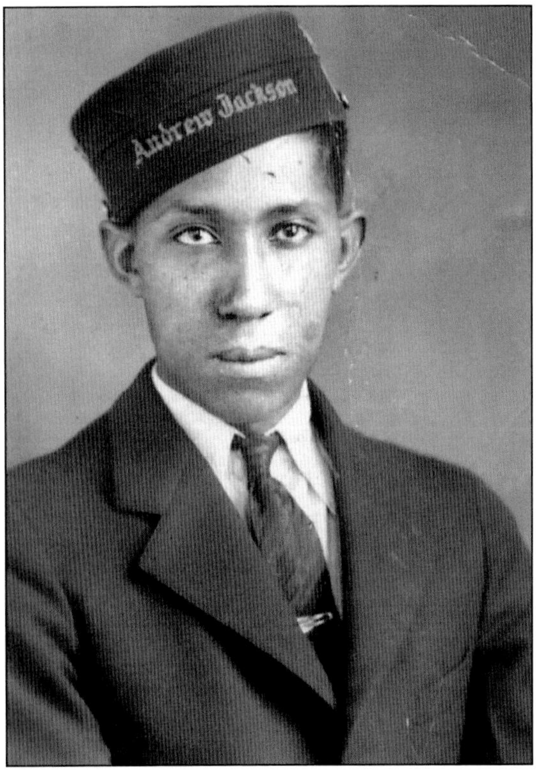

Gentry Fitzgerald (1912–1994) worked at the Andrew Jackson Tavern as a bellhop in the late 1920s and 1930s. He later became a pastor and ministered for 43 years. Gentry Fitzgerald's son Jerome has served as an alderman in Jonesborough since 1996. (Courtesy of Jerome Fitzgerald.)

Gabriel Morgan arrived from Virginia *c.* 1800 and built this grist mill on a cliff at the head of these beautiful, cascading falls. The family lived in a large frame house, which is still standing, near the mill. The large creek at the top of the 75-foot falls is fed by seven freshwater springs. (Courtesy of Jerry Deakins.)

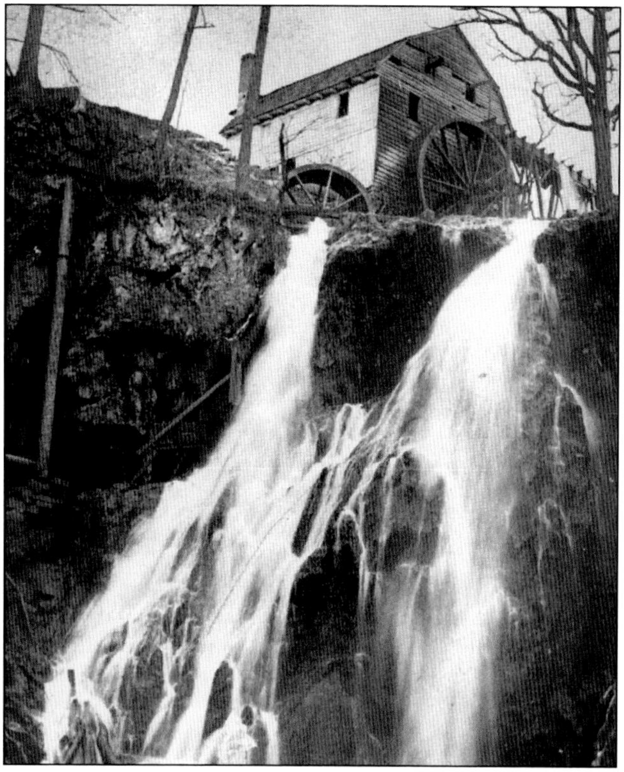

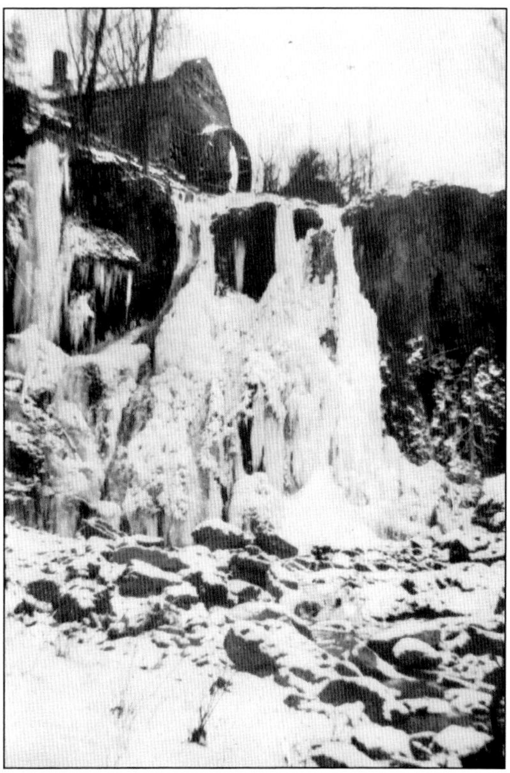

Here is a gorgeous shot of the mill atop the frozen falls in winter. The creek around Fall Branch Falls has been known as Horse Creek since the late 1700s. The story is told that a great flash flood carried some horses down the creek and over the falls, where they drowned at the base of the falls, thus named Horse Creek. (Courtesy of Jean Barnes Dawson.)

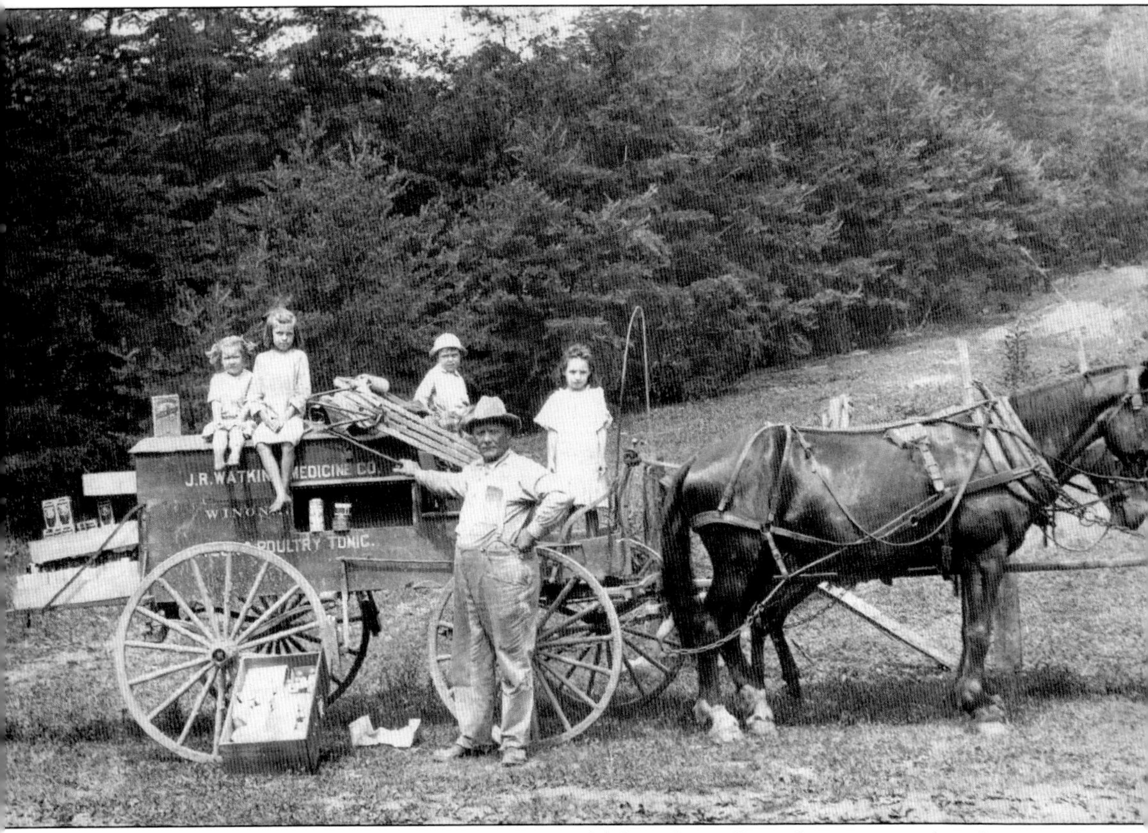

With his horse and buggy, an entrepreneur could drive his rolling pharmacy, and in this case, his children, throughout the countryside selling medicinal supplies to local farmers. The side of the buggy says, "J.R. Watkins Medicine Co." and lists poultry tonic as one item for sale, though it is certain he also carried supplies for human consumption as well. This photo was taken in the Garbers community, which is located on Little Cherokee Creek. (Courtesy of Chip White.)

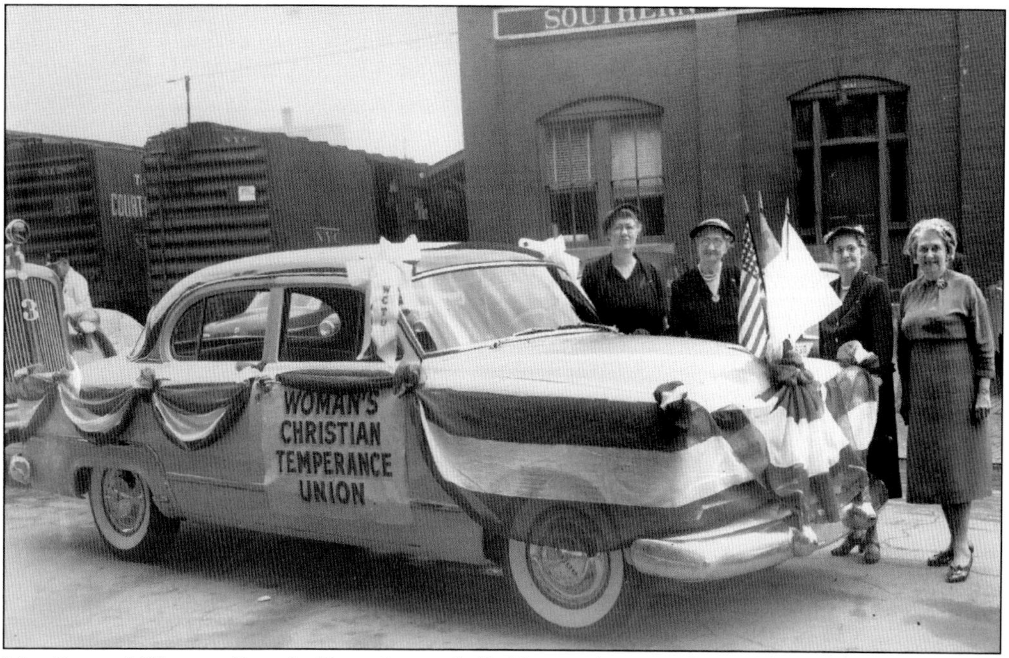

Mrs. Samuel Clemens Beard of Jonesborough (left) served as president of the Women's Christian Temperance Union. Mrs. Beard spoke throughout the state for the cause of prohibition, including a 15-minute presentation she gave to the state senate on February 12, 1953. (Courtesy of the Schubert Club and the Jonesborough Public Library.)

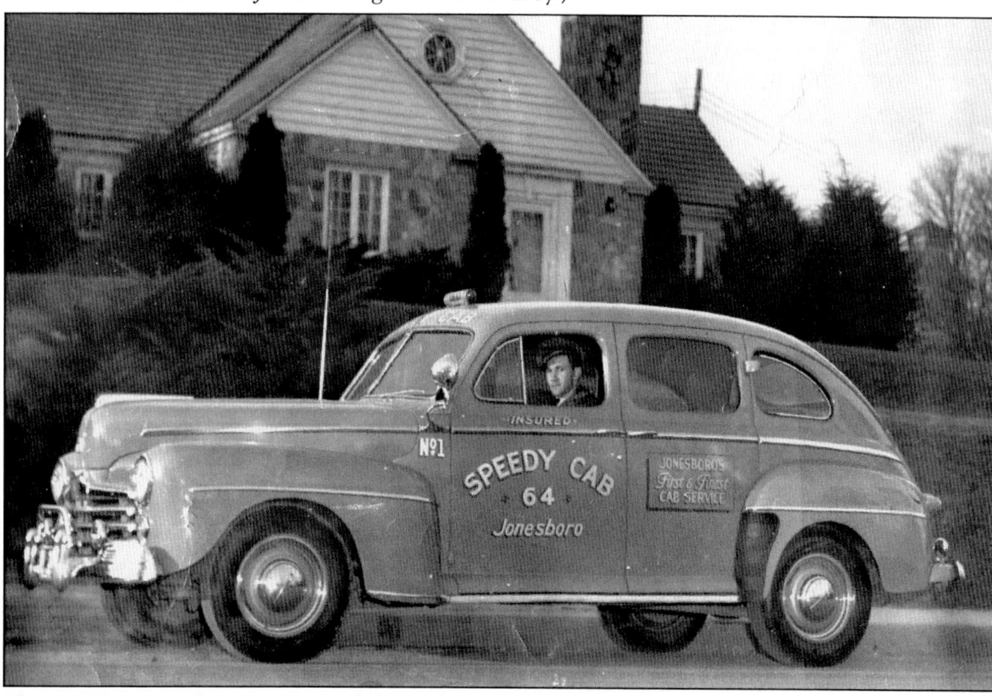

Elmer Mottern, known around Jonesborough as "Speedy," began Jonesborough's first automobile cab company. Shown here *c.* 1946, Mottern had five cabs in his business. (Courtesy of Rose Mottern.)

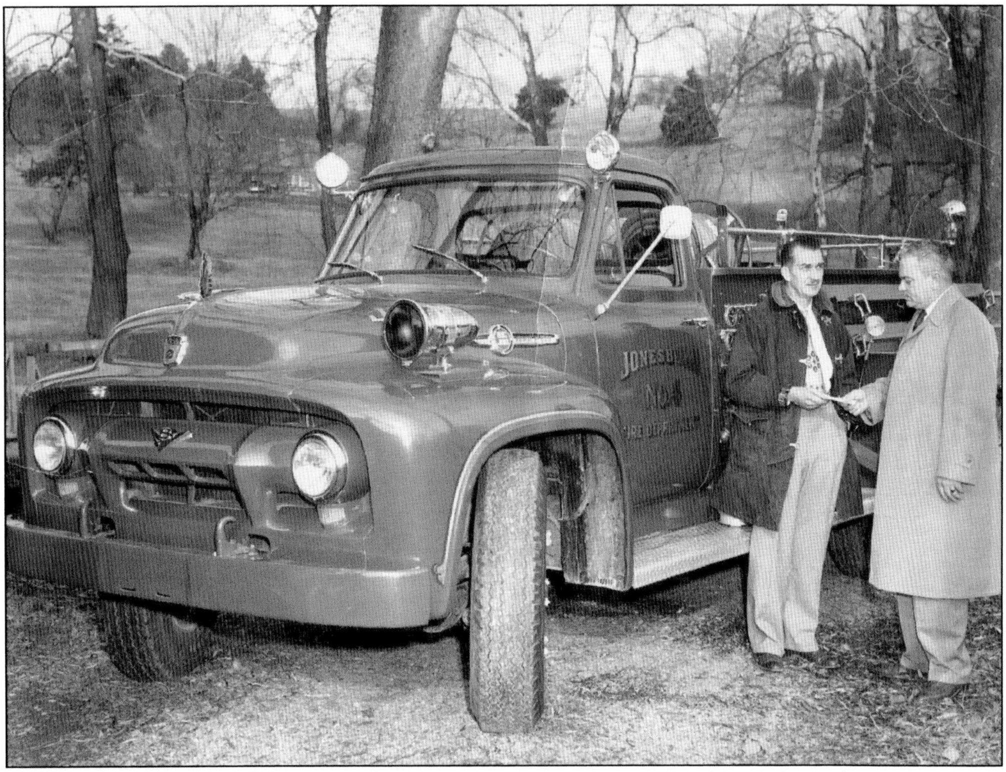

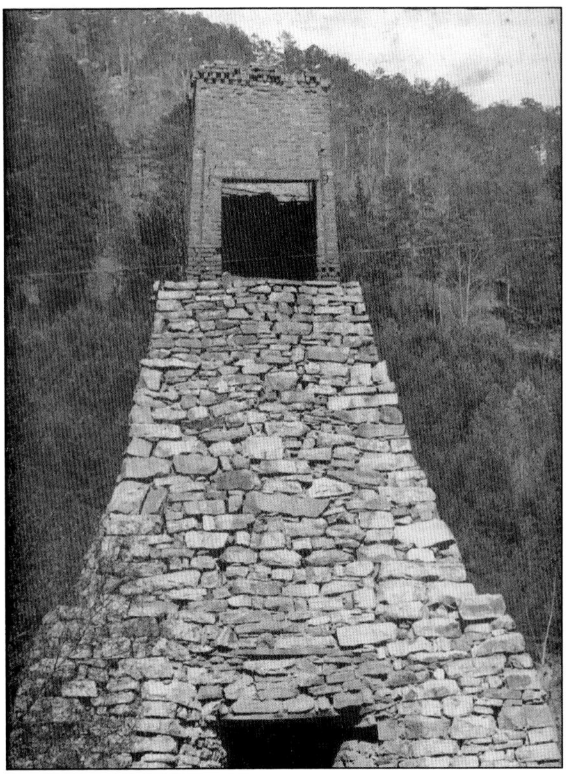

Ivan Good (right), with the Tennessee Motor Company, presents Wilber Weems, Jonesborough's fire chief, with the keys to a new fire truck for the town of Jonesborough. (Courtesy of Rose Mottern.)

William P. Chester purchased 260 acres of land near the mouth of Bumpass Cove in 1812 to forge for iron ore. He sold this forge to Elijah and Elihu Embree, from whom came the name of the Embreeville Iron Company and community. Shown here is a stone iron blast furnace. (Courtesy of Washington County Clerk's Office.)

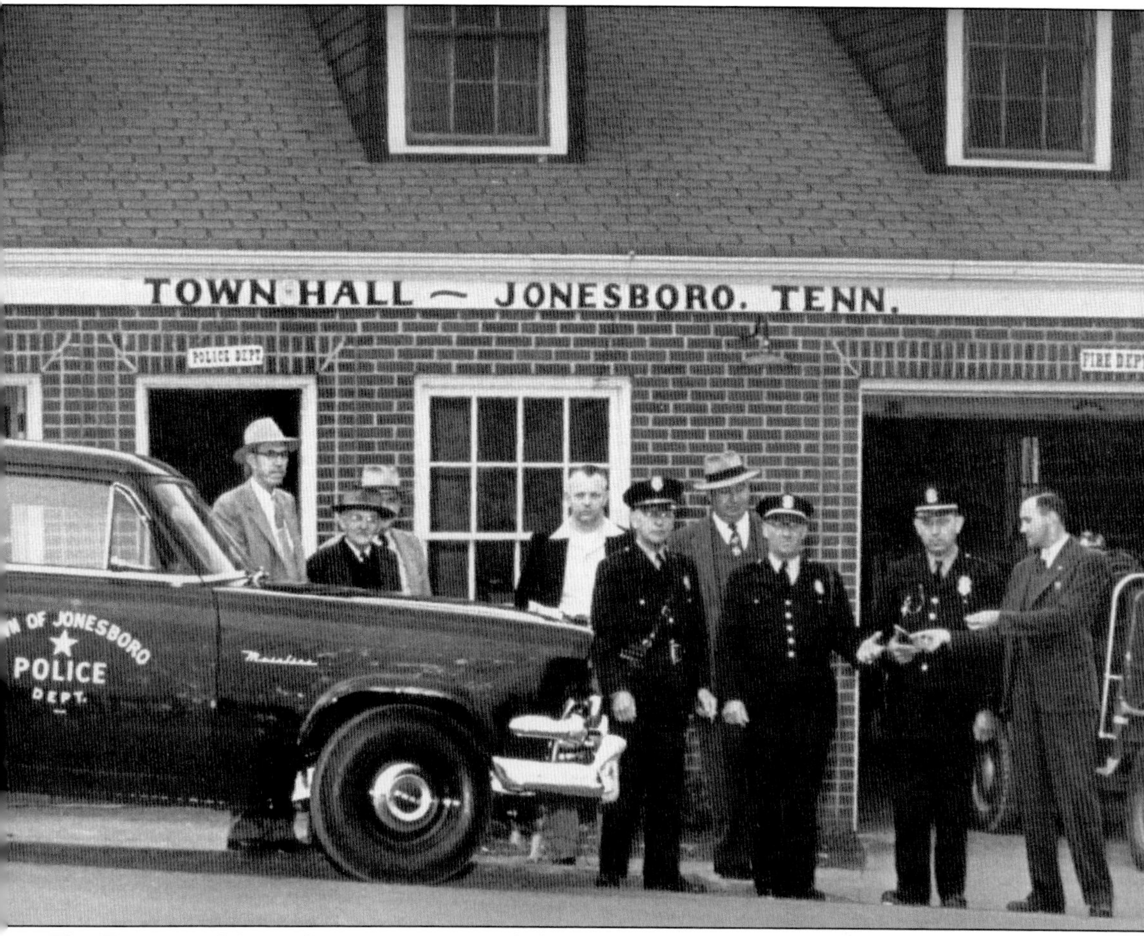

The Tennessee Motor Company presented the town of Jonesborough with its first cruiser in February 1954. In attendance, from left to right, were Dewey H. Byrd, Charley Deakins, Bob May (mayor), Niles Osburn, Bill Daniels, "Tiny" Hale, Scott Vines, Jim Shaw, and Speedy Mottern. (Courtesy of the Jonesborough Department of Public Safety, Haskel Greene, and D.H. Byrd.)

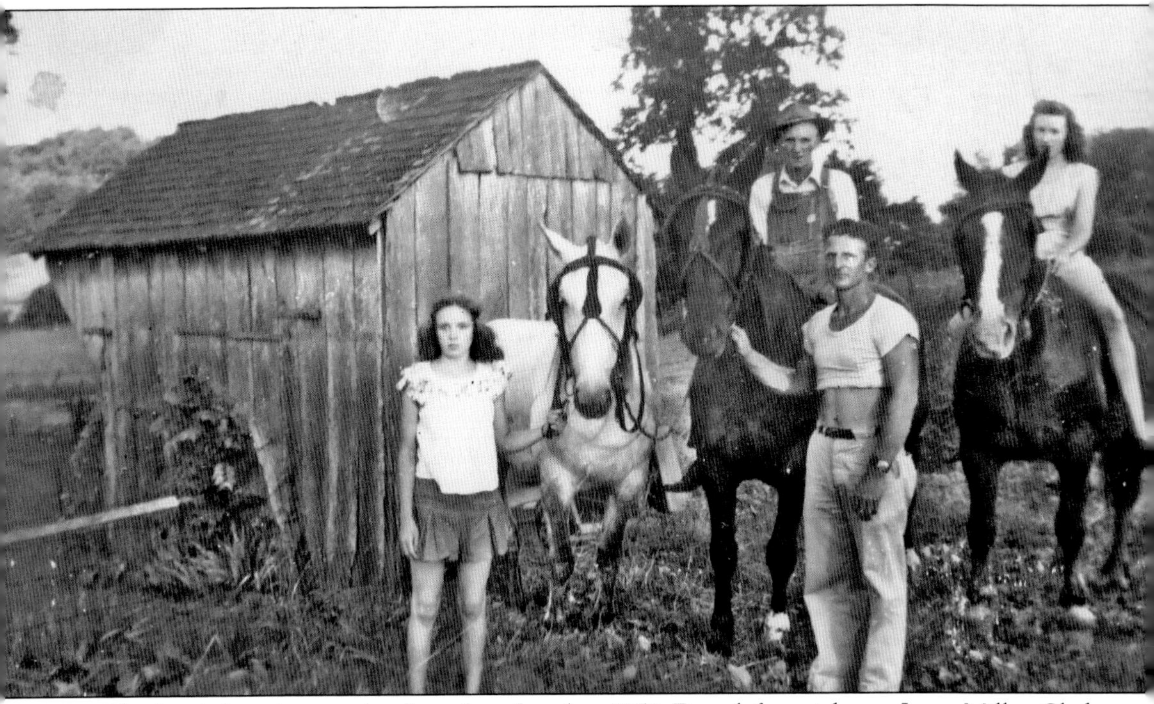

The family here is preparing for a day of work *c.* 1950. From left to right are Joyce Miller, Clyde Miller (on the horse), unidentified, and June Miller. The girls were teenagers; these must have been work clothes as they would not have been traveling around town dressed this way. (Courtesy of Clarence and Linda Bailey.)

Five

EDUCATION

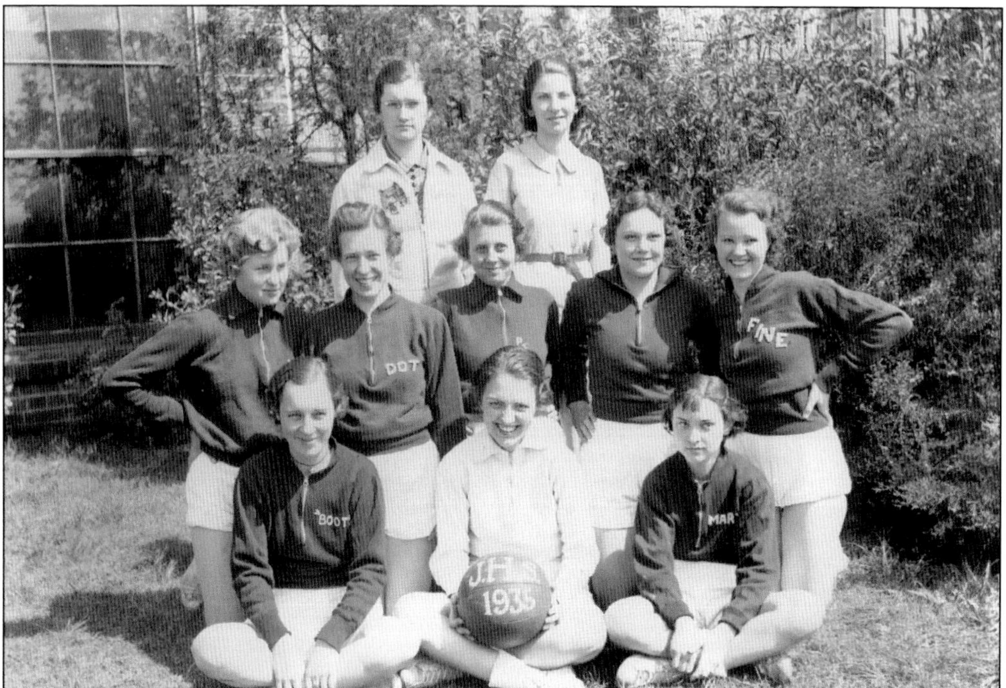

Members of the girls' basketball team for Jonesborough High School in 1935 flash charming smiles for the photographer. (Courtesy of Barbara G. Smith.)

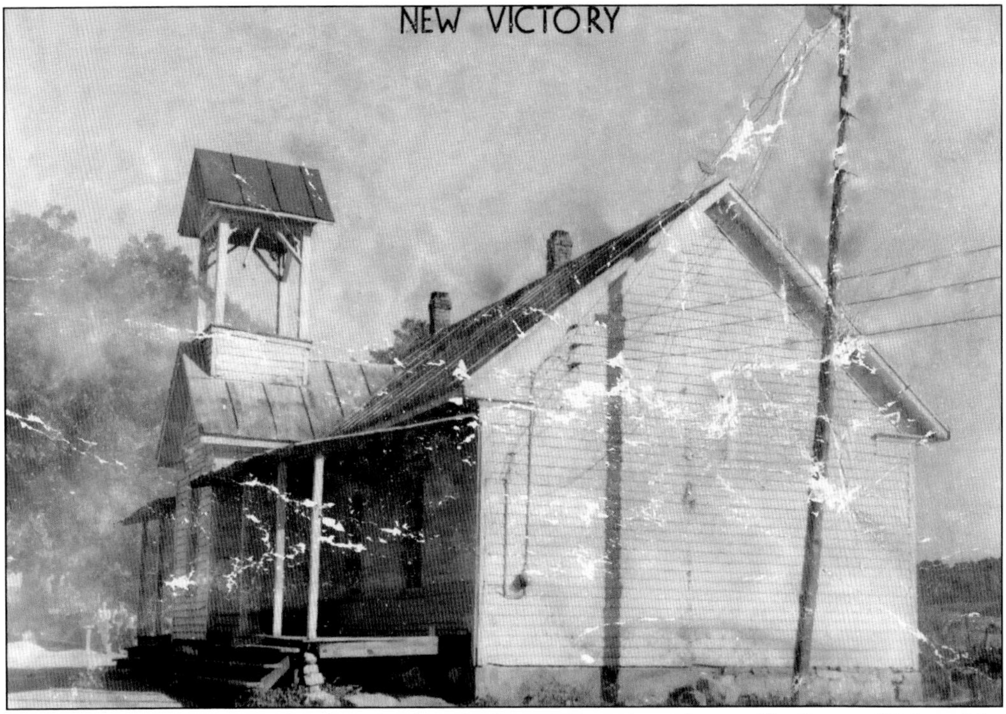

New Victory Elementary School was built in the late 1800s on land donated by George W. Sprinkle. The school was torn down in the 1950s. (Courtesy of Washington County Schools.)

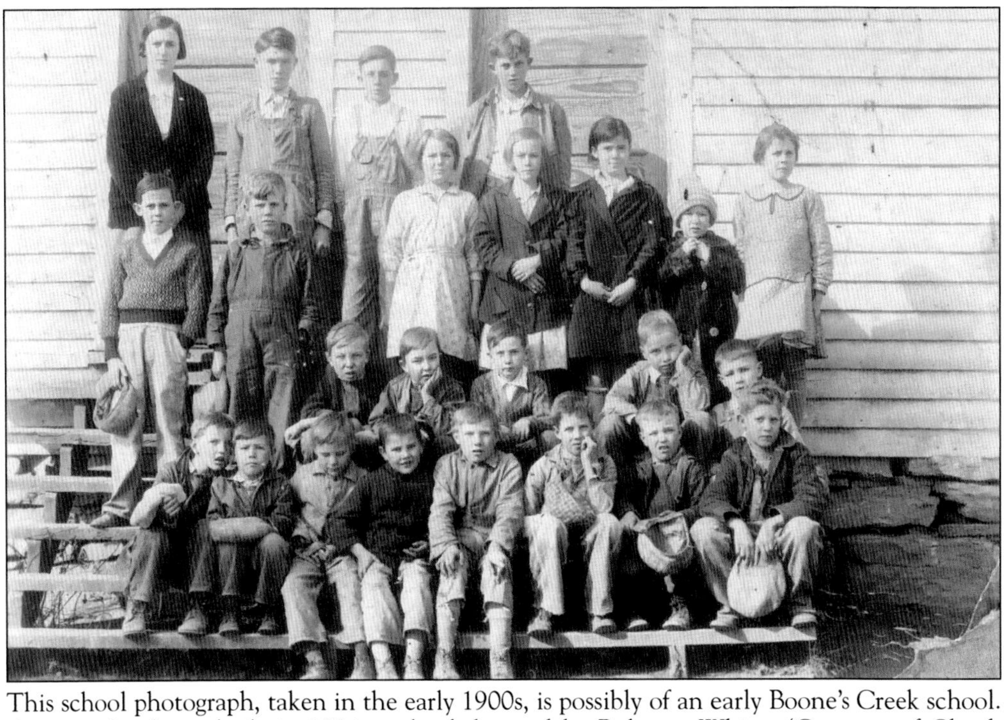

This school photograph, taken in the early 1900s, is possibly of an early Boone's Creek school. A new school was built in 1924 on land donated by Rebecca White. (Courtesy of Chuck and Nancy Mason.)

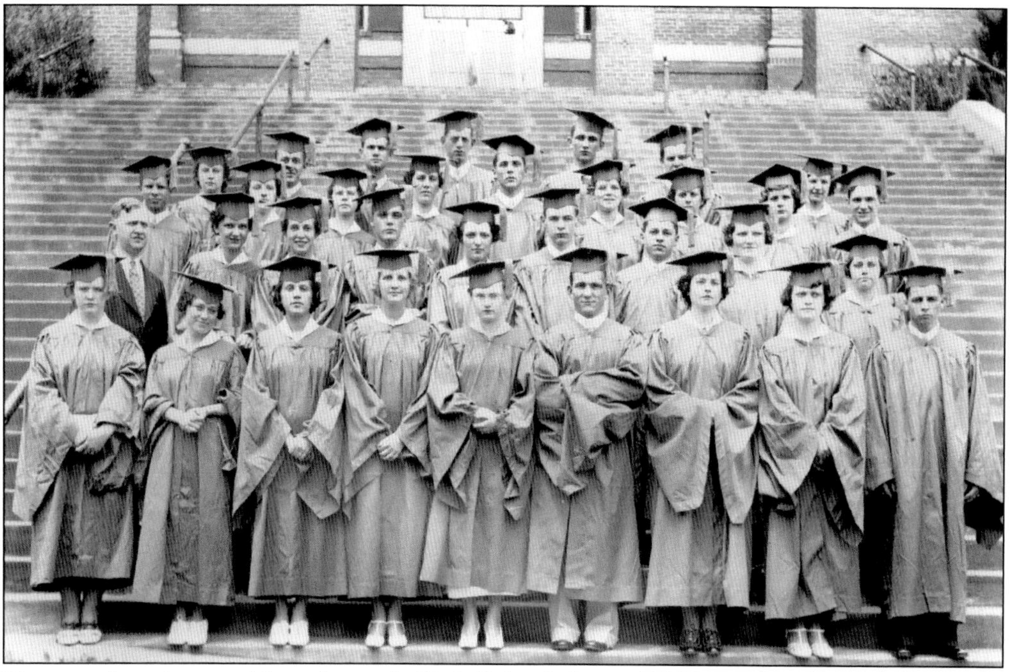

The proud graduates of Jonesborough High School class of 1935 stand in front of their alma mater. The man on the far left in the second row is W.C. Morrison, principal. (Courtesy of Barbara G. Smith.)

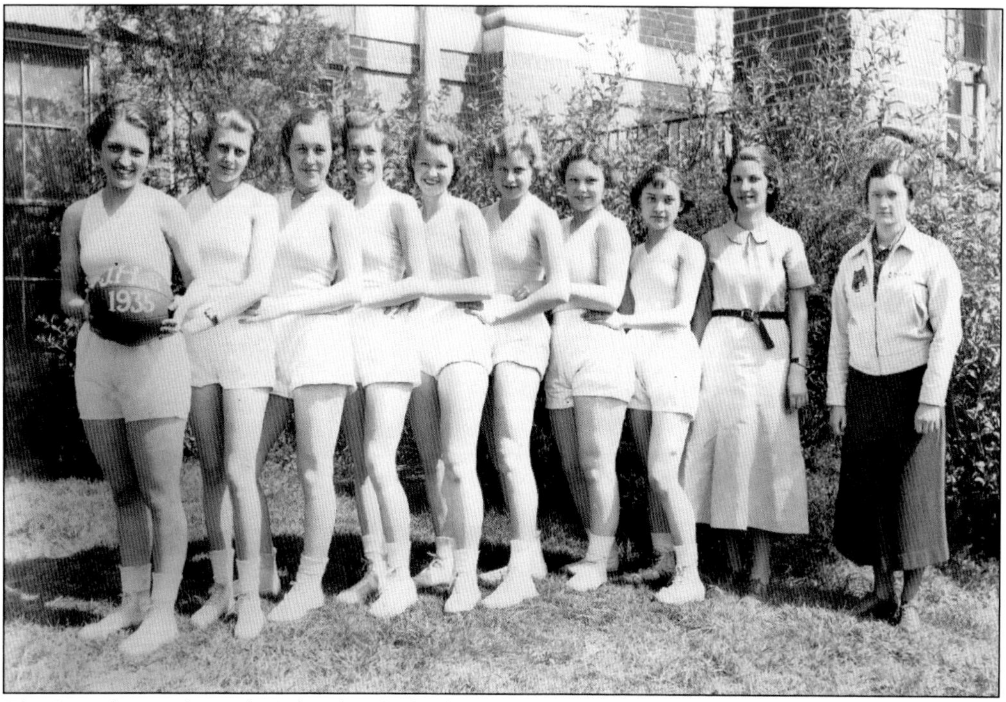

The Jonesborough High School girls' basketball team posed for this photo in 1935. Dorothy Landreth is the fourth player from the left. She lived from December 23, 1916, until December 12, 1996. (Courtesy of Barbara G. Smith.)

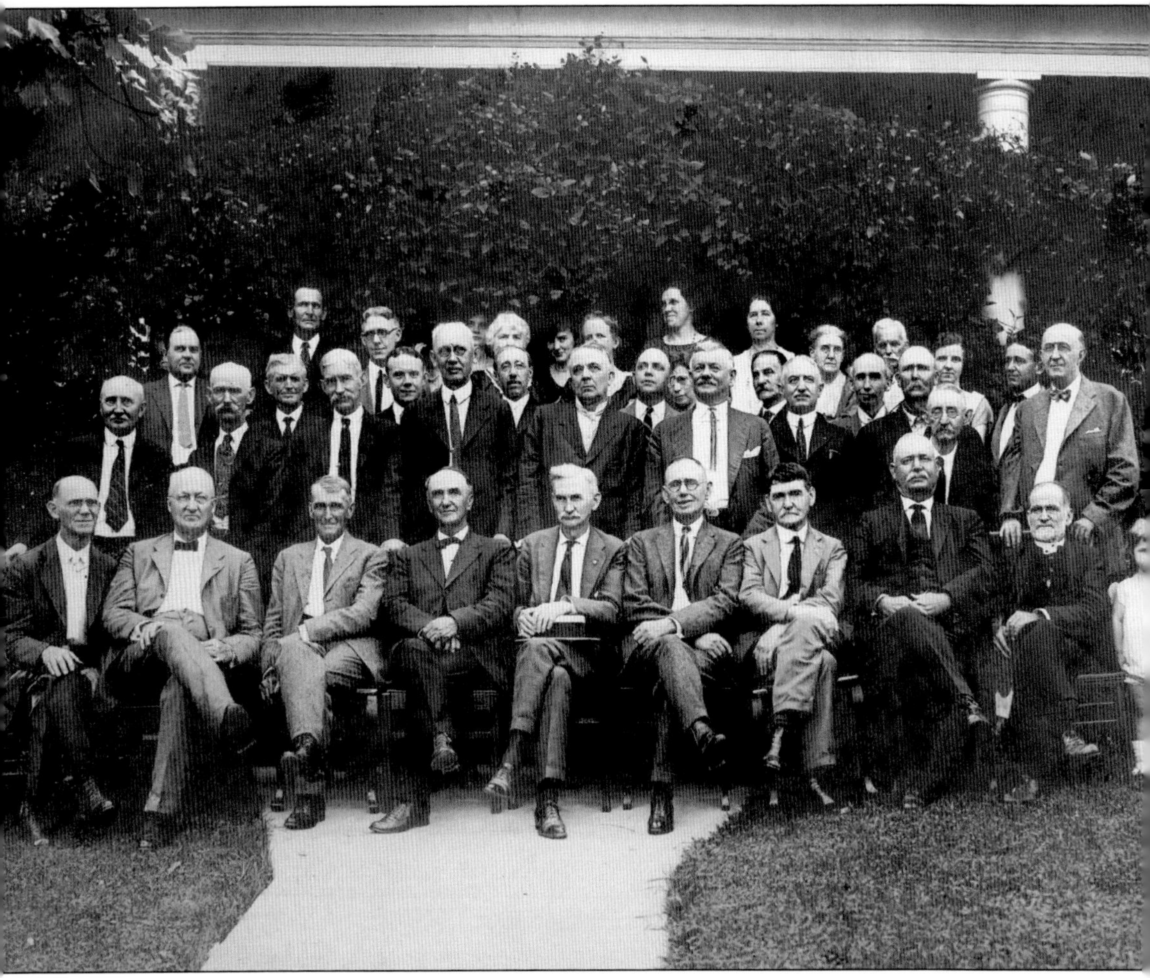

While most students call themselves after their alma maters, the Dungan boys called themselves after the man who established the school. Confederate colonel Robert Dungan established the Holston Male Institute, shown on the next page, in 1867, and it closed in 1875 when it was sold to Quakers to establish a school for freed African Americans. A few of the Dungan boys in this picture are Wright Hoss, John T. Wilds, W.S. Hickey, Frank S. Patton, and F.B. Poteat. The photo was taken during Jonesborough's sesquicentennial celebrations on July 4, 1930. (Courtesy of Caroline Metzgar May.)

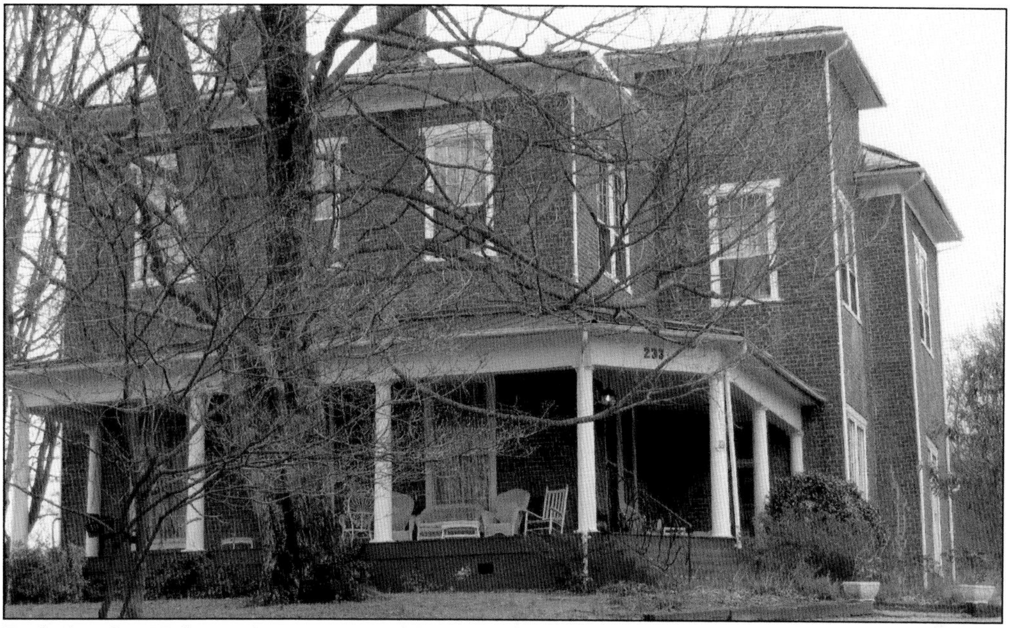

Built by the Holston Association of Baptist churches in 1854, this building served as the Holston Baptist Female Institute, Tadlock's School for Boys, and the Holston Male Institute, operated by Col. Robert Dungan. In 1876, Yardley Warner, a Quaker, purchased the building and established Warner Institute to educate freed African Americans. The school closed soon after the public school system began in 1910. (Photograph by the author.)

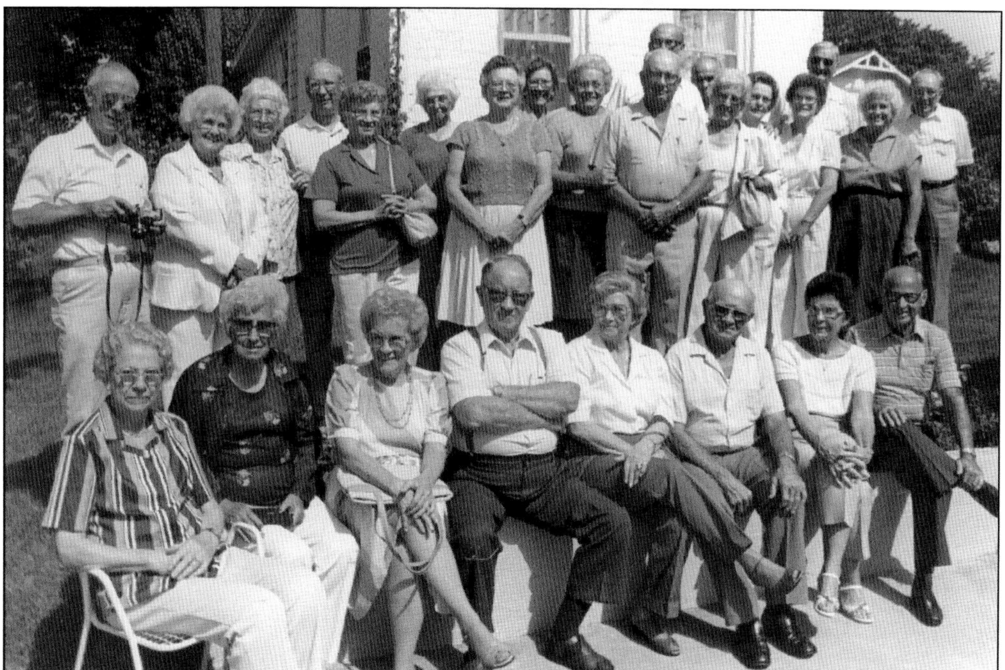

The Jonesborough High School class of 1932 held a 50-year reunion in 1982. Although most are unidentified, on the far left of the first row is Miriam Fink and the second man from the right in the back row is Lyle Haws. (Courtesy of Lyle Haws.)

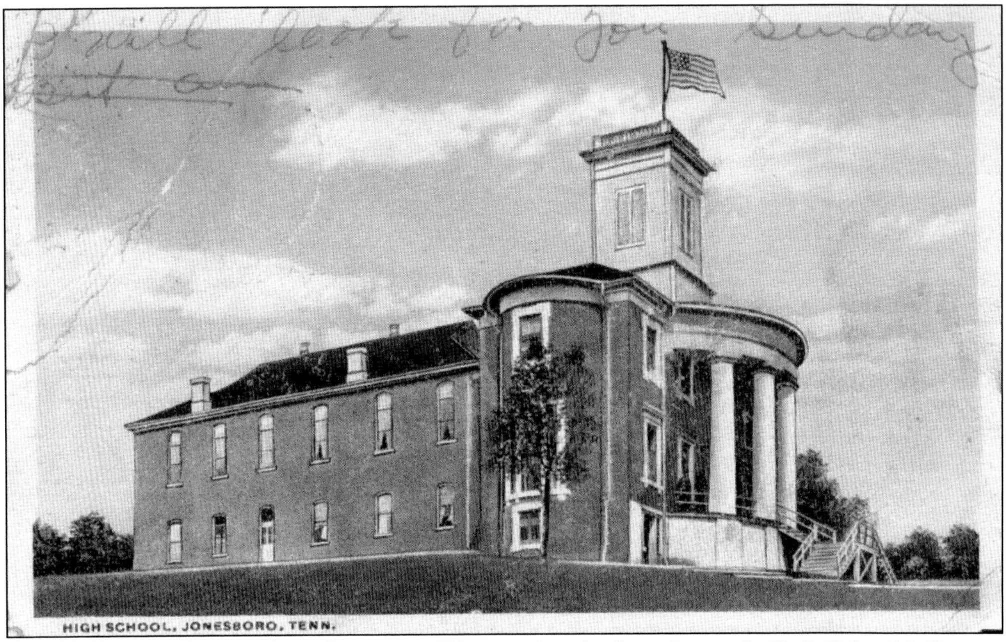

This building, which was torn down in 1927, served as the Jonesborough High School following the Civil War. A new school was built and put into use from 1926 to 1950, when what is now the Jonesborough Middle School was built to house grades 7 through 12. David Crockett High School opened in the fall of 1971. (Courtesy of Paul Stone.)

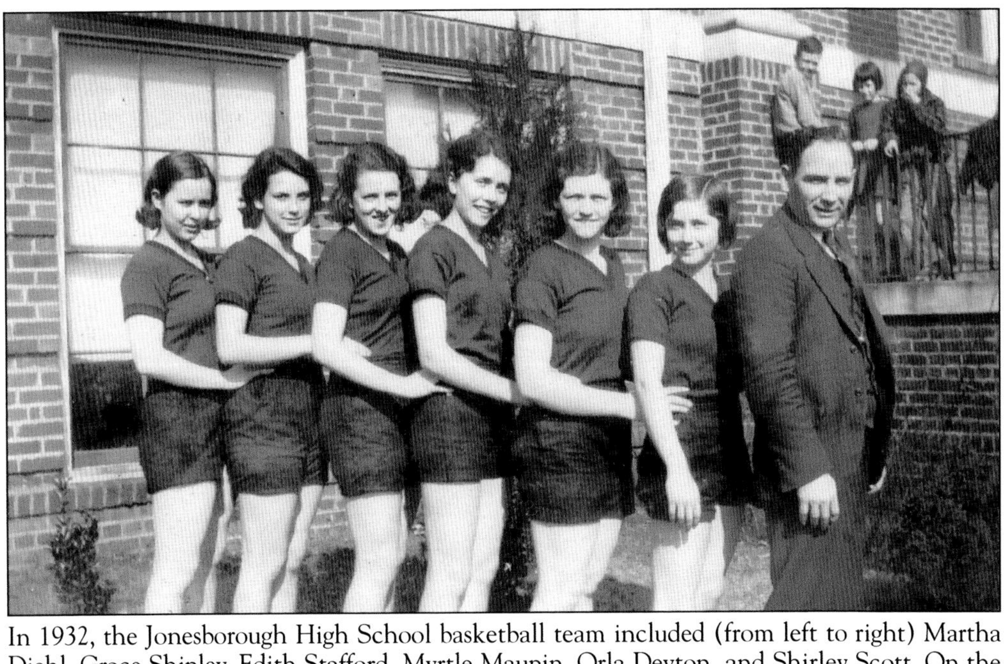

In 1932, the Jonesborough High School basketball team included (from left to right) Martha Diehl, Grace Shipley, Edith Stafford, Myrtle Maupin, Orla Deyton, and Shirley Scott. On the right is Coach Boswell. (Courtesy of Lyle Haws.)

The MacDowell Juvenile Music Club was quite popular among young residents of Jonesborough. Today, the participants' eyes still light up with joy and pride when discussing the club's events. (Courtesy of Jeanne Anne Alexander.)

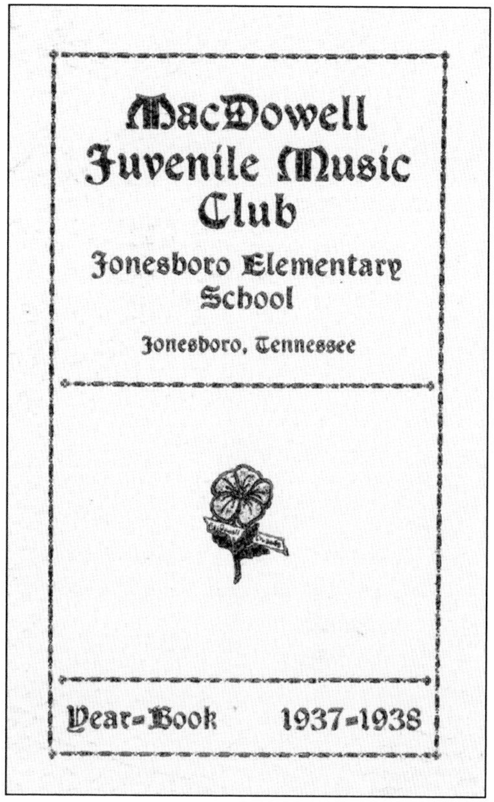

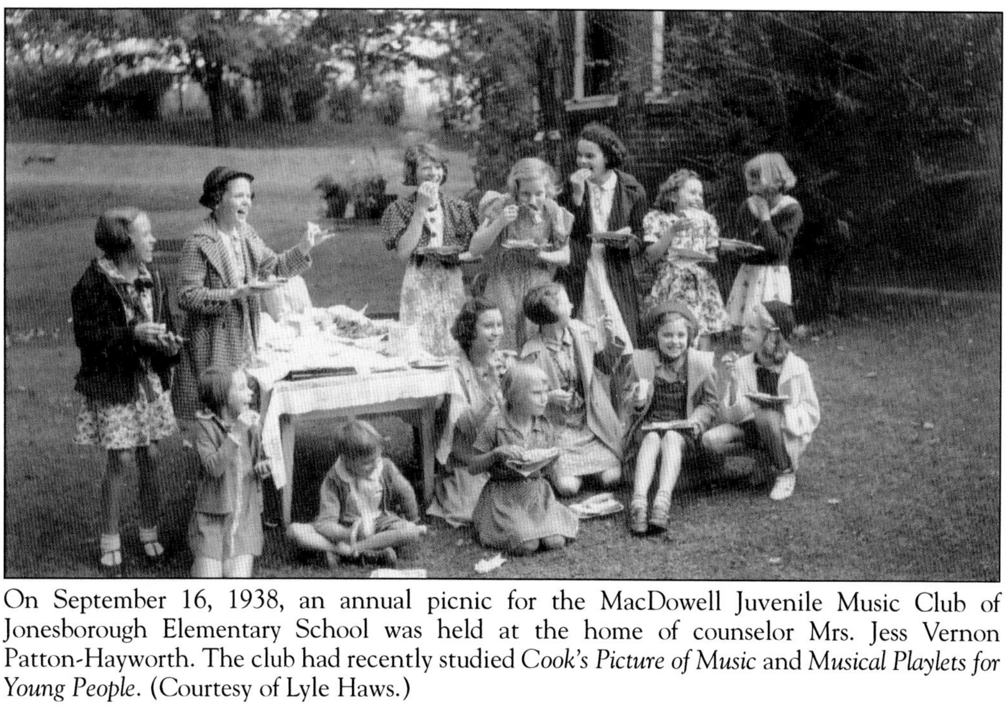

On September 16, 1938, an annual picnic for the MacDowell Juvenile Music Club of Jonesborough Elementary School was held at the home of counselor Mrs. Jess Vernon Patton-Hayworth. The club had recently studied *Cook's Picture of Music* and *Musical Playlets for Young People*. (Courtesy of Lyle Haws.)

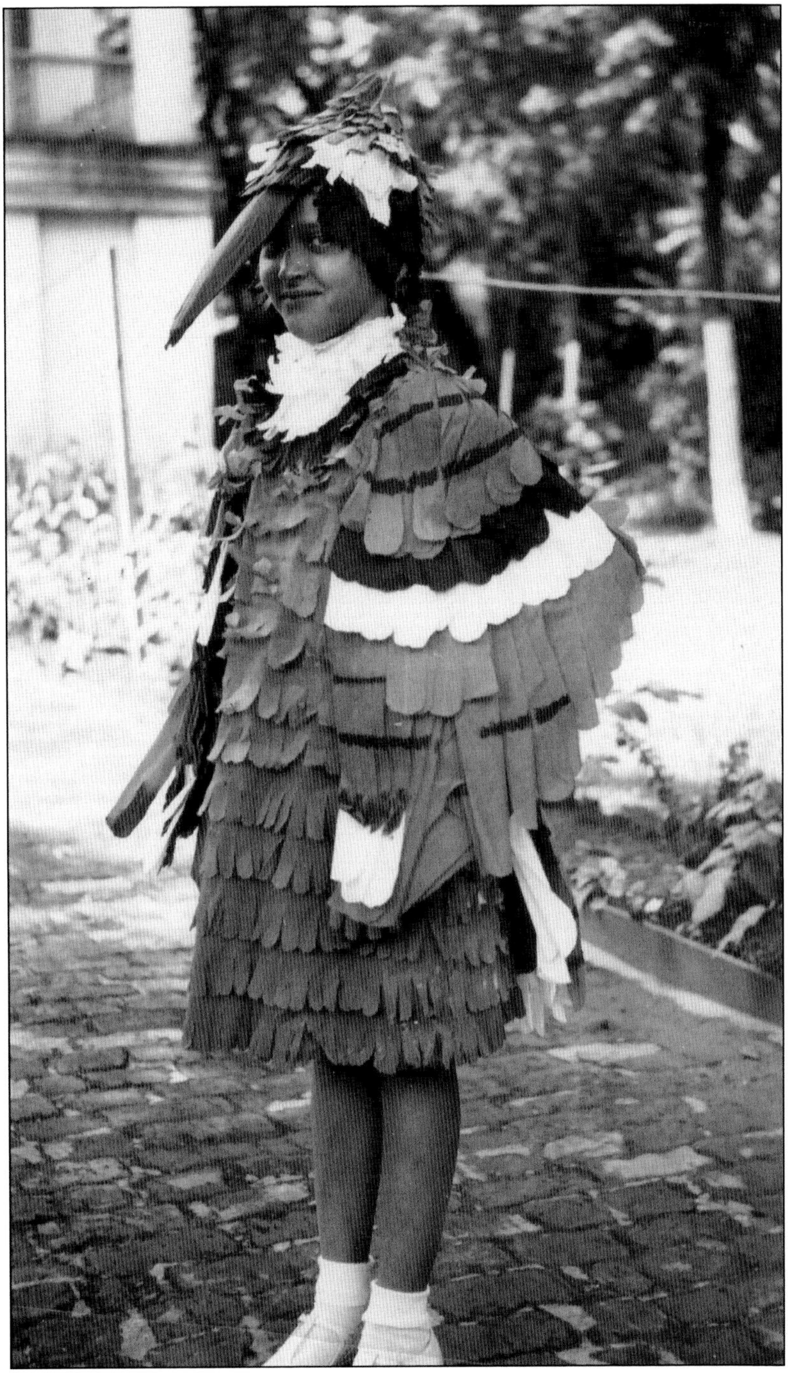

In May 1939, the MacDowell Juvenile Music Club held a bird program in costume at the Jonesborough High School auditorium. Norma Jean Dillow, pictured here, won first prize, a club pin, for the best costume. Elizabeth Fink and Janet Diehl tied for the prize of a junior gold pin for the best piano solo. The music club frequently held programs and events and studied various music-related topics. They also had an American composers program and a Tennessee composers program. (Courtesy of Lyle Haws.)

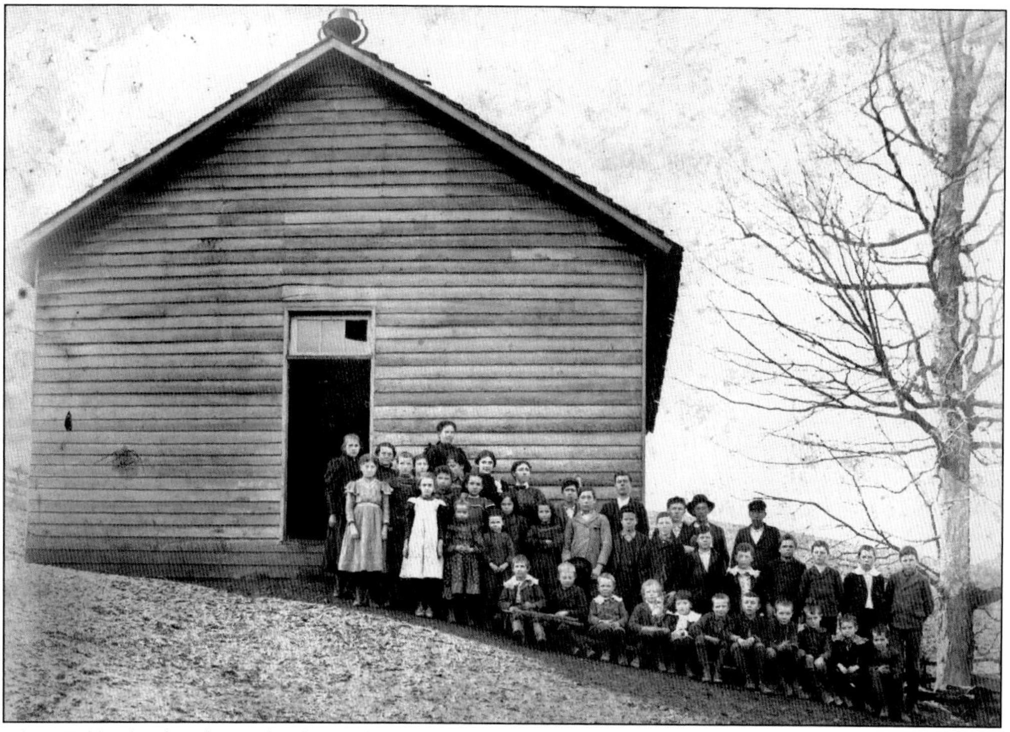

This Telford school was built in the late 1800s. Take note of the incline where the children are standing and especially the log bench the boys are sitting on. The building shown below replaced this one in 1936. (Courtesy of Elaine Cantrell.)

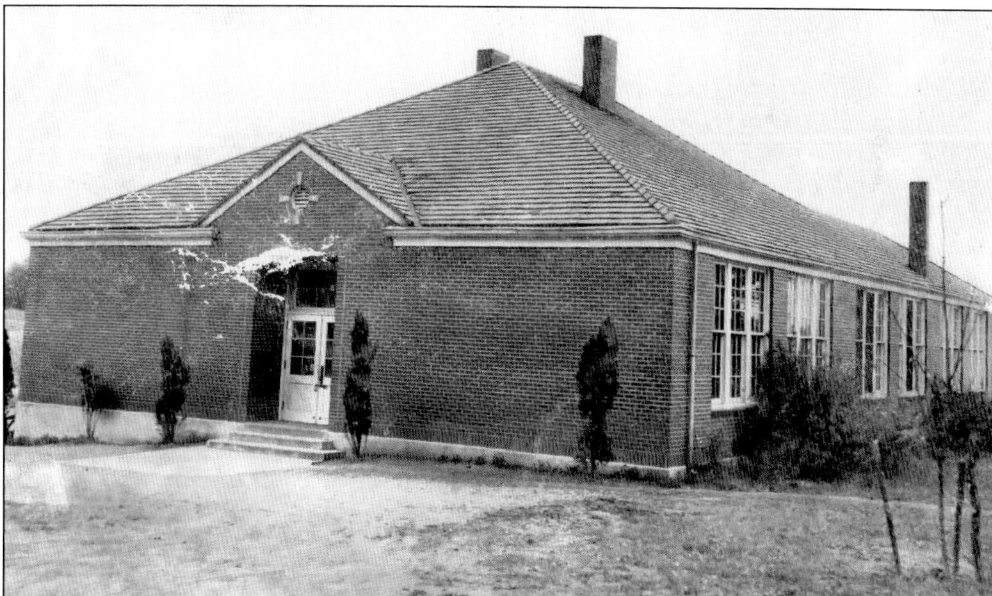

In the 1930s, following the Great Depression, President Roosevelt initiated the Works Progress Administration (WPA). Funds from this program were to be used to build schools, roads, airports, and other approved building projects within a community. This school building in Telford was built in 1936 under WPA. (Courtesy of Washington County Schools.)

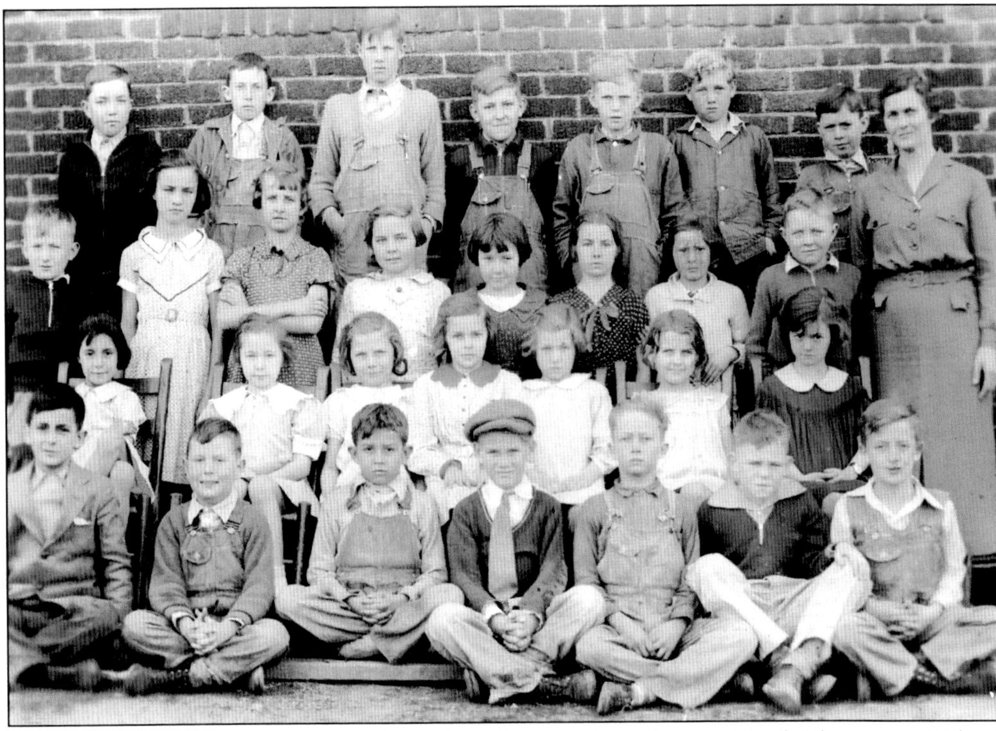

Nervous-looking students pose for their class photograph at Boones Creek Elementary School in 1936. (Courtesy of Chuck and Nancy Mason.)

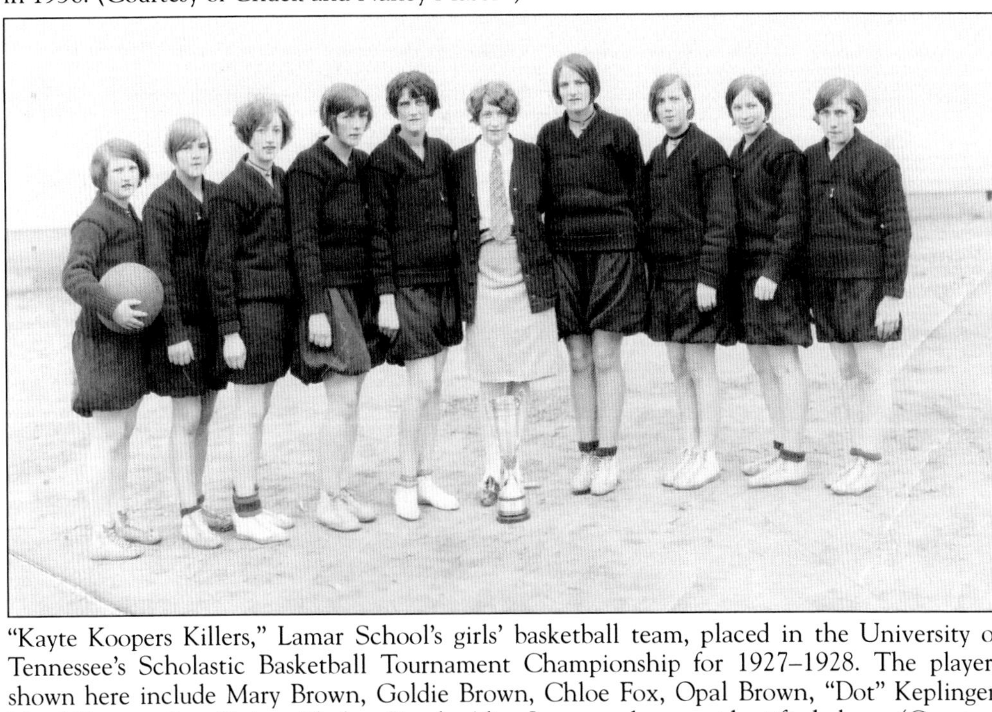

"Kayte Koopers Killers," Lamar School's girls' basketball team, placed in the University of Tennessee's Scholastic Basketball Tournament Championship for 1927–1928. The players shown here include Mary Brown, Goldie Brown, Chloe Fox, Opal Brown, "Dot" Keplinger, Hazel Howren, Inez Guinn, Thelma Booth, Alice Jones, and one unidentified player. (Courtesy of Chip White.)

Dave Howren served as the janitor of Lamar School in the 1930s and 1940s, when this photograph was taken. Many of the former students still remember him as a kind man. (Courtesy of Chip White.)

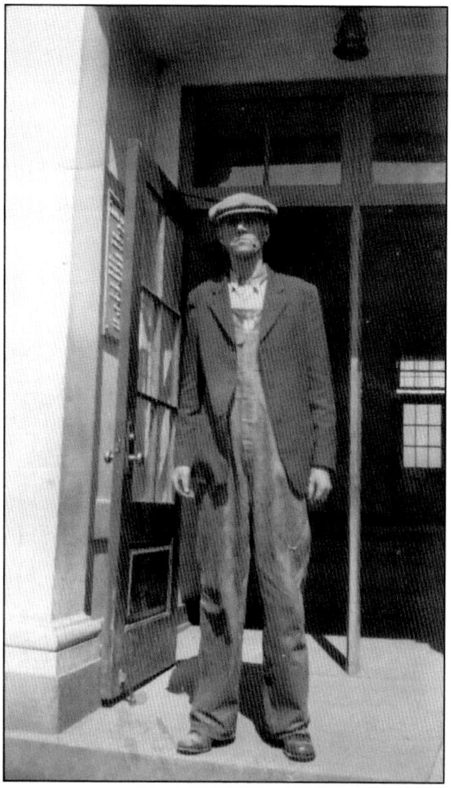

This building served as the Fall Branch Elementary and High School. (Courtesy of Washington County School System.)

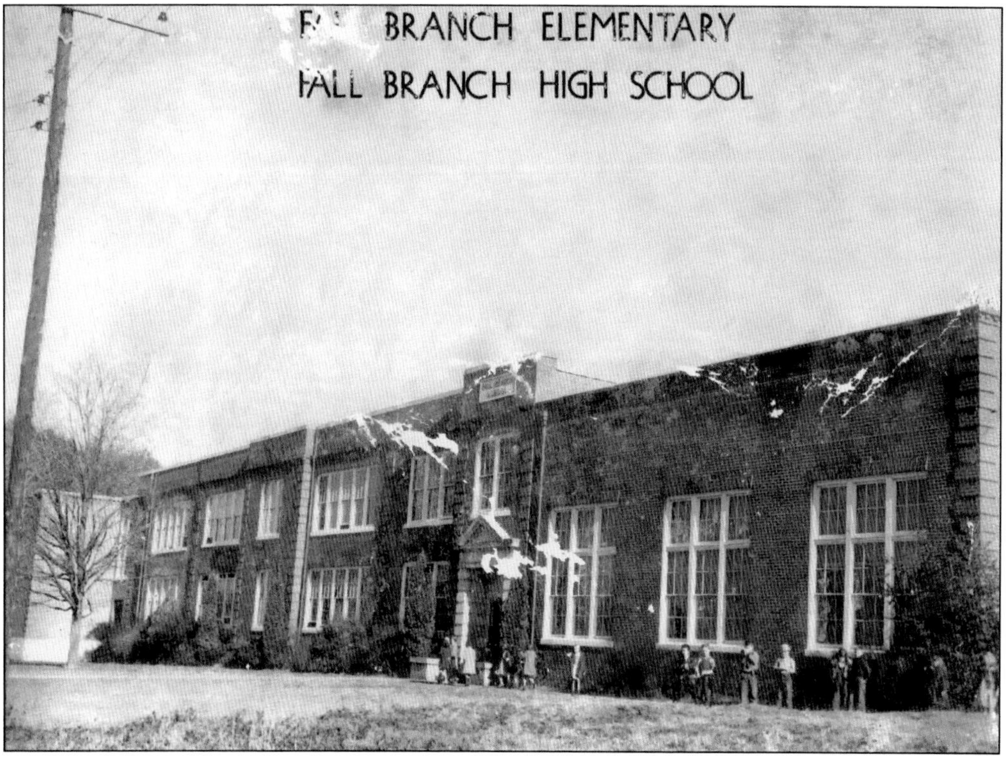

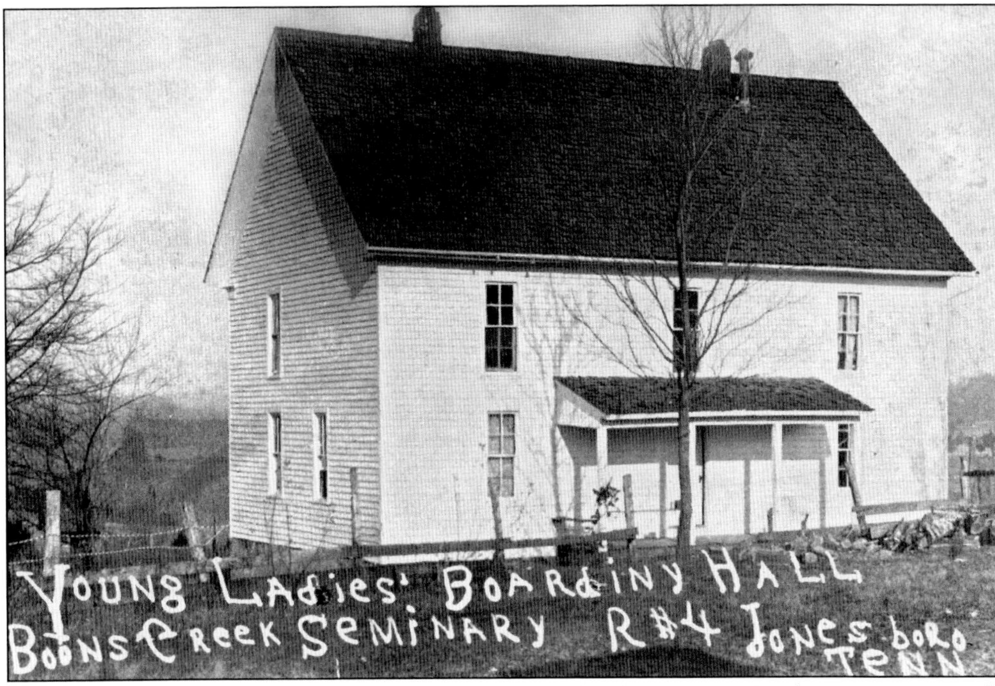

The Boon's Creek Seminary was established in 1851 by the Boone's Creek community. Male and female students attended together, possibly because in rural areas, there weren't enough students to separate them. Students stayed in the boarding house or in a local home that allowed boarders. Notice the spelling, "Boon," at the time the seminary was opened. (Courtesy of George and Margaret Holley.)

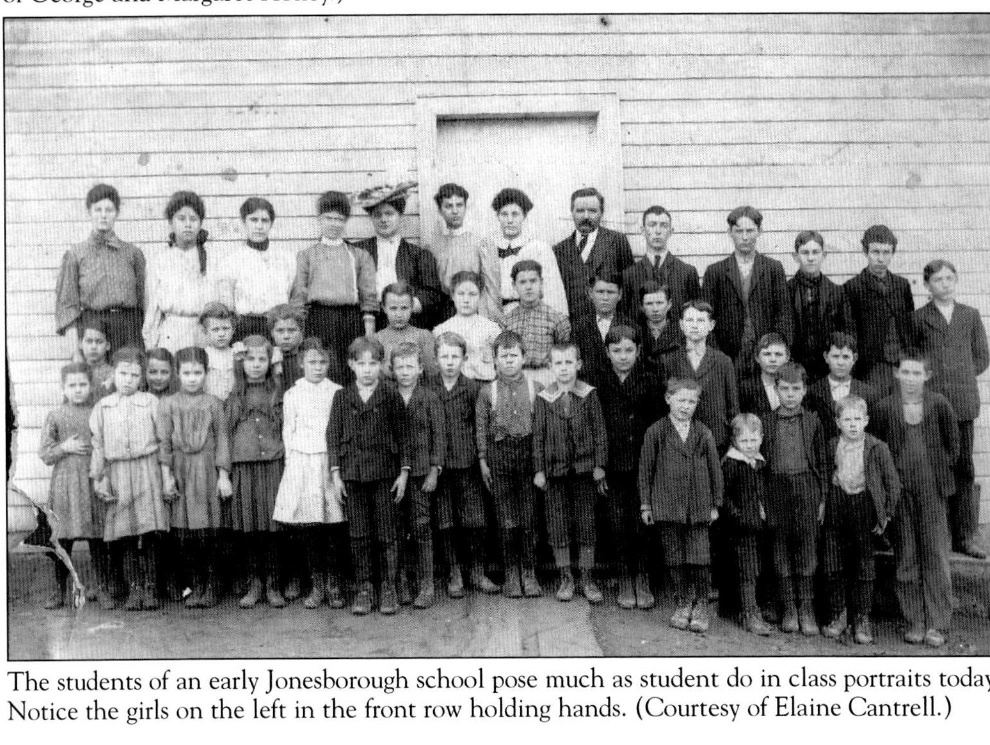

The students of an early Jonesborough school pose much as student do in class portraits today. Notice the girls on the left in the front row holding hands. (Courtesy of Elaine Cantrell.)

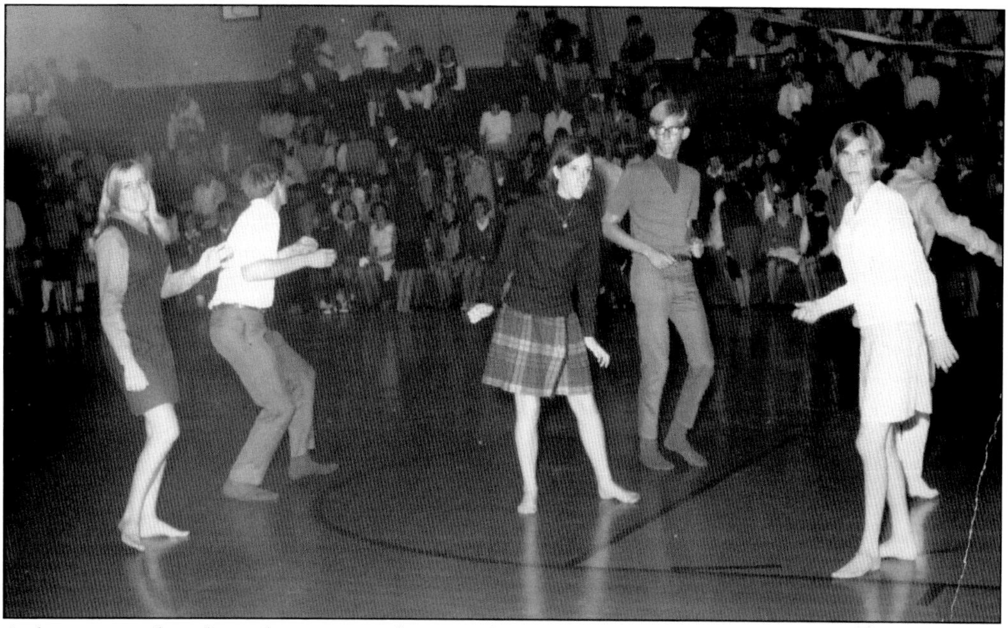

A dance marathon brought many students to the Jonesborough High School. The girls pictured in the foreground, from left to right, are Sue Green, Vickie Sauls, and Nancy Nelson. (Courtesy of Chuck and Nancy Mason.)

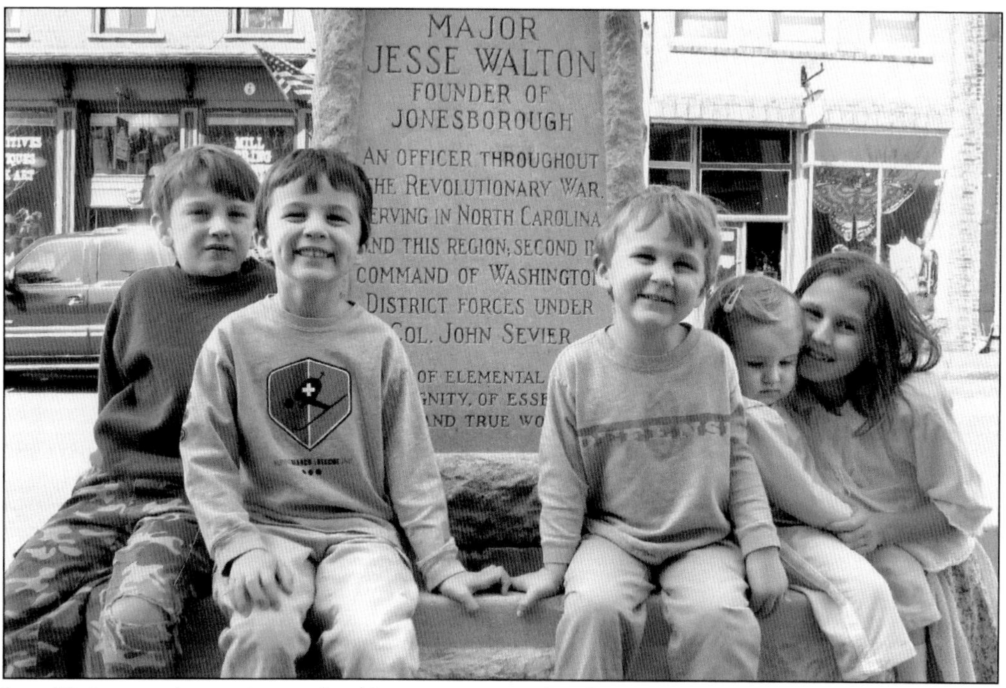

In addition to the options of public or private schools, many parents in the Tri-Cities are choosing to educate their children at home. Using their own funds and resources, parents focus on academic excellence, social training, and sharing positive character traits. The Haskins children are learning about Jonesborough from hands-on field trips. From left to right are Micah, Christopher, Daniel, Hannah, and Sarah. (Photograph by the author.)

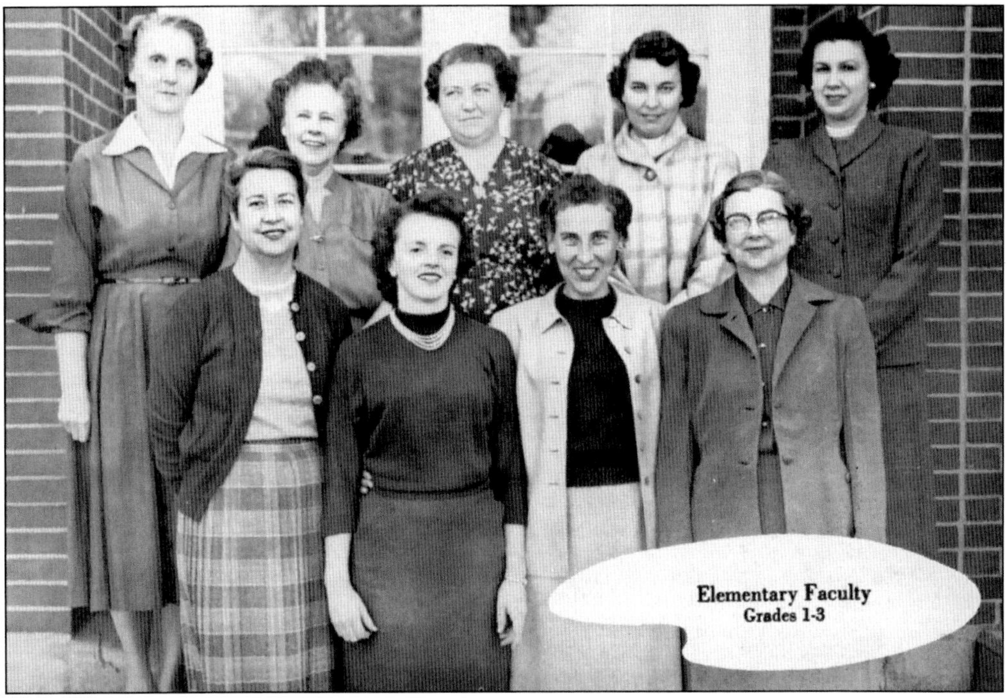

Shown here are the 1954–1955 faculty for grades one through three of Jonesborough Elementary. (Courtesy of William E. Wilson.)

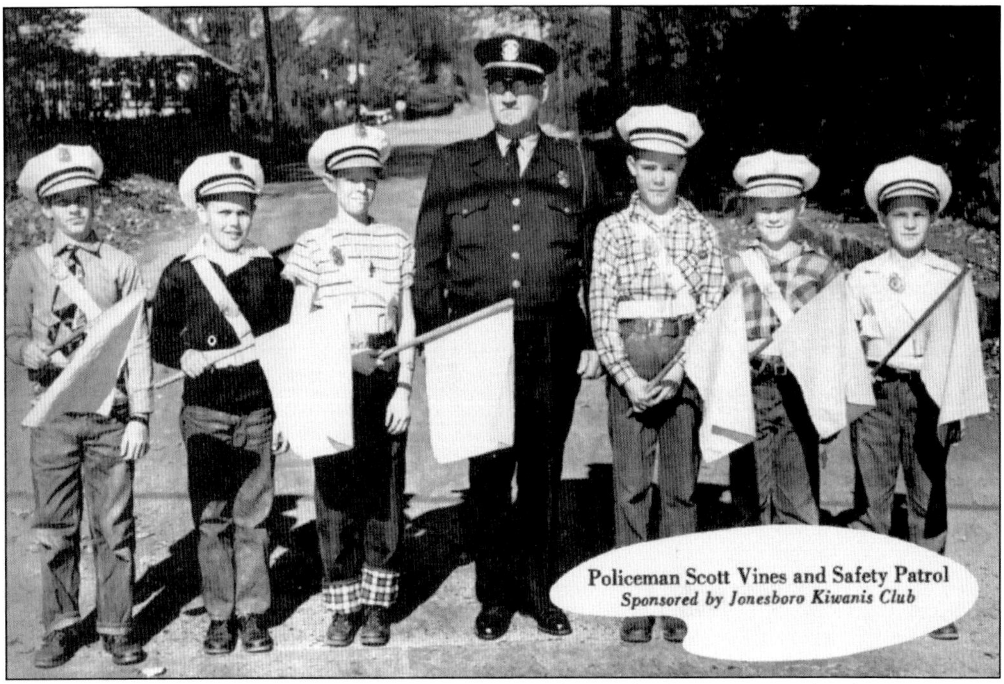

Policeman Scott Vines is shown here with the Jonesborough Elementary School safety patrol. (Courtesy of William E. Wilson.)

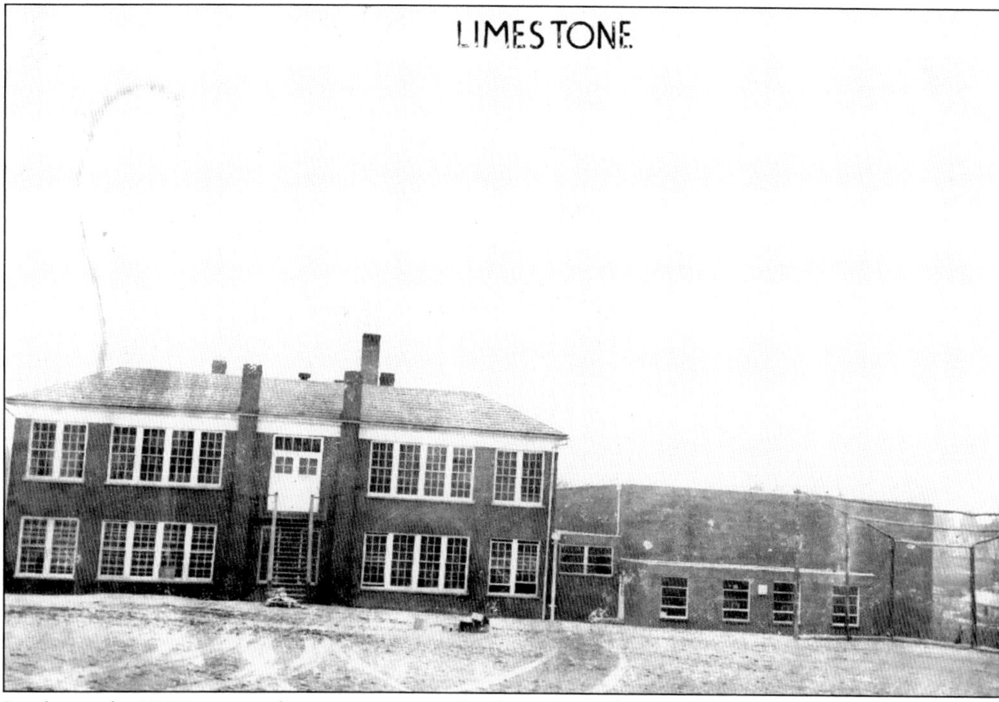

In the early 1900s, several acts were passed relating to education. In 1907, a free public high school system was created. This was important because before that time, many students had to stop attending school in the eighth grade. Congress also passed a compulsory attendance act in 1913. This is Limestone Elementary School. (Courtesy of Washington County Schools.)

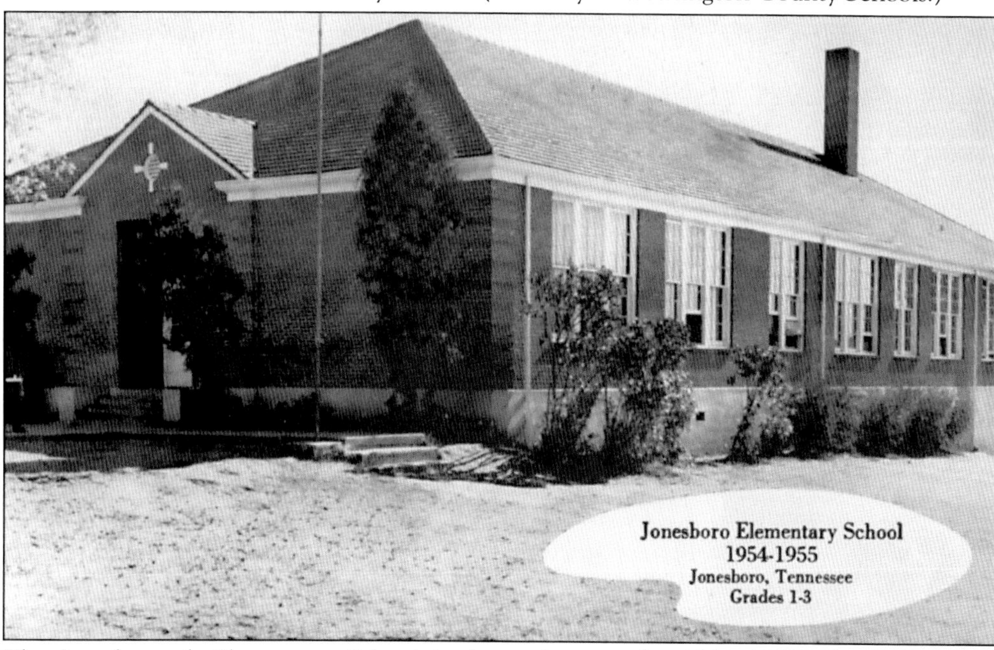

The Jonesborough Elementary School is shown here in the 1954–1955 school year. This building now serves as the central office for the Washington County School System. (Courtesy of William E. Wilson.)

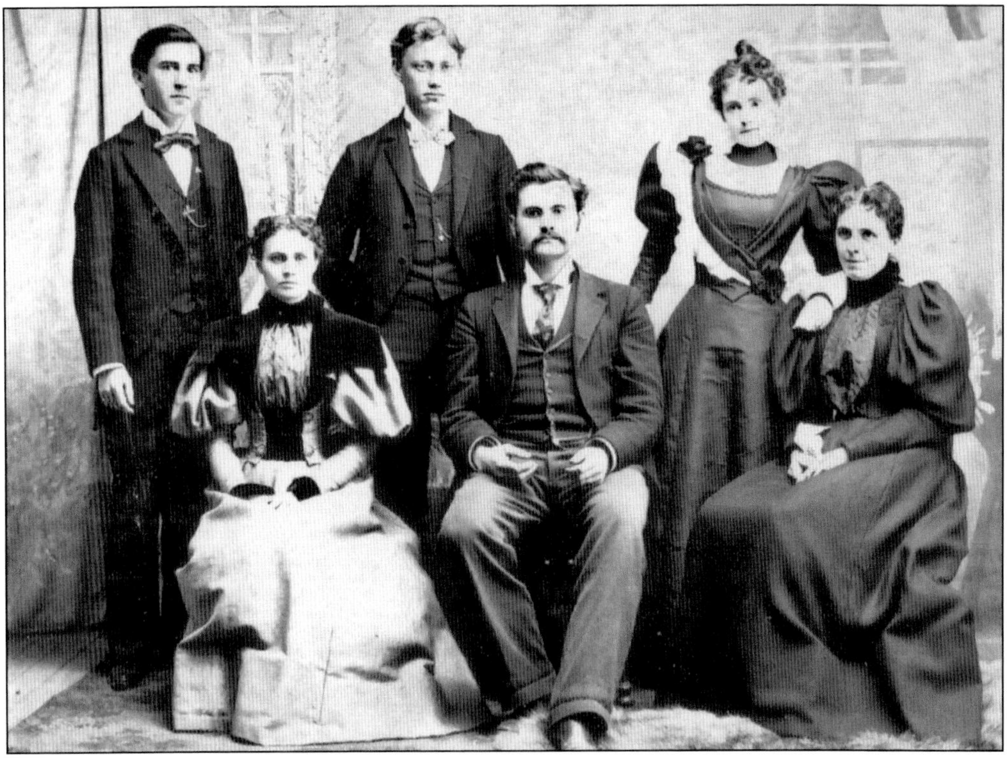

The Jonesborough School faculty from 1896 to 1898 for grades one through ten were (front row) Dora Crockett, third and fourth grades; superintendent S.W. Sherrill, ninth and tenth grades; and ? Park, music; (back row) either A.R. Hickam or Andy Nicholson, seventh and eighth grades; Calvin Waller, fifth and sixth grades; and Cora Kennedy, first and second grades. (Courtesy of the Jonesborough–Washington County Public Library.)

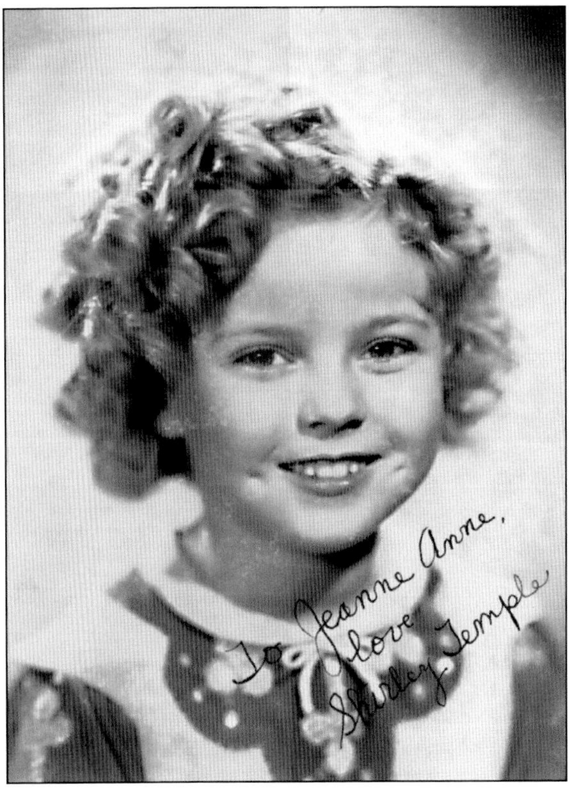

Shirley Temple sent this autographed picture to Jeanne Anne Taylor when she was a student at Jonesborough Elementary School. It was quite popular in the early part of the 20th century to request and receive autographs from movie stars and other well-known people. (Courtesy of Jeanne Anne Alexander.)

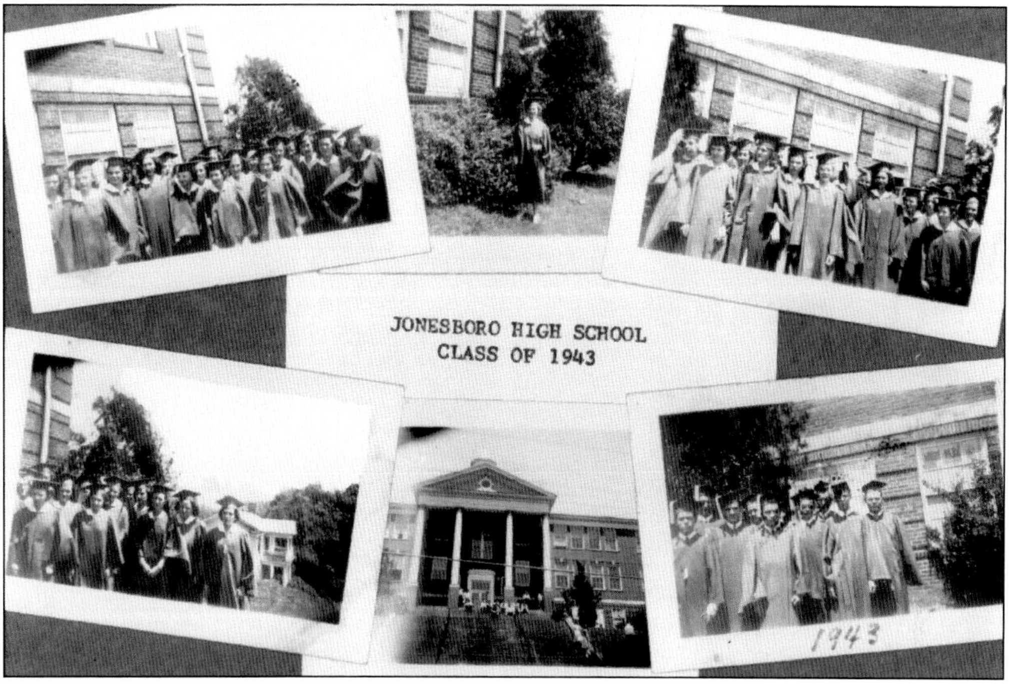

Mary Nelle Bacon, a member of the Jonesborough class of 1943, can remember when she walked to school each day, about a mile each way. She also remembers her first bicycle she received when she was 10. After that, she rode to school. (Courtesy of Bill and Mary Nelle Roberson.)

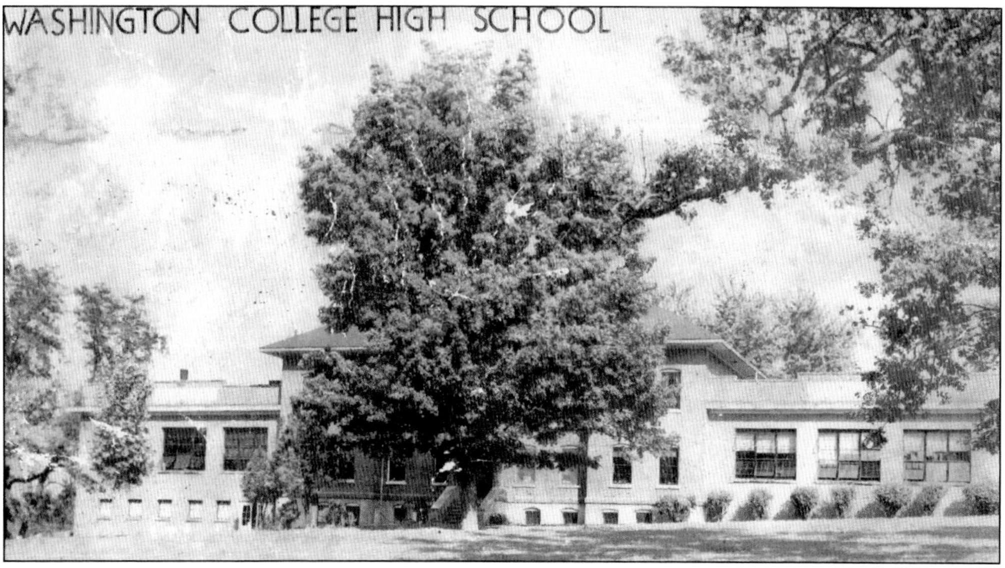

When David Crockett and Daniel Boone opened in the fall of 1971, numerous small community high schools, like Washington College High School shown here, were closed. This shifted people's focus from their primary community to the larger areas of Jonesborough, Johnson City, Boone's Creek, and Gray. While communities will remain important in Upper East Tennessee, there is a significant unification now as well. (Courtesy of Washington County Schools.)

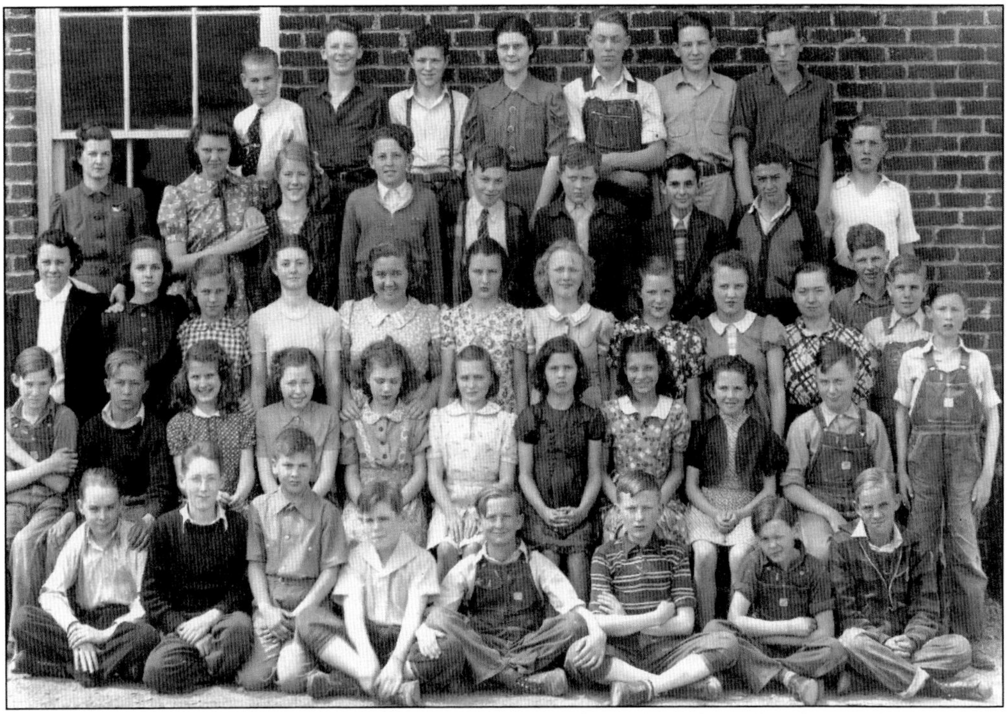

The 1940 Boones Creek seventh grade class included children from families such as Carter, Clark, Hensley, Whitaker, Shipley, Sanders, Gross, Martin, and Kelley. The teachers were Bernice Leonard, Thelma White, and Olivia Bowman. (Courtesy of Chuck and Nancy Mason.)

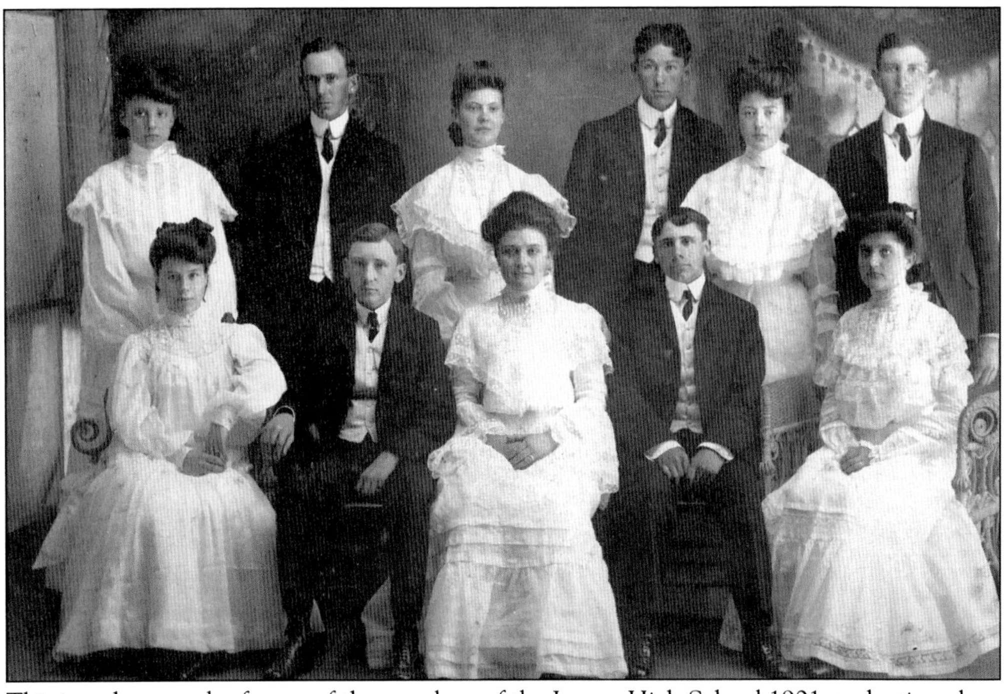

This is a photograph of some of the members of the Lamar High School 1901 graduating class. (Courtesy of John G. and Etta Love.)

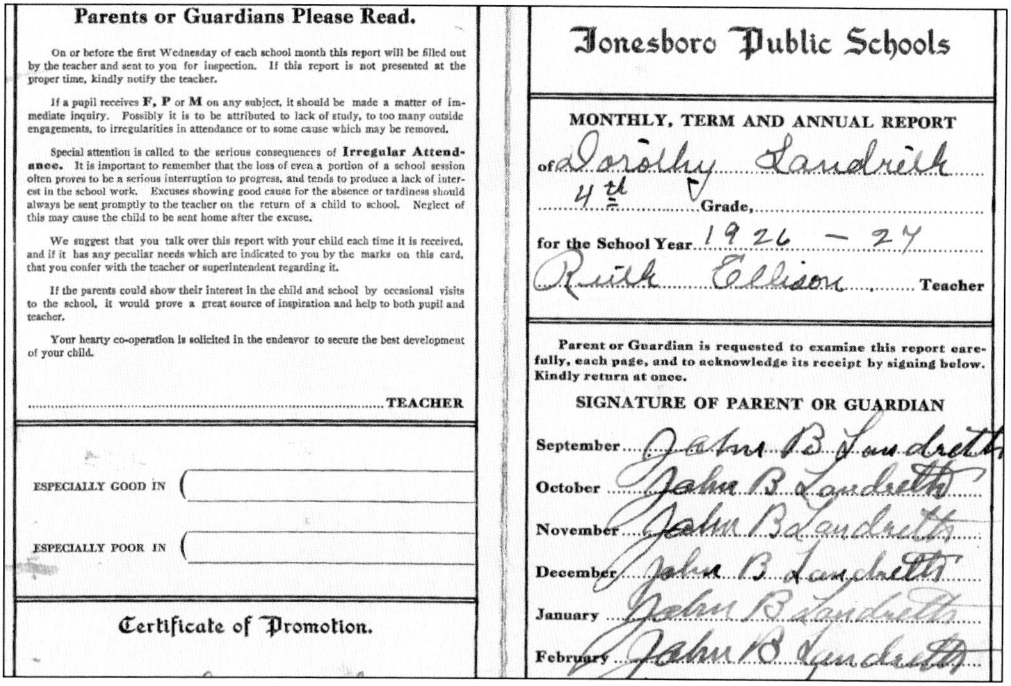

Parents or Guardians Please Read.

On or before the first Wednesday of each school month this report will be filled out by the teacher and sent to you for inspection. If this report is not presented at the proper time, kindly notify the teacher.

If a pupil receives **F**, **P** or **M** on any subject, it should be made a matter of immediate inquiry. Possibly it is to be attributed to lack of study, to too many outside engagements, to irregularities in attendance or to some cause which may be removed.

Special attention is called to the serious consequences of **Irregular Attendance.** It is important to remember that the loss of even a portion of a school session often proves to be a serious interruption to progress, and tends to produce a lack of interest in the school work. Excuses showing good cause for the absence or tardiness should always be sent promptly to the teacher on the return of a child to school. Neglect of this may cause the child to be sent home after the excuse.

We suggest that you talk over this report with your child each time it is received, and if it has any peculiar needs which are indicated to you by the marks on this card, that you confer with the teacher or superintendent regarding it.

If the parents could show their interest in the child and school by occasional visits to the school, it would prove a great source of inspiration and help to both pupil and teacher.

Your hearty co-operation is solicited in the endeavor to secure the best development of your child.

.... TEACHER

ESPECIALLY GOOD IN

ESPECIALLY POOR IN

Certificate of Promotion.

Jonesboro Public Schools

MONTHLY, TERM AND ANNUAL REPORT

of Dorothy Landreth

4th Grade,

for the School Year 1926 – 27

Ruth Ellison, Teacher

Parent or Guardian is requested to examine this report carefully, each page, and to acknowledge its receipt by signing below. Kindly return at once.

SIGNATURE OF PARENT OR GUARDIAN

September John B. Landreth

October John B. Landreth

November John B. Landreth

December John B. Landreth

January John B. Landreth

February John B. Landreth

The back of this 1926–1927 report card for fourth-grader Dorothy Landreth emphasizes the importance of school attendance, stating that "the loss of even a portion of a school session often proves to be a serious interruption to progress, and tends to produce a lack of interest in the school work." (Courtesy of Barbara G. Smith.)

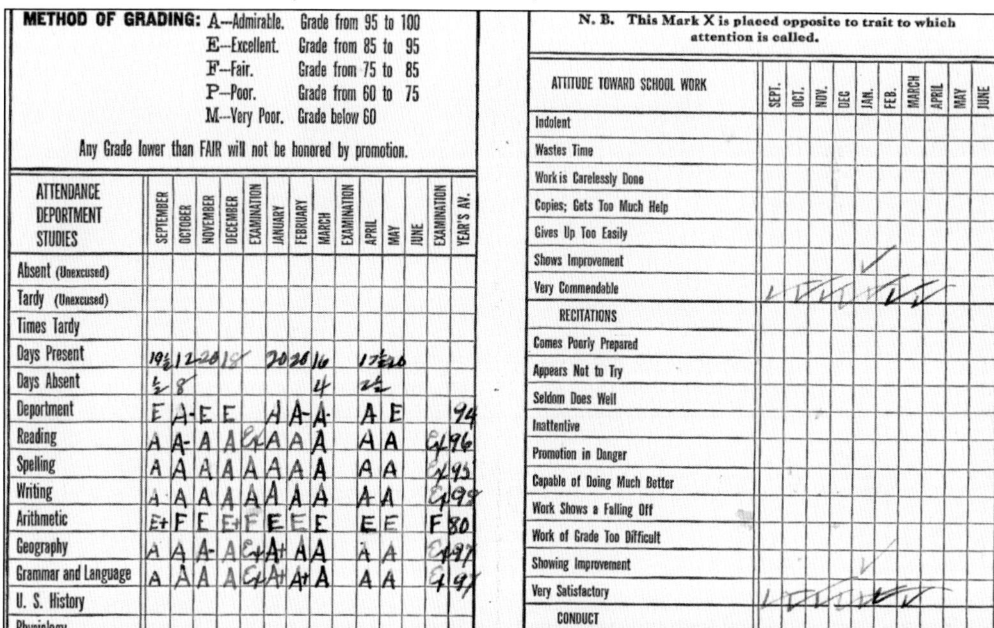

METHOD OF GRADING: A—Admirable. Grade from 95 to 100
E—Excellent. Grade from 85 to 95
F—Fair. Grade from 75 to 85
P—Poor. Grade from 60 to 75
M—Very Poor. Grade below 60

Any Grade lower than FAIR will not be honored by promotion.

ATTENDANCE DEPORTMENT STUDIES	September	October	November	December	Examination	January	February	March	Examination	April	May	June	Examination	Year's Av.
Absent (Unexcused)														
Tardy (Unexcused)														
Times Tardy														
Days Present	19½	12	20	18		20	20	16		17½	20			
Days Absent	½	8						4		2½				
Deportment	E	A-	E	E		A	A-	A-		A	E			94
Reading	A	A-	A	A	E+	A	A	A		A	A		E+	96
Spelling	A	A	A	A	A	A	A	A		A	A		E+	95
Writing	A	A	A	A	A	A	A	A		A	A		E	95
Arithmetic	E+	F	E	E+	F	E	E	E		E	E		F	80
Geography	A	A	A-	A	E+	A+	A	A		A	A		E	97
Grammar and Language	A	A	A	A	E+	A+	A+	A		A	A		E	97
U. S. History														
Physiology														

N. B. This Mark X is placed opposite to trait to which attention is called.

ATTITUDE TOWARD SCHOOL WORK	SEPT.	OCT.	NOV.	DEC.	JAN.	FEB.	MARCH	APRIL	MAY	JUNE
Indolent										
Wastes Time										
Work is Carelessly Done										
Copies; Gets Too Much Help										
Gives Up Too Easily										
Shows Improvement					✓					
Very Commendable	✓	✓	✓	✓	✓	✓	✓			
RECITATIONS										
Comes Poorly Prepared										
Appears Not to Try										
Seldom Does Well										
Inattentive										
Promotion in Danger										
Capable of Doing Much Better										
Work Shows a Falling Off										
Work of Grade Too Difficult										
Showing Improvement					✓					
Very Satisfactory	✓	✓	✓	✓	✓	✓	✓			
CONDUCT										
Restless; Inattentive										

Dorothy Landreth studied the following subjects in the fourth grade: deportment (conduct), reading, spelling, writing, arithmetic, geography, health, and grammar/language. The school year went from September through May. (Courtesy of Barbara G. Smith.)

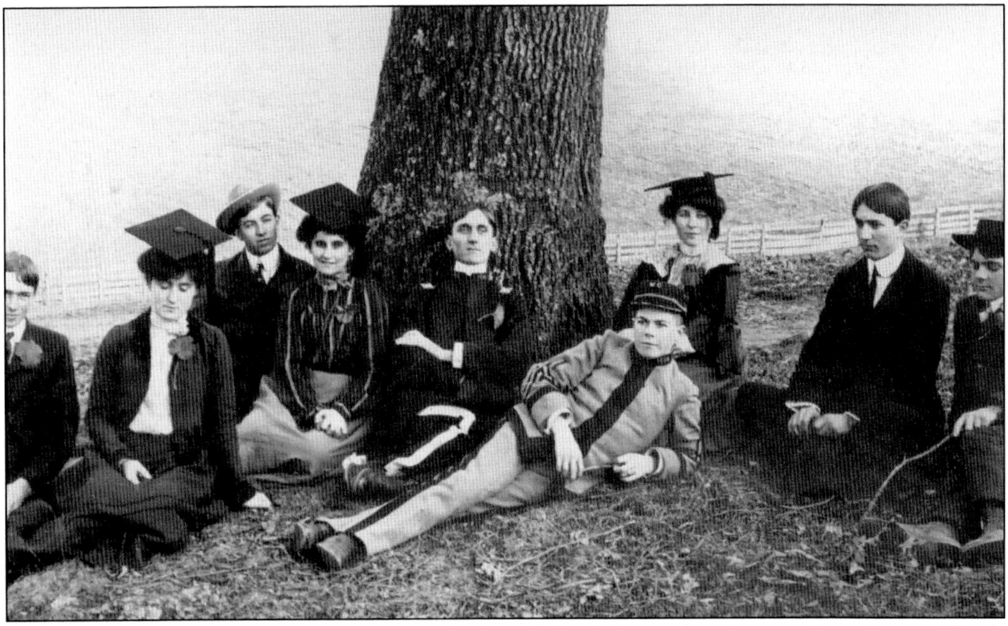

Washington College Academy was originally founded as Martin Academy by Rev. Samuel Doak in 1780. Martin Academy was the earliest institution of higher education west of the Allegany Mountains. Substantial damage during the Civil War forced the college to close for several years. Shown here is a photograph of a graduating class, probably in the early 1900s. (Courtesy of Washington College Academy.)

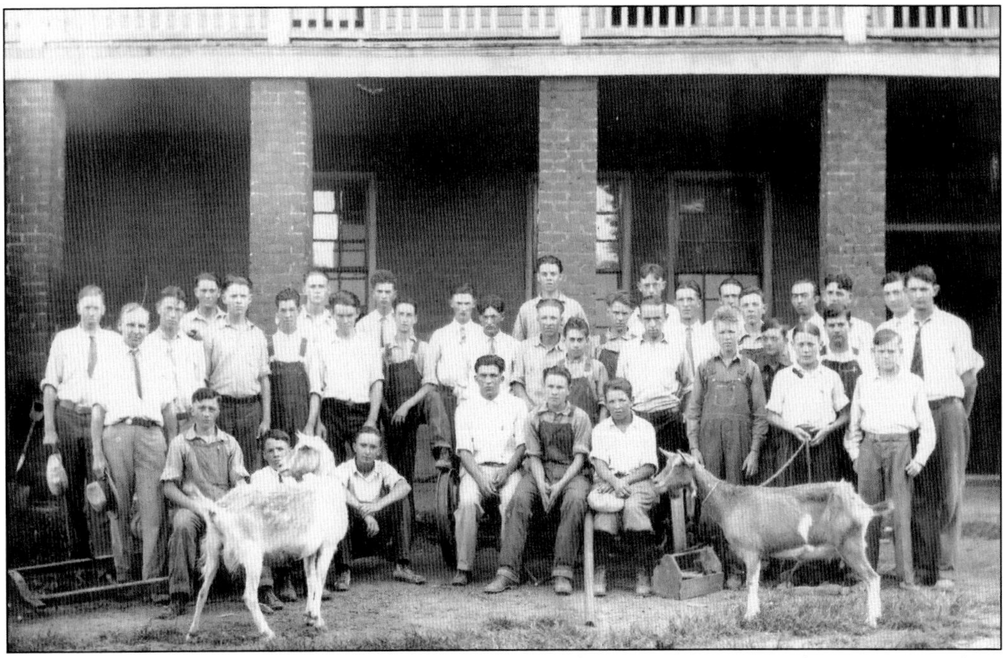

Students at Washington College Academy maintained a fully functioning farm, growing their own food and raising animals to provide meat and dairy products. This not only helped provide food for the students, but also taught them useful skills. Pictured here are some boys in the agricultural department in 1920. (Courtesy of Washington College Academy.)

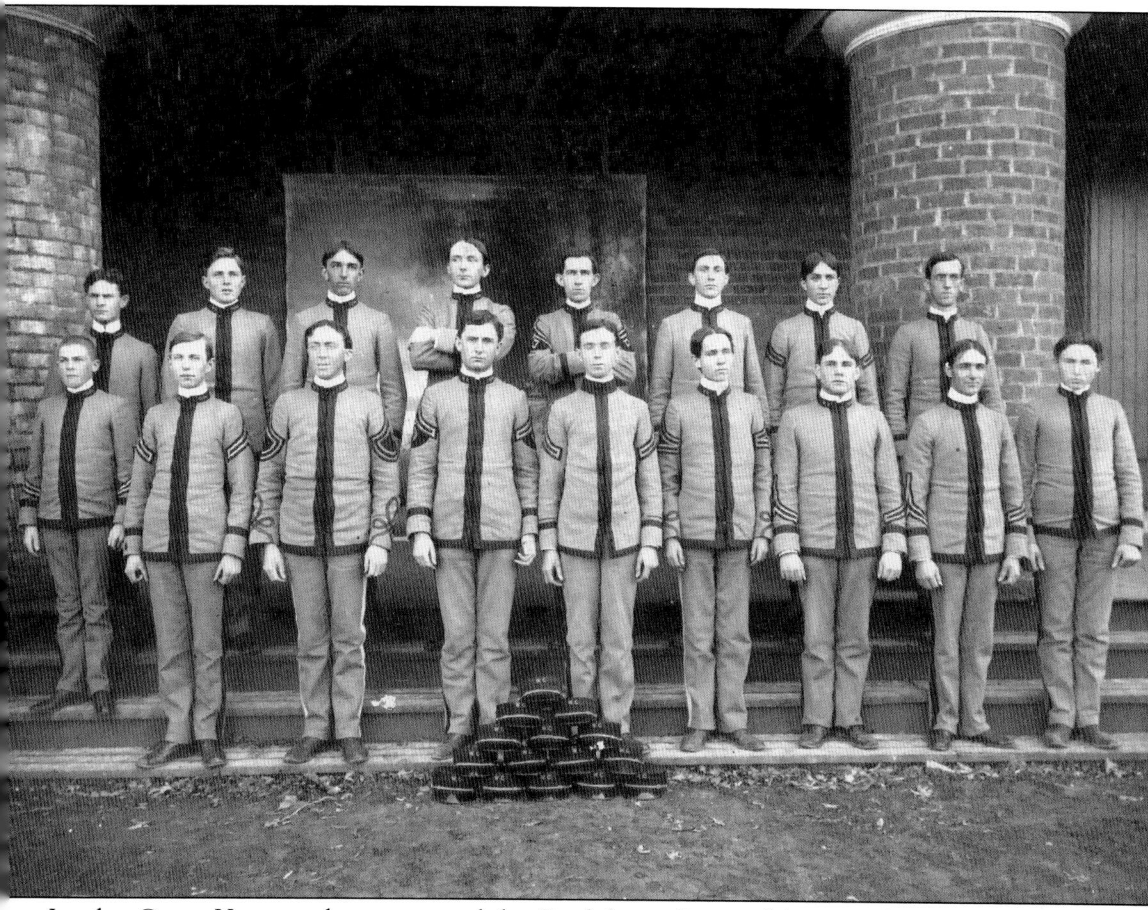

Landon Carter Haynes, who represented the Confederate States of America during the Civil War, was an 1838 graduate of Washington College Academy. Oliver Perry Temple, who graduated in 1844, supported the Unionists. The school was as divided in loyalties as was the rest of Upper East Tennessee. These boys are not in war uniforms, however, but college uniforms. Notice the "WC" on their hats. (Courtesy of Washington College Academy.)

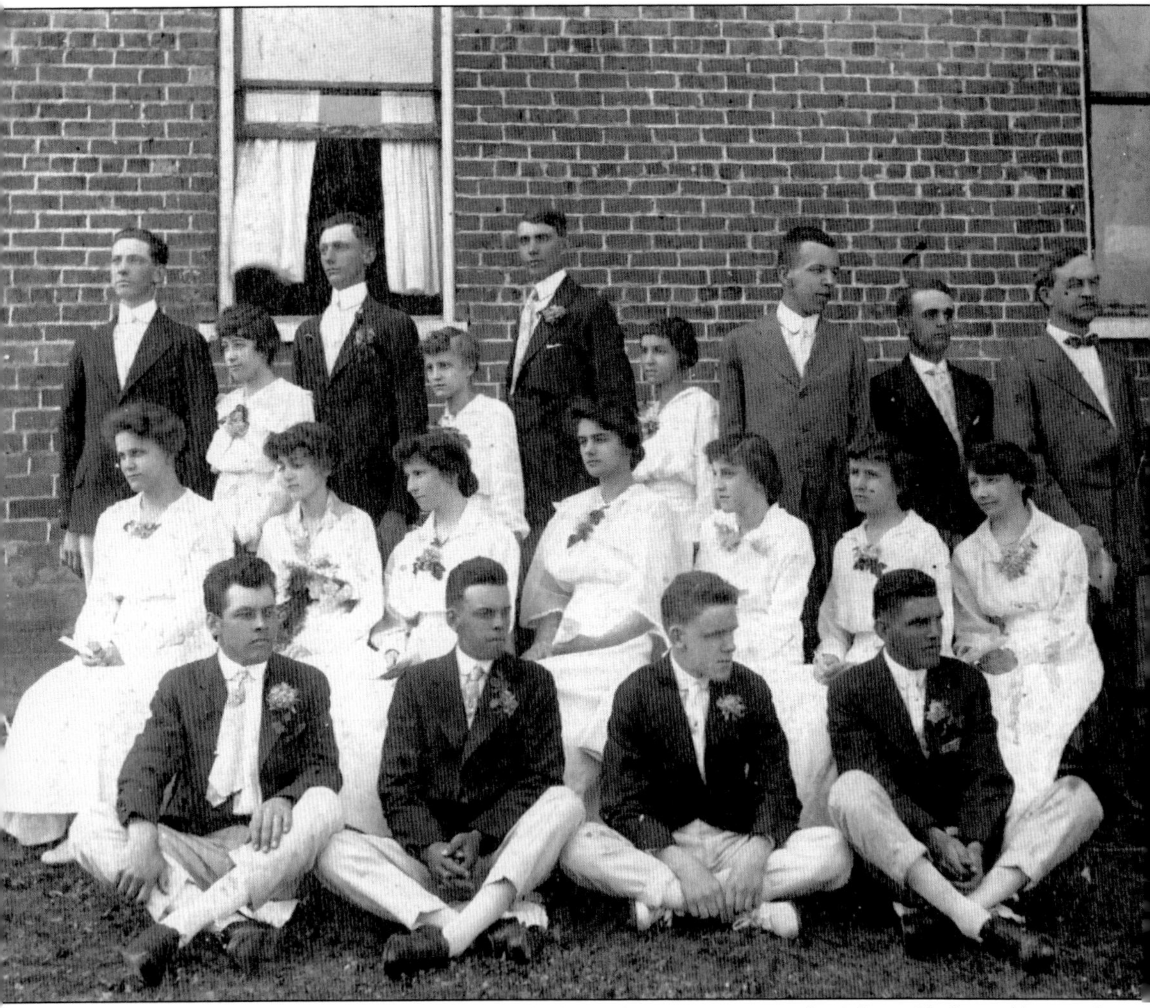

Among this Jonesborough High School class of 1916 were Pearl Miller, Clyde Miller, and Mary Keyes, who later married a Carter. Their son owned Carter Equipment Company in Boone's Creek. (Courtesy of Ruth May Robinson.)

Six

Religion

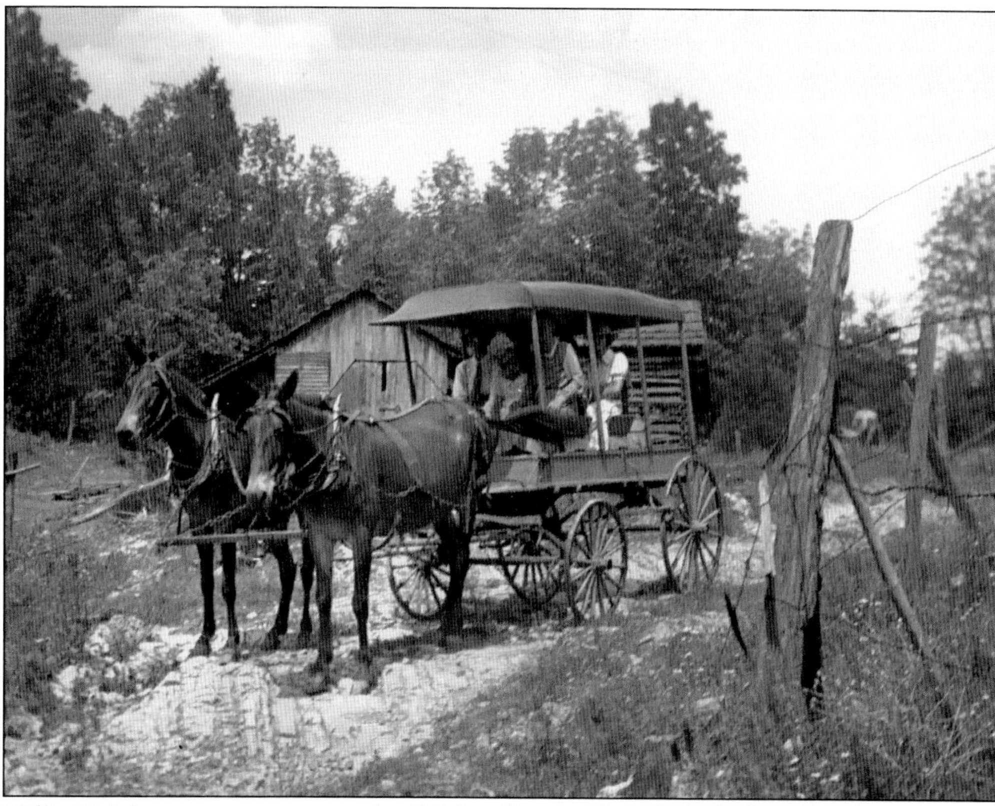

Willis H. Johnson was a pastor at the Sulphur Springs United Methodist Church in the early 1900s. Johnson is shown here with his family in a beautiful carriage. (Courtesy of Sulphur Springs United Methodist Church.)

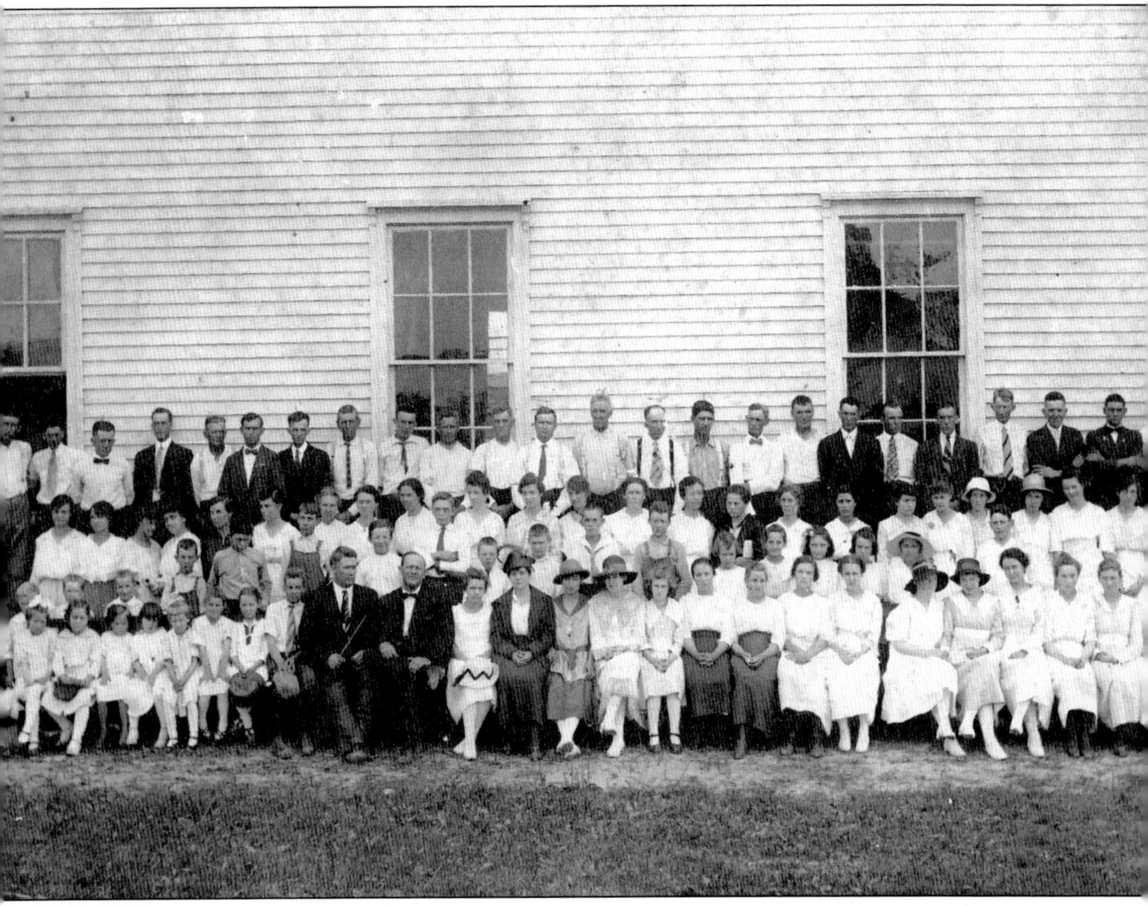

Early families put a lot of emphasis on community activities. Community gatherings were used to share information, provide entertainment, and find ways to build up the community. Much of the early entertainment centered around the area's churches and school. Shown here is a singing school that took place in Sulphur Springs in the summer of 1916. Notice that the man on the left in the front row is holding a baton. (Courtesy of Sulphur Springs United Methodist Church.)

This page is from *The Intermediate Quarterly*, second quarter 1884. It lists various publications available to aid teachers. *The Intermediate Quarterly* was published by the American Baptist Publication Society "to help the boys and girls study the international lessons." (Courtesy of Bill and Mary Nelle Roberson.)

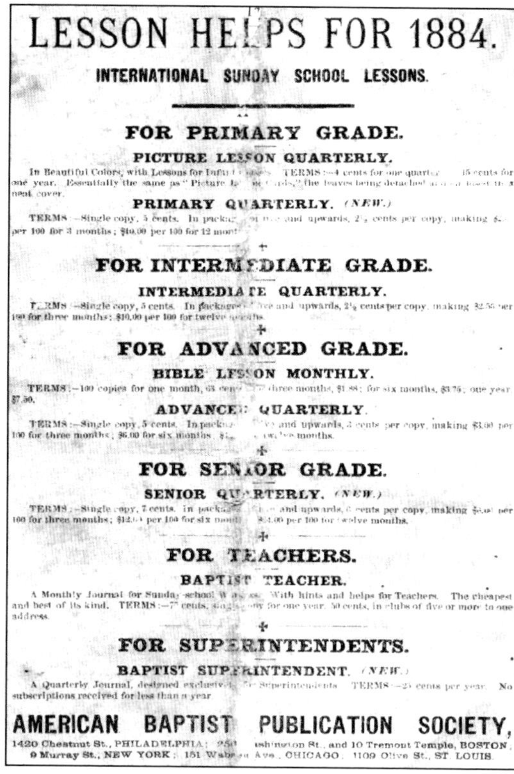

LESSON HELPS FOR 1884.

INTERNATIONAL SUNDAY SCHOOL LESSONS.

FOR PRIMARY GRADE.

PICTURE LESSON QUARTERLY.

In Beautiful Colors, with Lessons for Infant [illegible]. TERMS:—4 cents for one quarter [illegible] 15 cents for one year. Essentially the same as "Picture Lesson Cards," the leaves being detached [illegible] in a neat cover.

PRIMARY QUARTERLY. *(NEW.)*

TERMS:—Single copy, 5 cents. In packages [illegible] and upwards, 2½ cents per copy, making $2[illegible] per 100 for 3 months; $10.00 per 100 for 12 months.

FOR INTERMEDIATE GRADE.

INTERMEDIATE QUARTERLY.

TERMS:—Single copy, 5 cents. In packages [illegible] and upwards, 2½ cents per copy, making $2.50 per 100 for three months; $10.00 per 100 for twelve months.

FOR ADVANCED GRADE.

BIBLE LESSON MONTHLY.

TERMS:—100 copies for one month, 63 cents; [illegible] three months, $1.88; for six months, $3.75; one year $7.50.

ADVANCED QUARTERLY.

TERMS:—Single copy, 5 cents. In packages [illegible] and upwards, 3 cents per copy, making $3.00 per 100 for three months; $6.00 for six months, $[illegible] twelve months.

FOR SENIOR GRADE.

SENIOR QUARTERLY. *(NEW.)*

TERMS:—Single copy, 7 cents. In packages [illegible] and upwards, 6 cents per copy, making $6.00 per 100 for three months; $12.00 per 100 for six months; $24.00 per 100 for twelve months.

FOR TEACHERS.

BAPTIST TEACHER.

A Monthly Journal for Sunday-school Workers. With hints and helps for Teachers. The cheapest and best of its kind. TERMS:—75 cents, single copy for one year. 50 cents, in clubs of five or more to one address.

FOR SUPERINTENDENTS.

BAPTIST SUPERINTENDENT. *(NEW.)*

A Quarterly Journal, designed exclusively for Superintendents. TERMS:—25 cents per year. No subscriptions received for less than a year.

AMERICAN BAPTIST PUBLICATION SOCIETY,

1420 Chestnut St., PHILADELPHIA; [illegible] Washington St., and 10 Tremont Temple, BOSTON; 9 Murray St., NEW YORK; 151 Wabash Ave., CHICAGO; 1109 Olive St., ST. LOUIS.

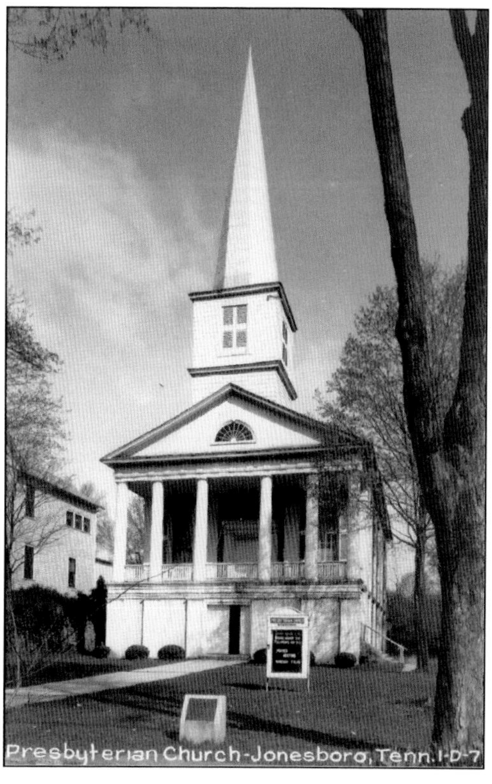

The Jonesborough Presbyterian Church was established in 1790. The church, with its massive columns customary of Greek-Revival influence, was erected in 1845. The church still contains the original pulpit, pews, and slave gallery and is located on Main Street. (From the author's collection.)

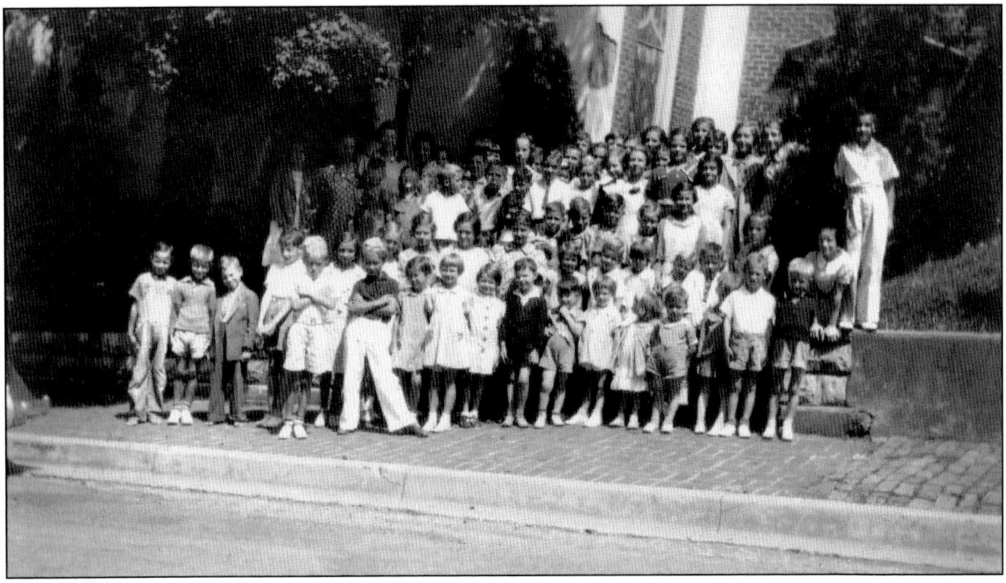

Recreation in the early 20th century was frequently combined with religious activities, and Bible schools became more common. This is a Bible school at the First Baptist Church in Jonesborough in the early 1930s. (Courtesy of Jeanne Anne Alexander.)

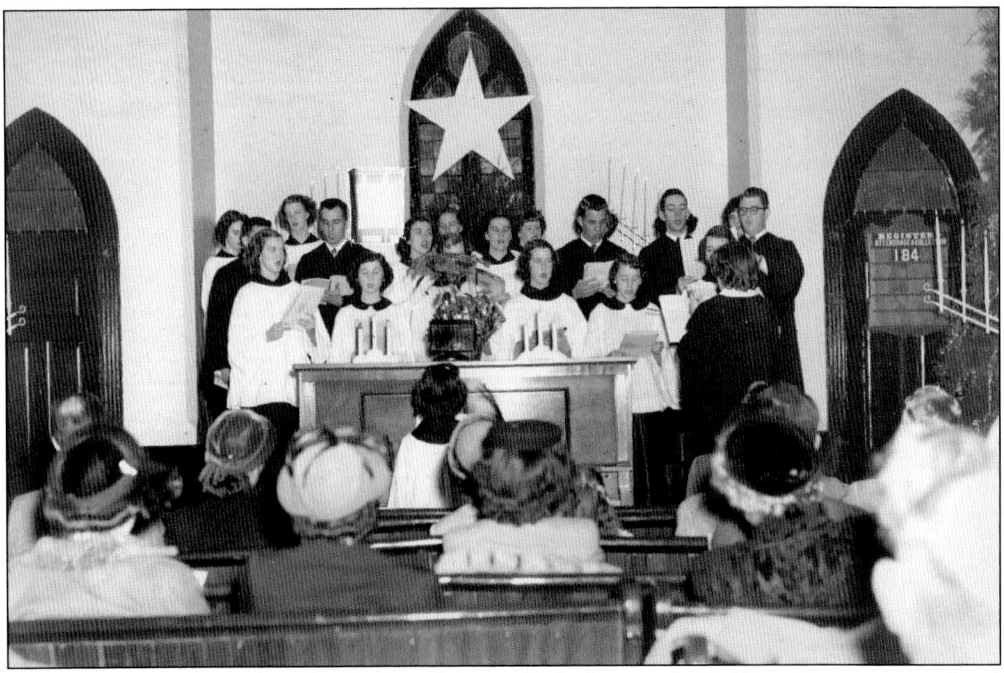

The Jonesborough High School Opus Music Club frequently held performances at local churches. (Courtesy of Lyle Haws.)

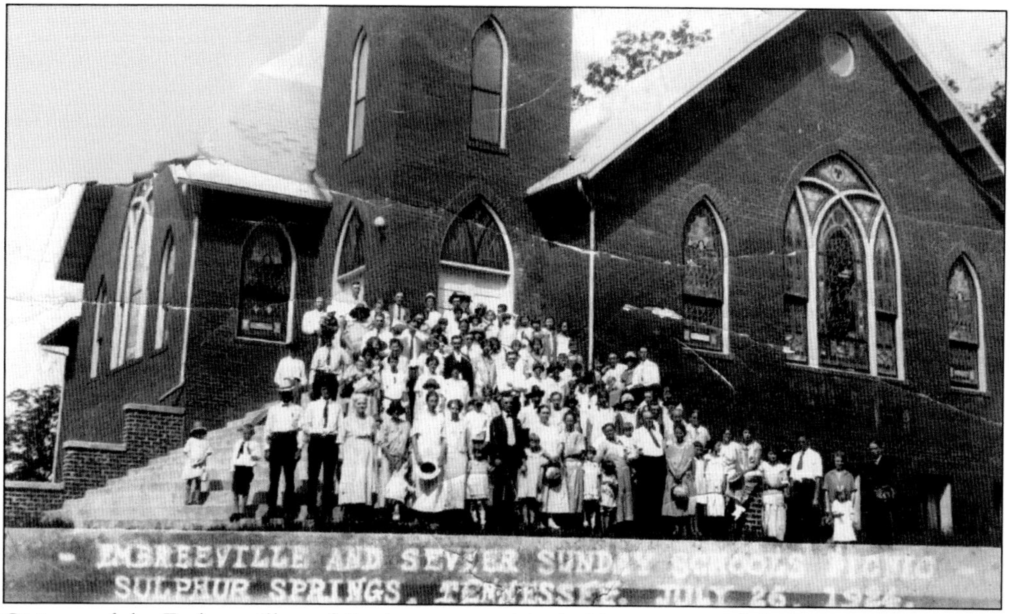

Citizens of the Embreeville and Sevier communities held a picnic on July 26, 1924, in Sulphur Springs, Tennessee. (Courtesy of Chip White.)

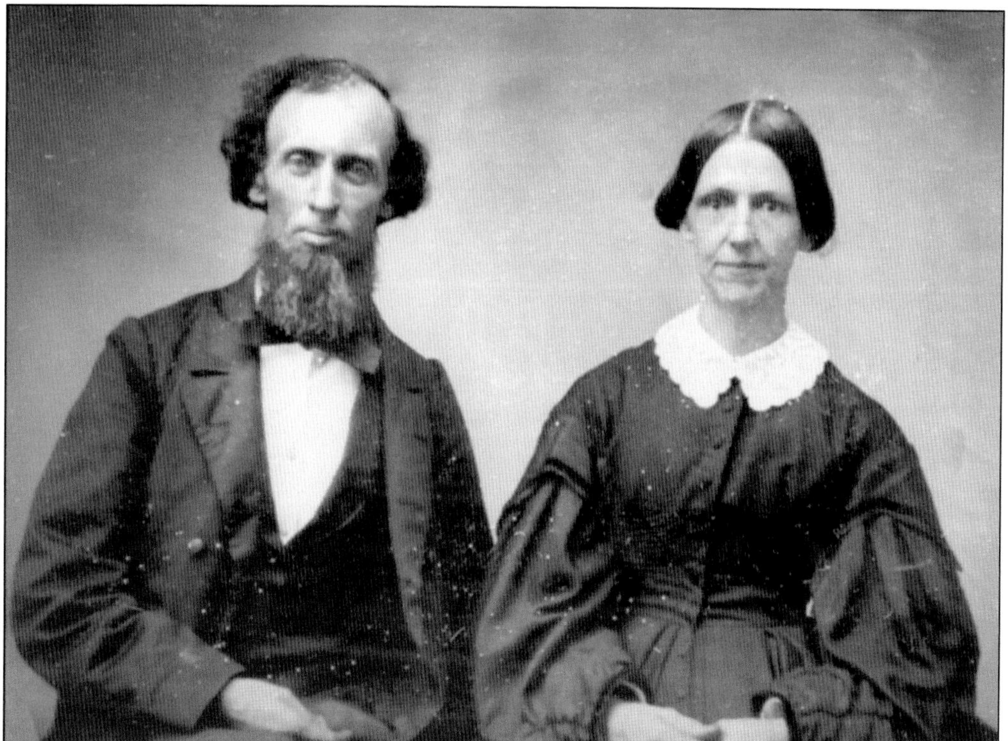

Rufus Wells served as pastor of the Jonesborough Presbyterian Church from 1845 through 1862. Wells encouraged parishioners to construct a new church building, which was eventually completed and is shown on page 91. Wells is shown here with his wife in this tintype photograph. (Courtesy of Caroline M. May.)

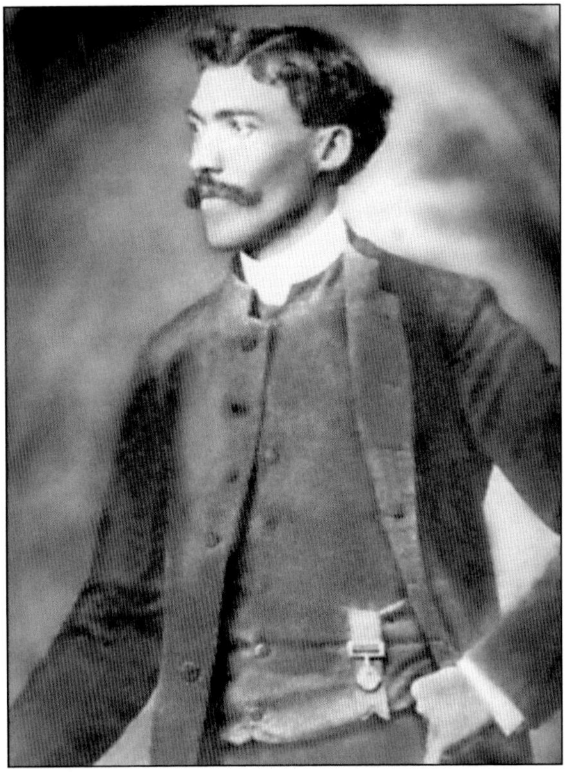

Samuel A. Russell was a minister at Bethel Christian Church in Jonesborough. Shortly after his first wife's death in 1924, Russell married Carrie Stuart Perry, also a widow. With the children from both previous unions and the two children they had together, the couple reared 11 children in a small house on Spring Street. Russell died on January 15, 1951, at age 82. (Courtesy of Alfred and Gwendolyn Greenlee.)

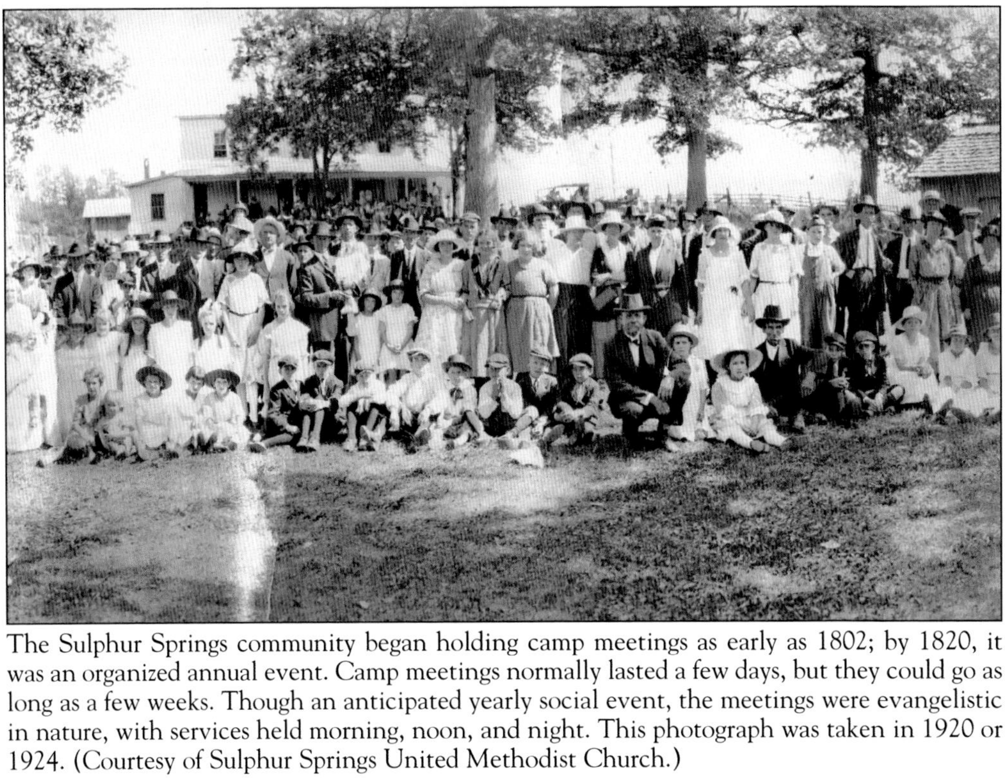

The Sulphur Springs community began holding camp meetings as early as 1802; by 1820, it was an organized annual event. Camp meetings normally lasted a few days, but they could go as long as a few weeks. Though an anticipated yearly social event, the meetings were evangelistic in nature, with services held morning, noon, and night. This photograph was taken in 1920 or 1924. (Courtesy of Sulphur Springs United Methodist Church.)

Seven

CHILDREN

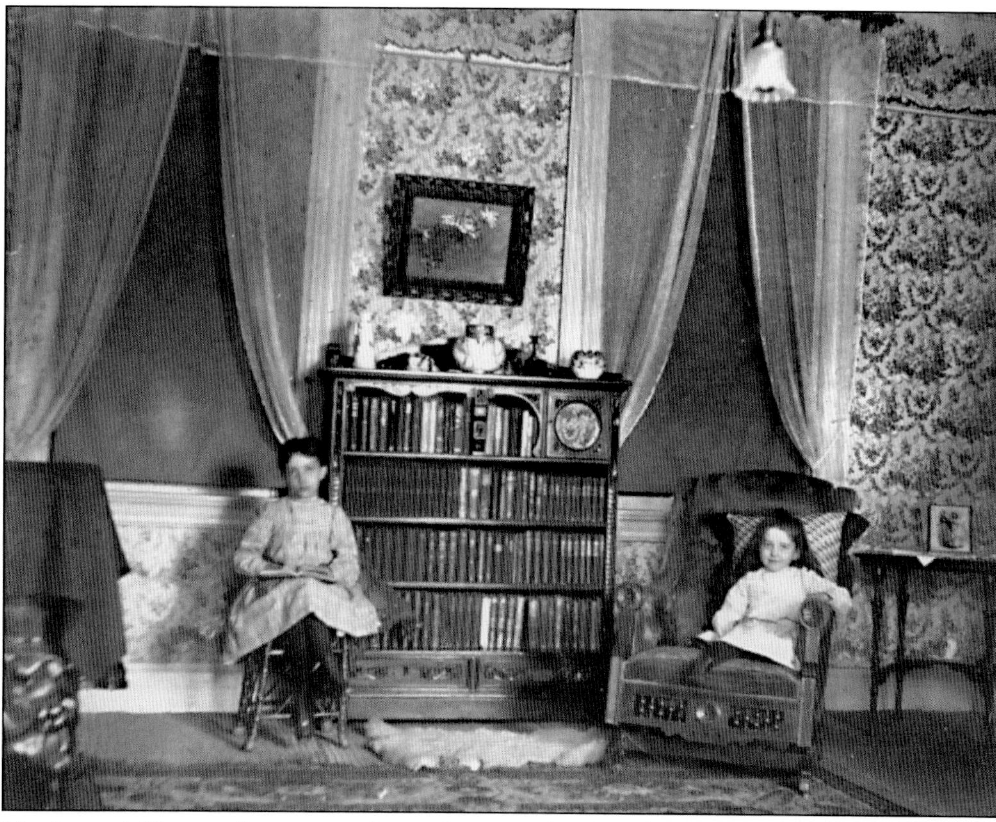

Martha and Eleanor Baxter are shown here in the formal sitting room of their home at 127 East Main Street. An outside view of the house can be seen on page nine. (Courtesy of Sue Henley.)

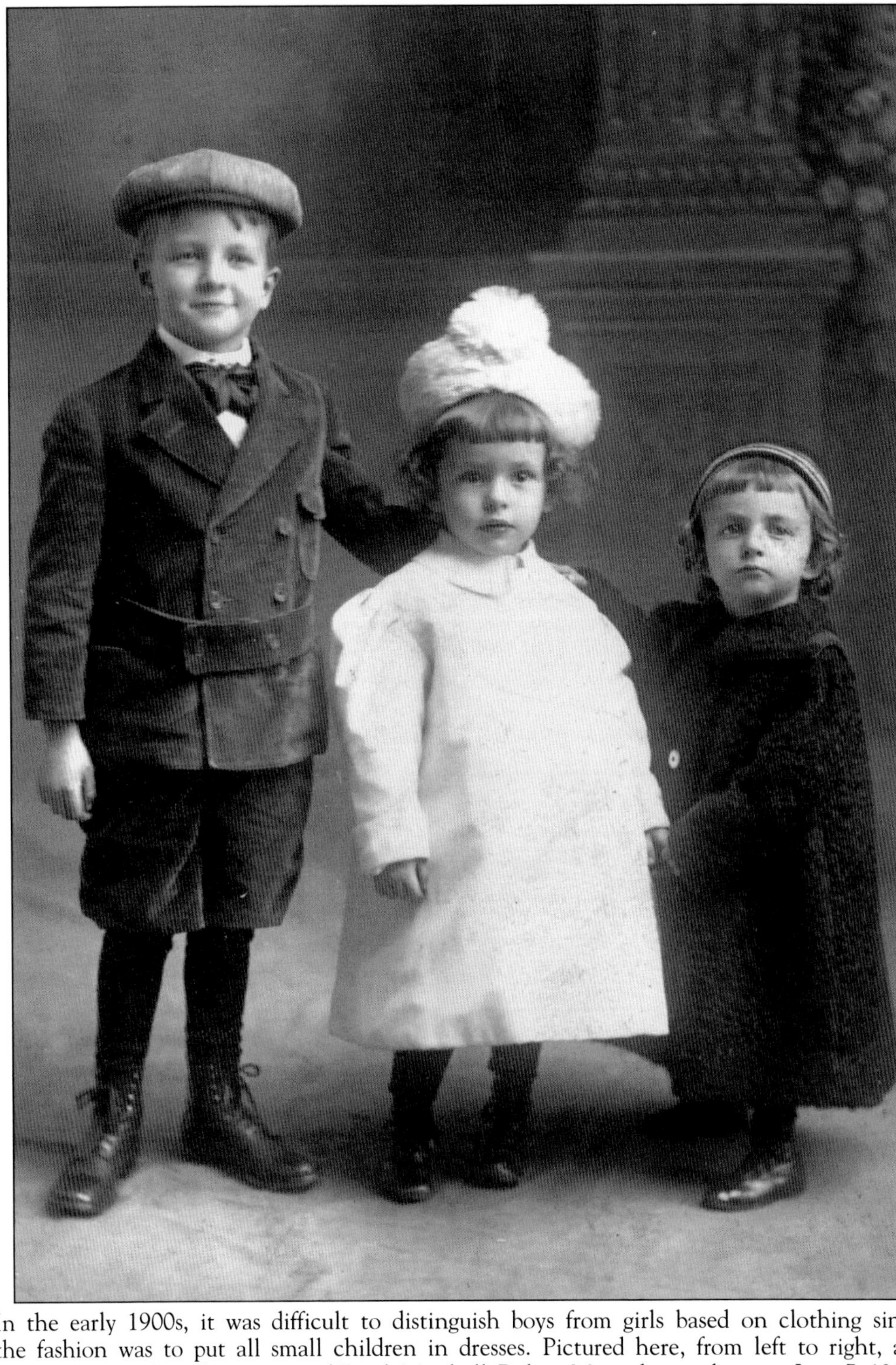

In the early 1900s, it was difficult to distinguish boys from girls based on clothing since the fashion was to put all small children in dresses. Pictured here, from left to right, are William Mitchell, Robert May, and Frank Mitchell. Robert May, who was born on June 7, 1904, eventually became a prominent attorney in Jonesborough and served as mayor from 1936 until 1950. William and Frank were his cousins. May died in 1985. (Courtesy of Caroline M. May.)

Edith Margaret McCracken was raised in Telford, just outside of Jonesborough. Although Edith appeared on the 1910 census and the family Bible lists her birth date as November 19, 1907, her birth certificate states her date of birth as November 19, 1911. No one knows the reason for the delay except possibly that it was issued later and they put the wrong date. (Courtesy of Betty Jane Hylton.)

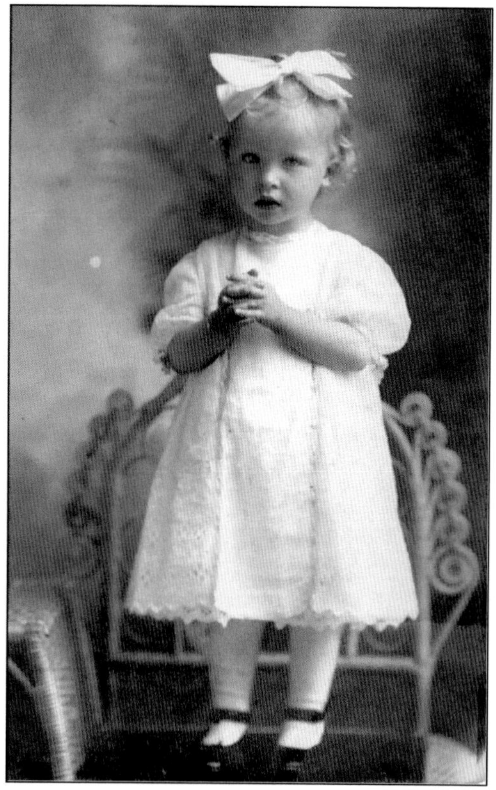

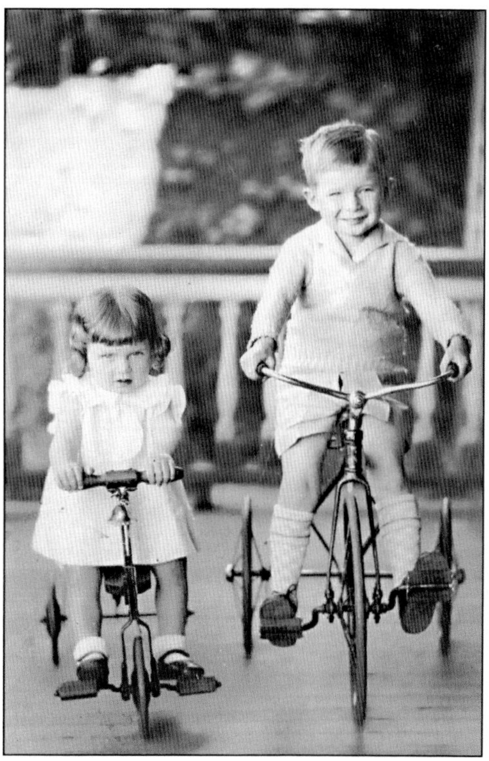

Mary Nelle Bacon and Frank M. Bacon (November 3, 1923–September 1, 1957) ride tricycles on their porch c. 1928. Frank later graduated from the Naval Academy, but he died young of a coronary blockage. (Courtesy of Bill and Mary Nelle Roberson.)

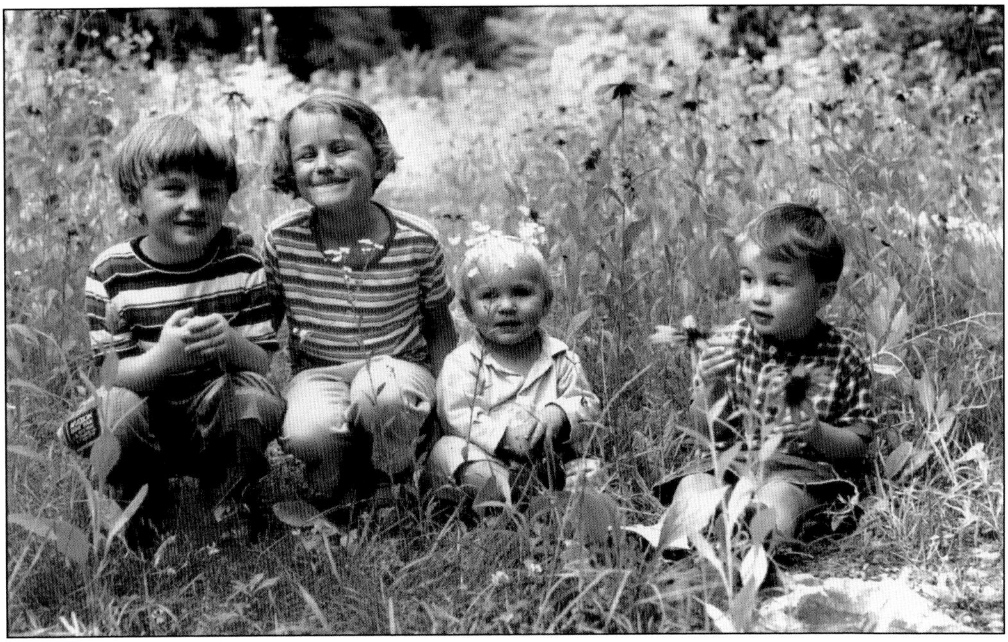

For visitors, the Tri-Cities area offers storytelling in Jonesborough, the racetrack in Bristol, and the opportunity to unwind in local parks. Doe River Gorge in Elizabethton is one area attraction, which includes a mountain lake and a restored 19th-century railroad. Shown here on a gorge outing in 2002, from left to right, are Micah, Sarah, Daniel, and Christopher Haskins. (Photograph by the author.)

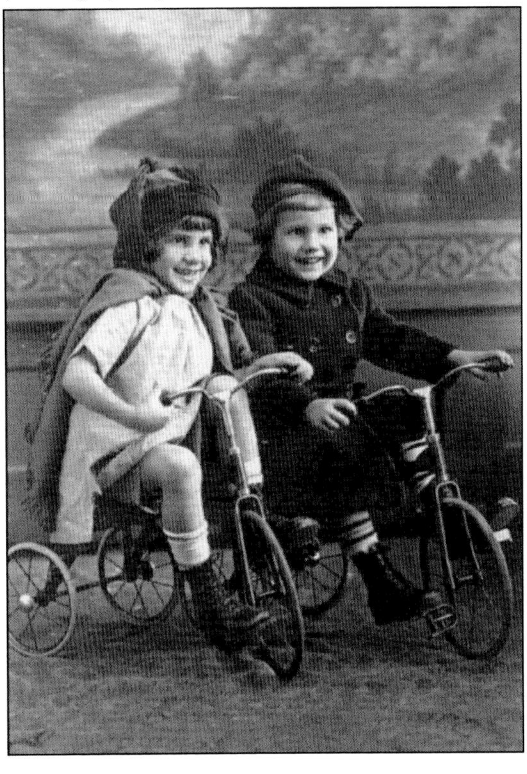

These unidentified children are adorable nonetheless. They were possibly related to the Nat Miller family, who lived in Embreeville in the late 1800s. They also could have been friends of the family. (Courtesy of John G. and Etta Love.)

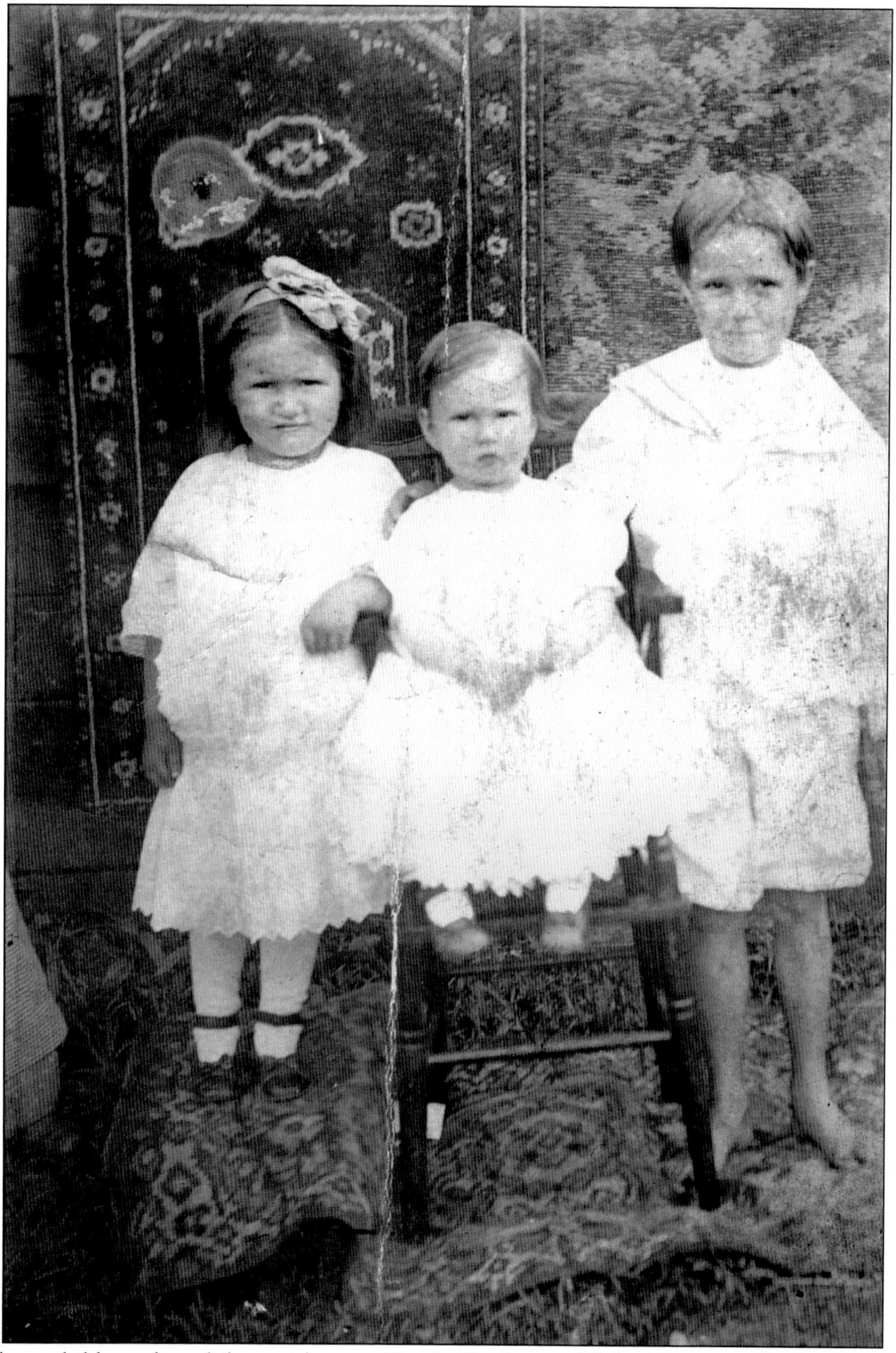

These children, from left to right, are Hazel, Charles, and John Howren. Charles died in October 1916, shortly after this photo was taken. The children are from the Embreeville community. (Courtesy of Chip White.)

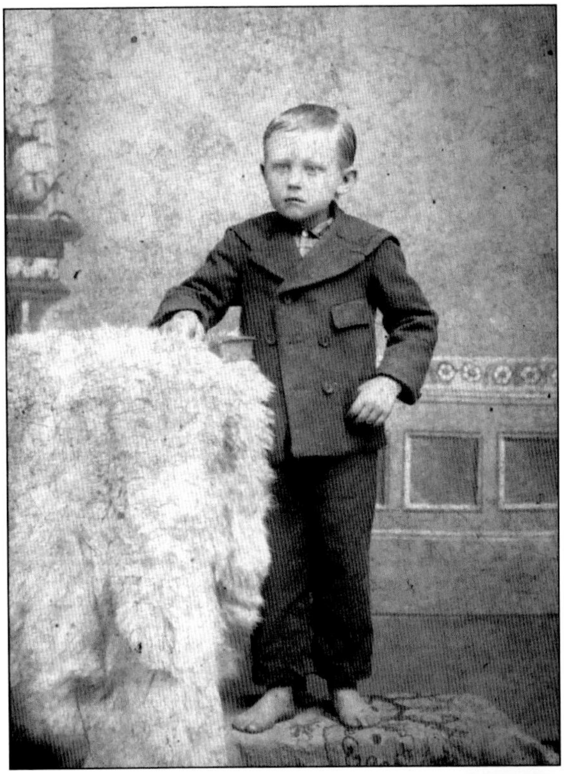

This photograph of Moses Miller was taken in Jonesborough by L.W. Keen. Moses was born September 2, 1892. He worked for a lumber mill in Johnson City as an adult and died young on January 11, 1925. (Courtesy of Barbara S. Hilton.)

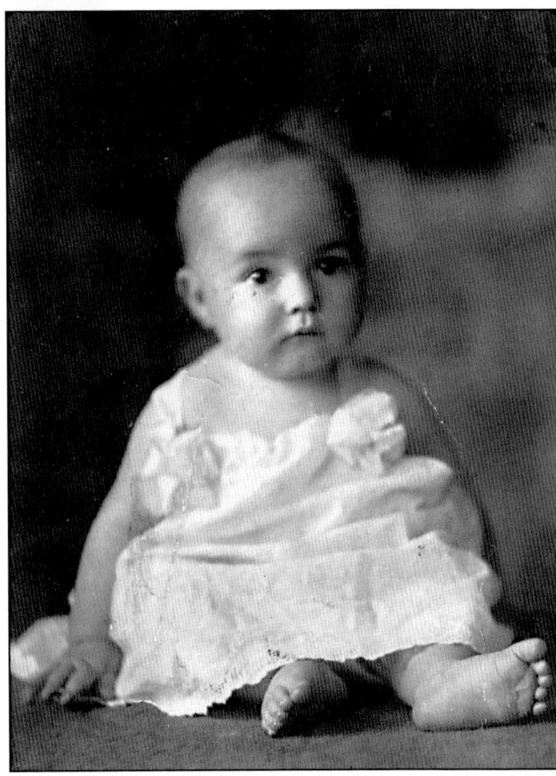

Robert Floyd Saylor was born November 20, 1918. He worked as a fireman in Johnson City and also worked at the nuclear plant in Oak Ridge for a while. He died on November 19, 1991. (Courtesy of Barbara S. Hilton.)

Lucille Huffine is pictured here with her tricycle in the late 1920s. Lucy was raised by her grandmother, Sophronia Young Huffine, upon the death of her mother one month after Lucy's birth. Lucy's mom died after surgery to remove a place from her eye. (Courtesy of Barbara S. Hilton.)

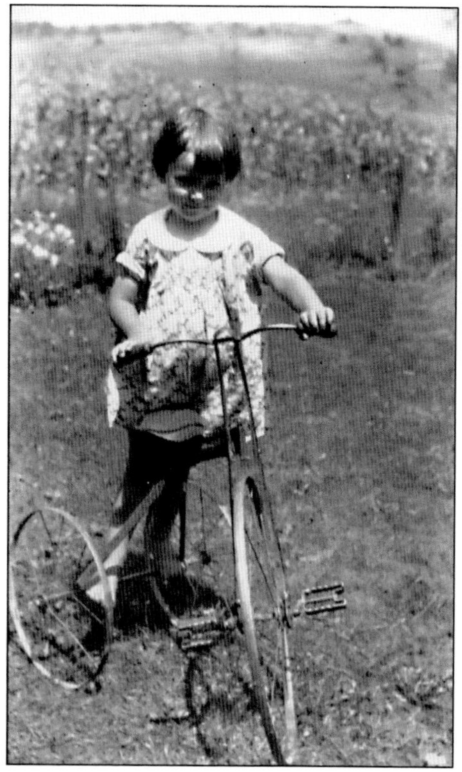

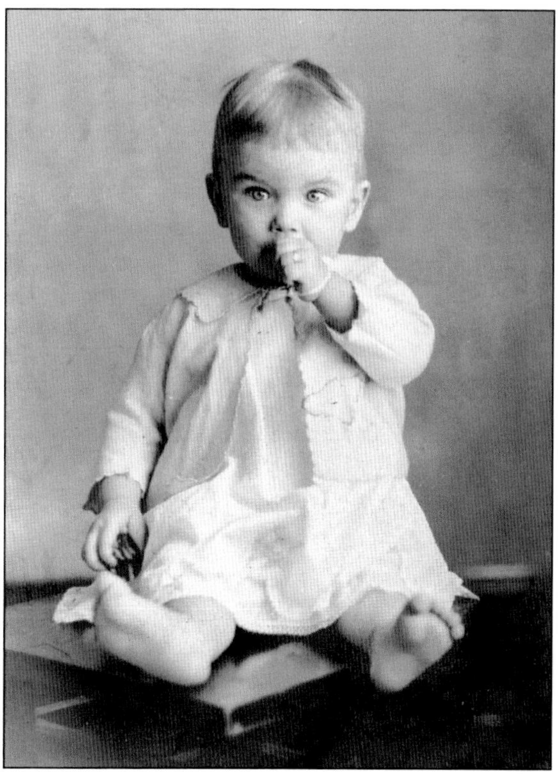

One-year-old Nicolas Patton posed for this photo in the early 1900s. Notice the pacifier, which fit over his thumb, is attached to his left hand. (Courtesy of Martha Stephenson.)

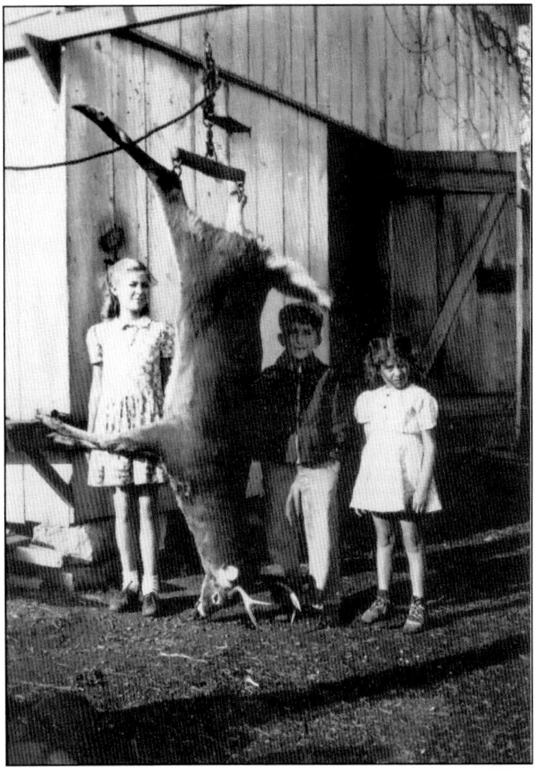

Emma Sue Campbell, George Robert Campbell, and Dottie Kyker stand behind a deer killed in the area by Hugh Harriman Campbell in 1944. (Courtesy of George R. Campbell.)

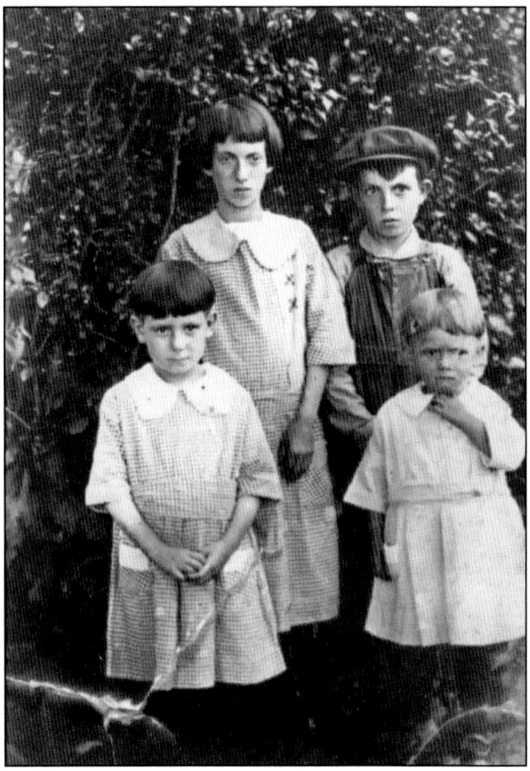

Benjamin and Mona Mitchell had a total of seven children. Pictured here, from left to right, are Cassie, Hazel, Ross, and Edith, c. 1923. (Courtesy of Dennis and Jean Mitchell.)

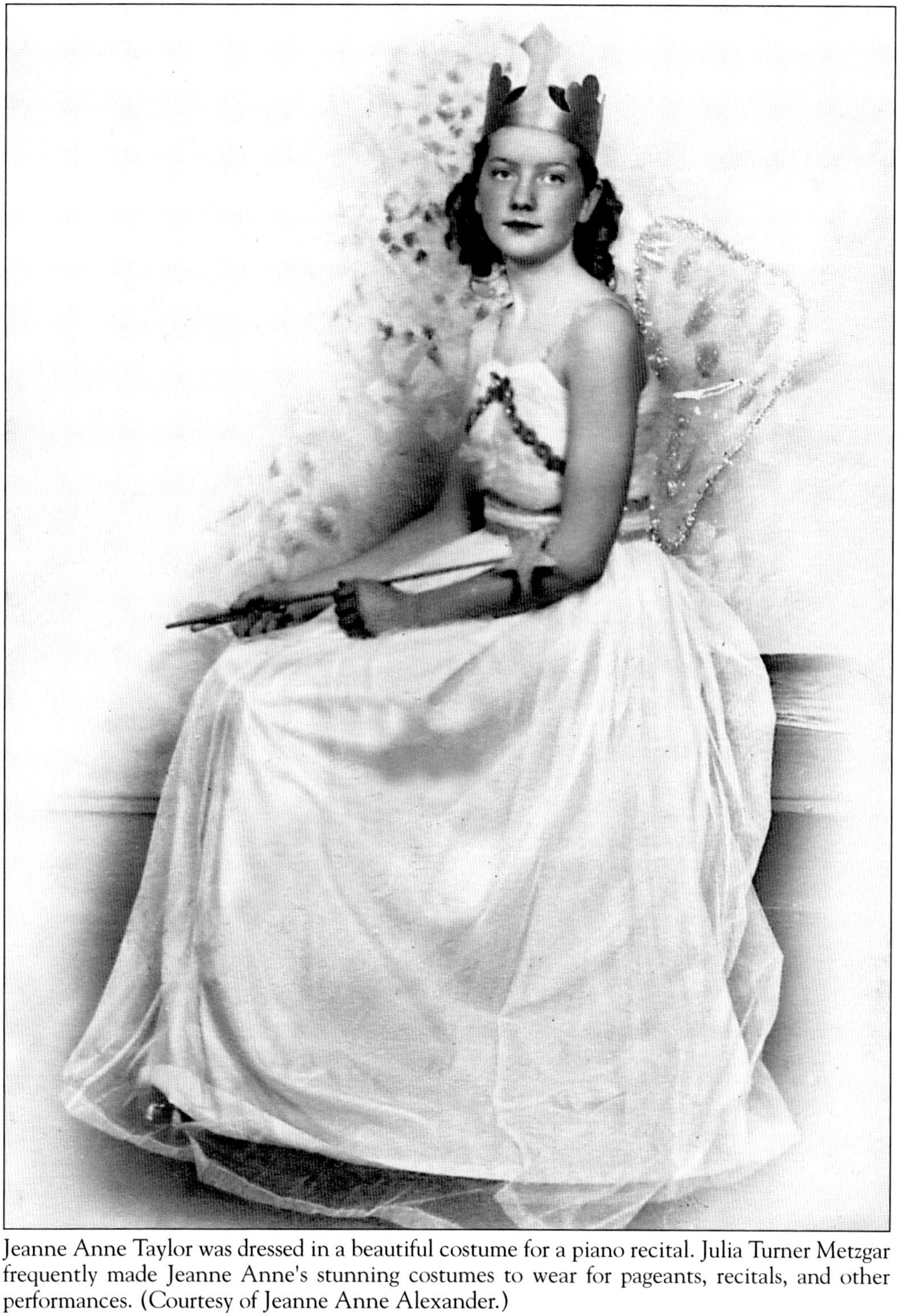

Jeanne Anne Taylor was dressed in a beautiful costume for a piano recital. Julia Turner Metzgar frequently made Jeanne Anne's stunning costumes to wear for pageants, recitals, and other performances. (Courtesy of Jeanne Anne Alexander.)

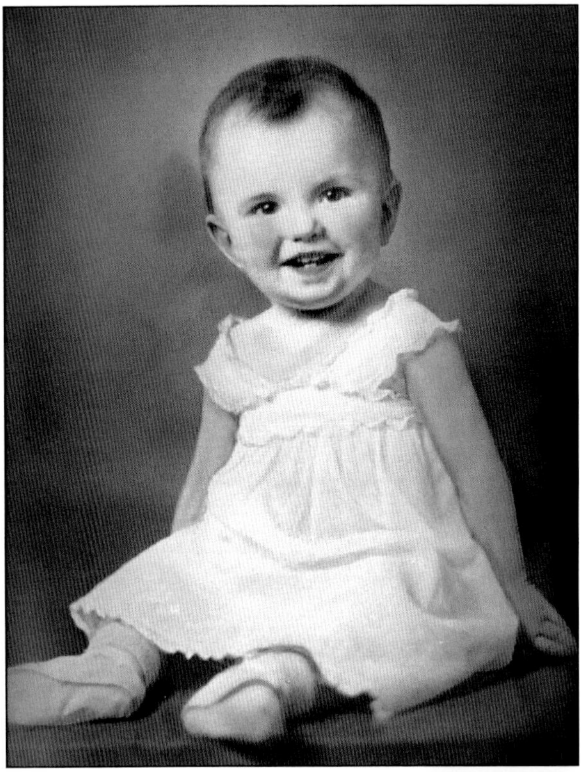

Helen Deakins, born August 22, 1924, was about one year old when this photograph was taken. She married Joseph Roy McCrary and still lives in Jonesborough. (Courtesy of Helen Deakins McCrary.)

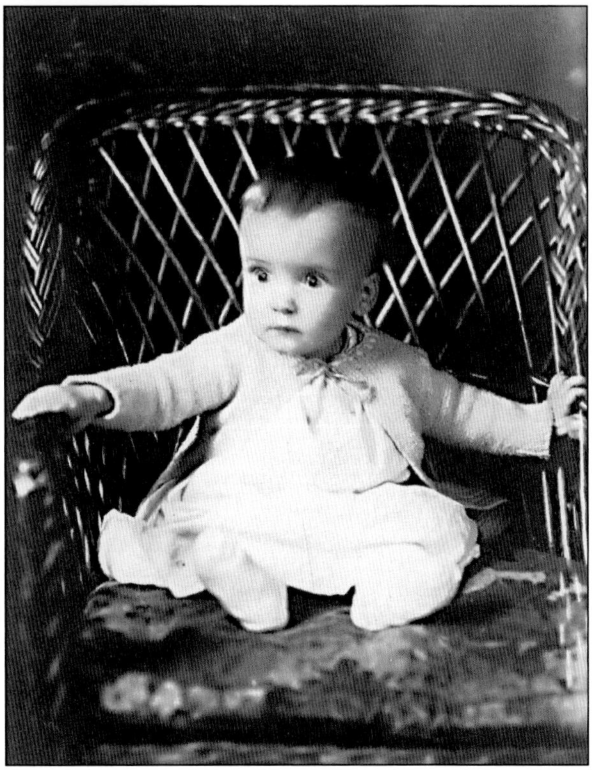

F.B. Poteat's family has lived in Jonesborough as farmers for several generations. F.B. was born in 1921 and is more commonly known as "June." When his hay barn caught fire in 2004, June said the outpouring of community support was remarkable. (Courtesy of June and Ruby Poteat.)

These giddy-looking girls are Ruby Saxon and Irene Clevenger. (Courtesy of June and Ruby Poteat.)

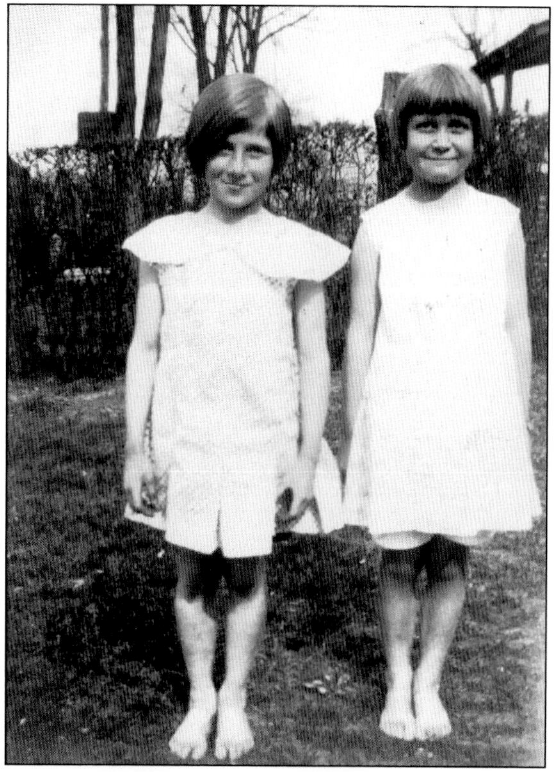

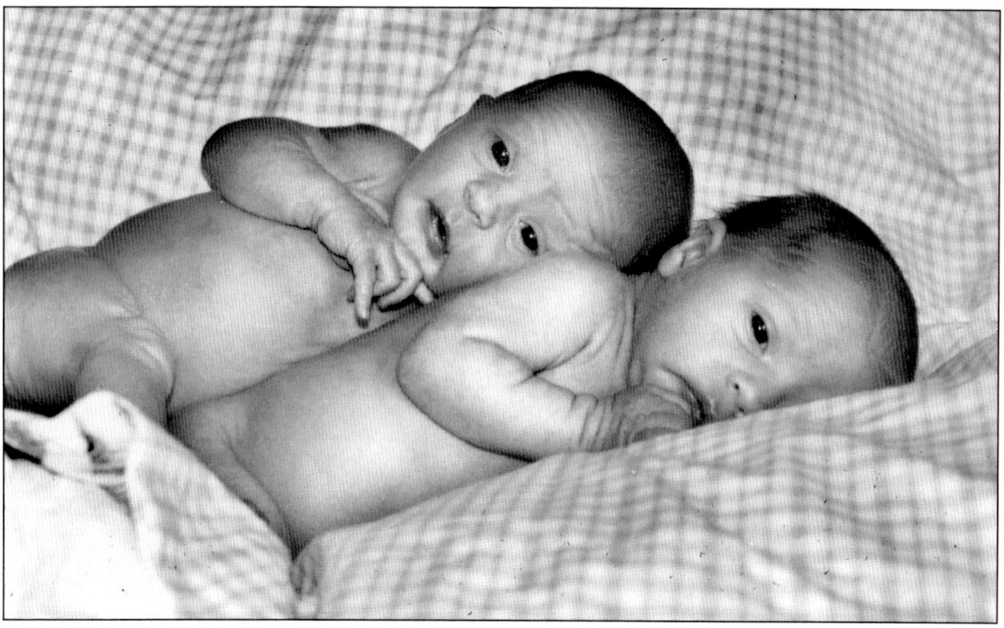

Haven Abigail and Olivia Hope, born on December 13, 2003, are the daughters of Kenny and Lori Keck. The girls join brothers Elijah and Noah as part of a whole new generation of Jonesborough residents who will enjoy all the area has to offer, including parks, museums, storytelling, hiking trails, art exhibits, and more. Kenny serves the area as a fireman for the Johnson City Fire Department.(Photograph by the author.)

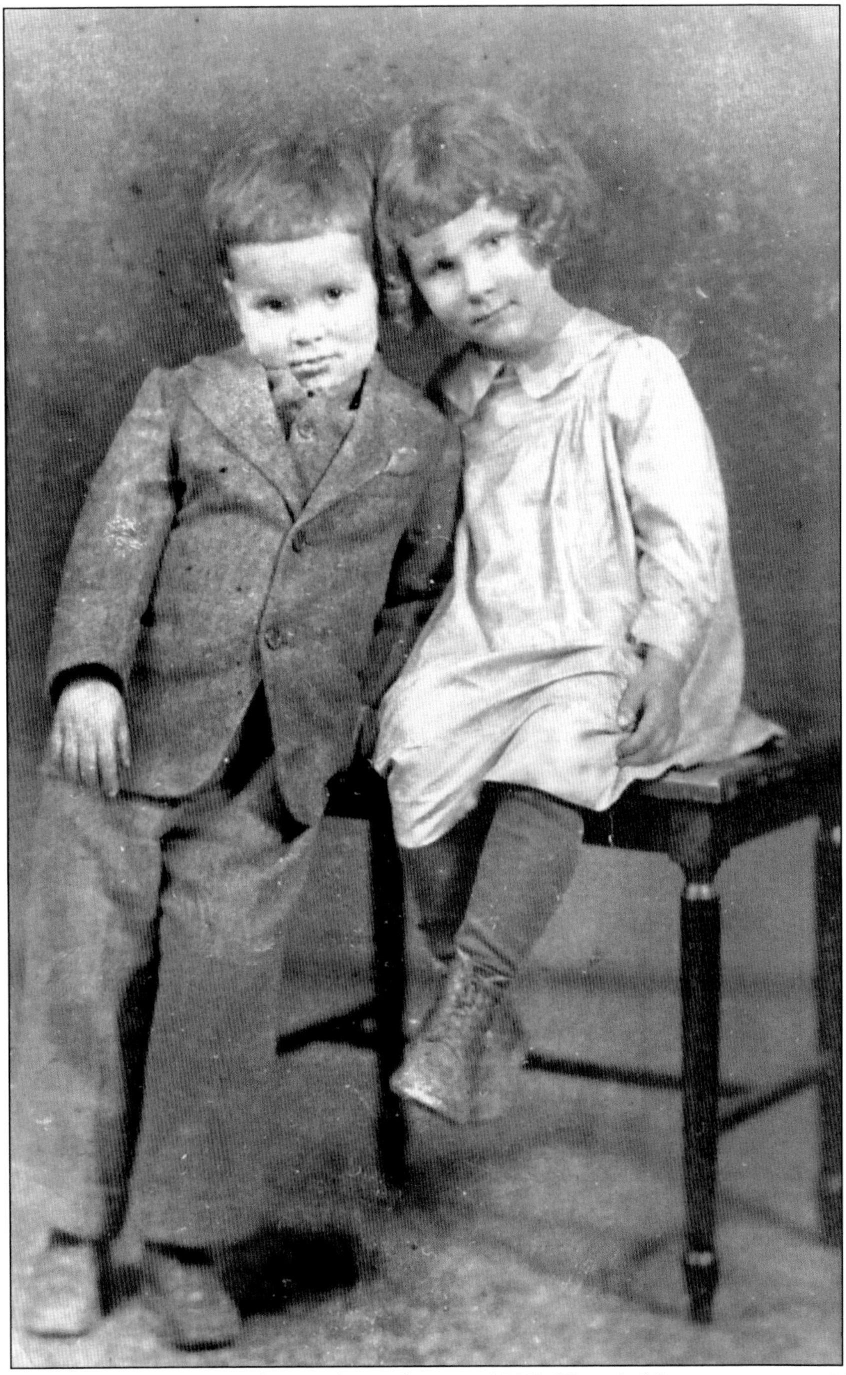

Sam D. May and his sister Ruth are shown here *c.* 1925. The children grew up at 280 May Road on the family homestead, near the New Victory Church. As an adult, Ruth married Palma L. Robinson, who was elected to the Tennessee House of Representatives. When her husband died in office, the Washington County commission appointed her to complete his term as state representative. She served from 1982 until 1992. The road from Jonesborough to Boones Creek is now known as the Palma L. Robinson Parkway. (Courtesy of Jane May.)

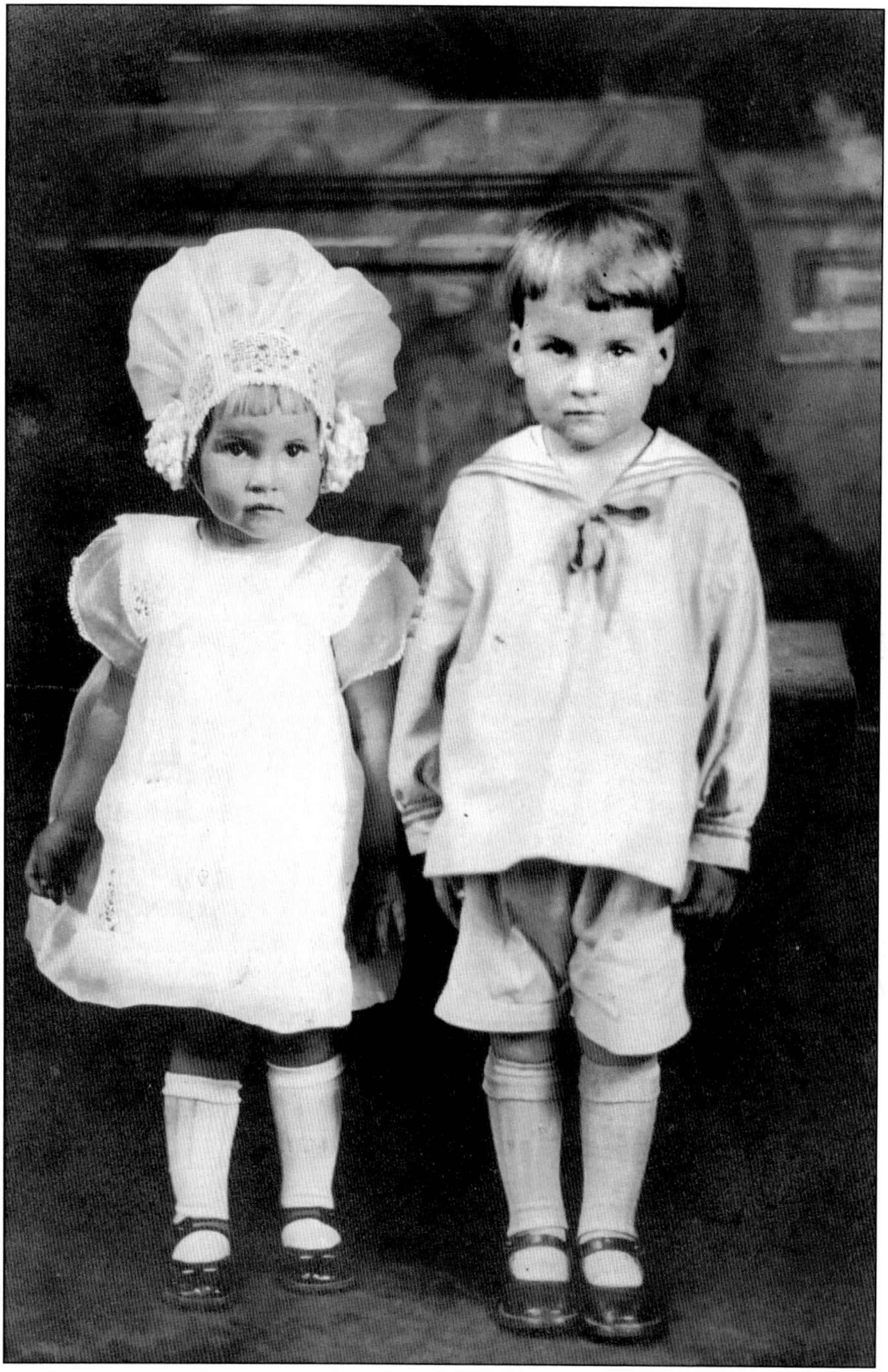

Photography came to the area early when L.W. Keen opened a photography studio in Jonesborough in 1847. Later, D.L. Hensley opened a studio, but amazingly enough, there were also excellent individual photographers. Eva Taylor, co-owner of Dillow-Taylor Funeral Home, enjoyed photography as a hobby, according to her daughter, Jeanne Anne. This adorable photograph of two unidentified children was taken by Taylor, probably in the early 1900s. (Courtesy of Jeanne Anne Taylor.)

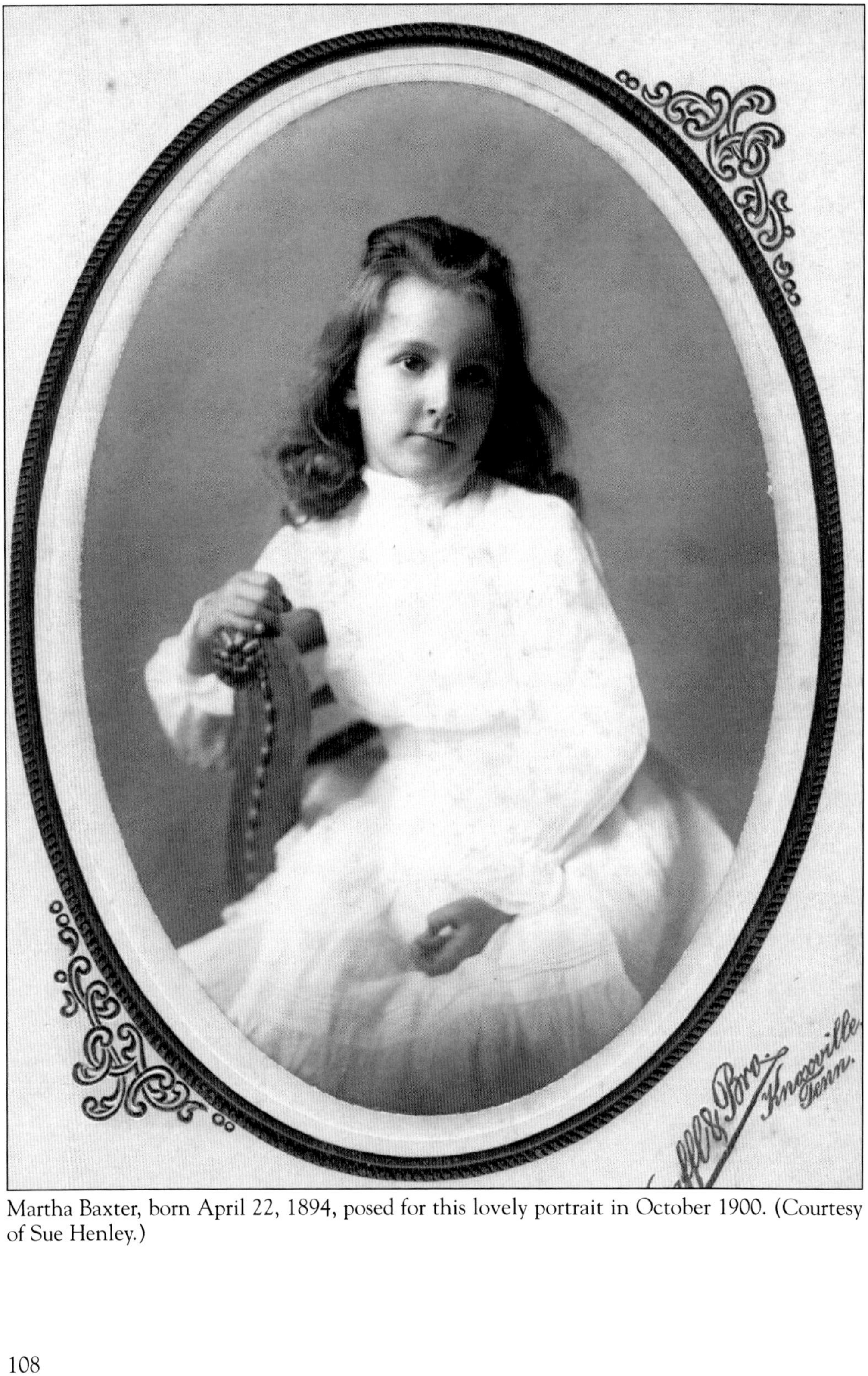

Martha Baxter, born April 22, 1894, posed for this lovely portrait in October 1900. (Courtesy of Sue Henley.)

Eight

MILITARY

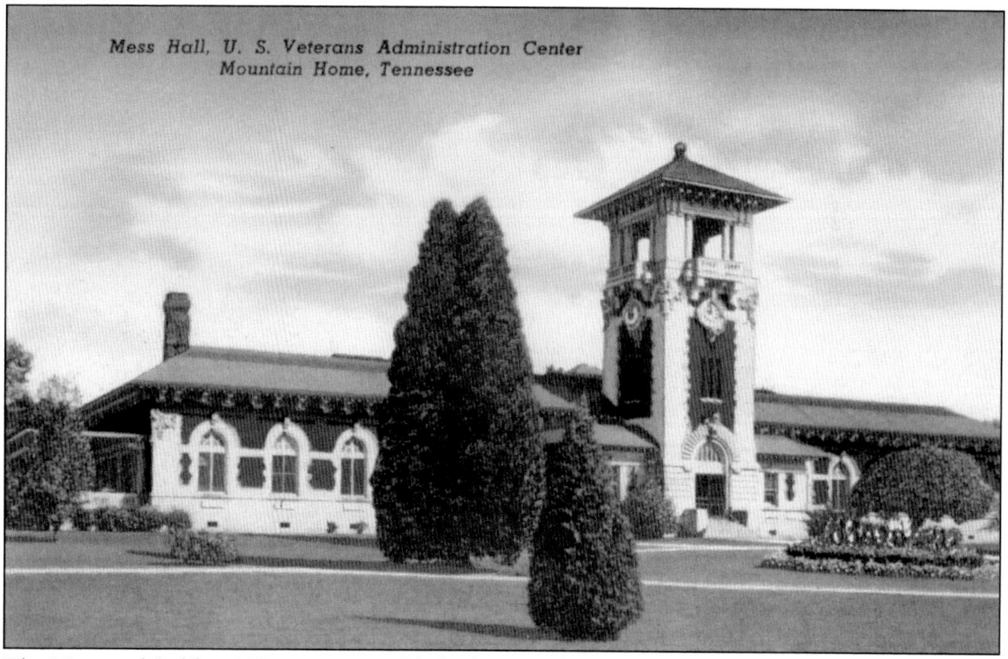

The National Soldiers' Home was established in nearby Johnson City in 1901 as a self-sufficient city. The home provided services for soldiers, including veterans of the Spanish-American War, the Civil War, and the War of 1812. The National Soldiers' Home became known as the Veterans Administration Center at Mountain Home in 1930, and this was later changed to the Veterans Affairs Medical Center. (Courtesy of Paul Stone.)

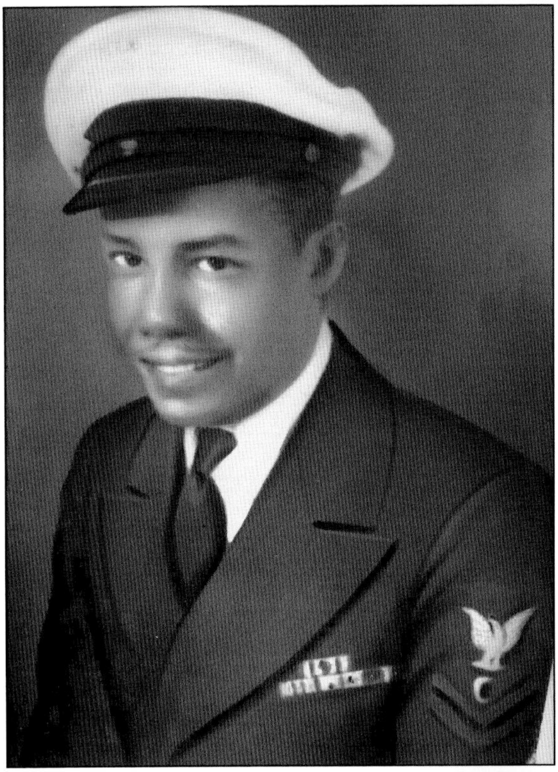

Curtis Franklin Russell, born February 28, 1924, joined the U.S. Navy on December 17, 1941, after the attack on Pearl Harbor. Russell was awarded a Purple Heart for injuries received on a ship in World War I. He is buried in Jonesborough's New Victory Cemetery. (Courtesy of Alfred and Gwendolyn Greenlee.)

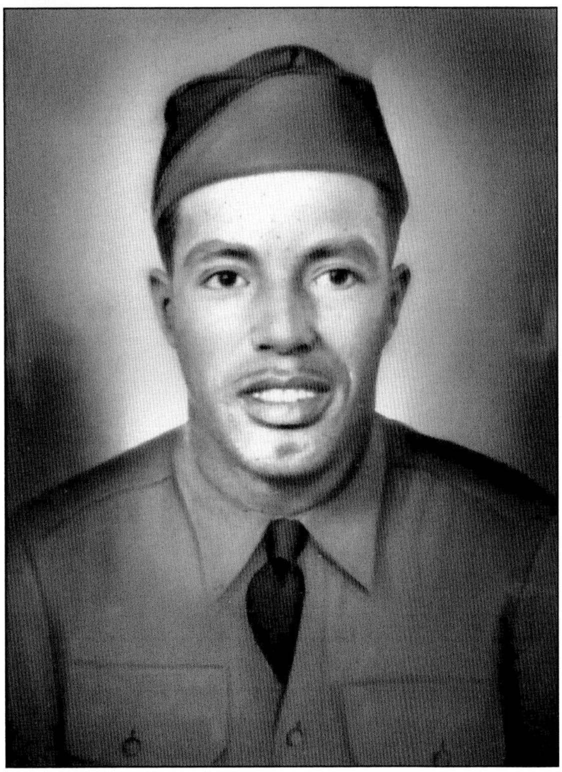

Hiawatha L.E. Perry, known as "Bud," died on October 19, 1944, in Normandy, France. He had been serving in the United States Army as a staff sergeant. (Courtesy of Alfred and Gwendolyn Greenlee.)

Deo Nacomus Russell was the daughter of Samuel and Carrie Russell. Like her brother Curtis, Deo also attended Jonesborough's segregated elementary school Booker T. Washington through the eighth grade and then the segregated Langston High School. Deo graduated in May 1950 and joined the U.S. Navy in December 1950. She served until June 1971 and died on December 5 that same year. (Courtesy of Alfred and Gwendolyn Greenlee.)

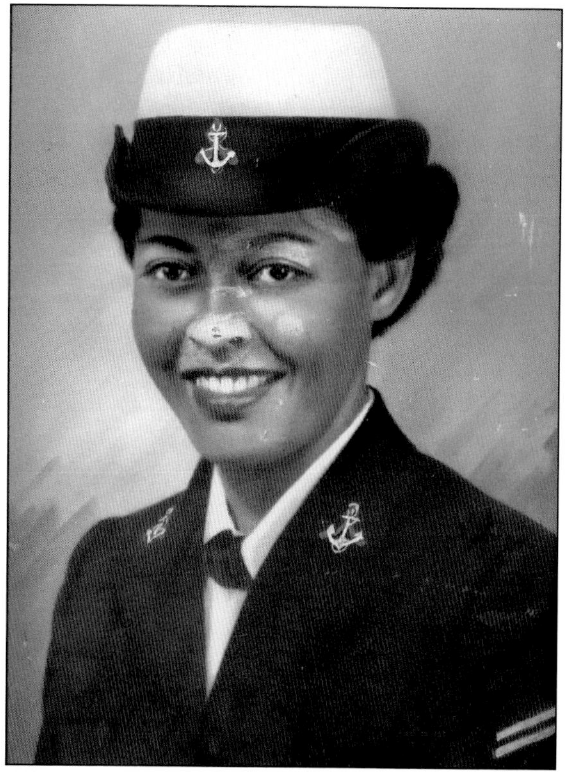

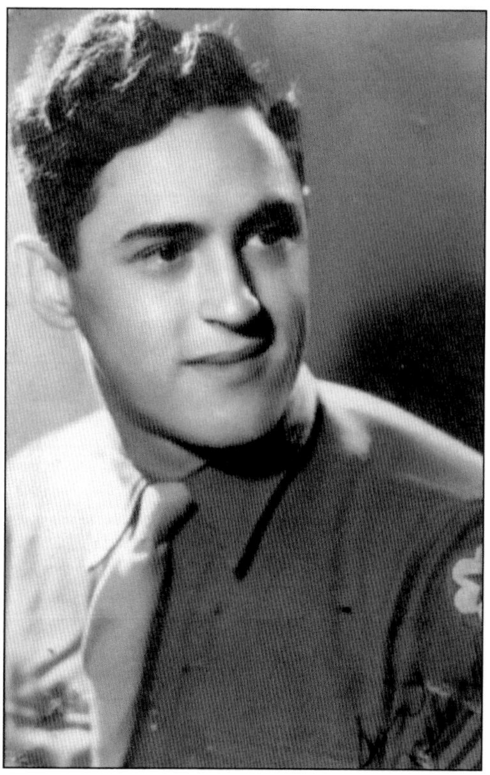

Walter Ballard Tyree was the son of Sally and Doc Tyree. The family lived on Bugaboo Springs Road in Jonesborough. Walter joined the military and served in World War II. This photograph was taken in France on June 12, 1944. (Courtesy of Barbara S. Hilton.)

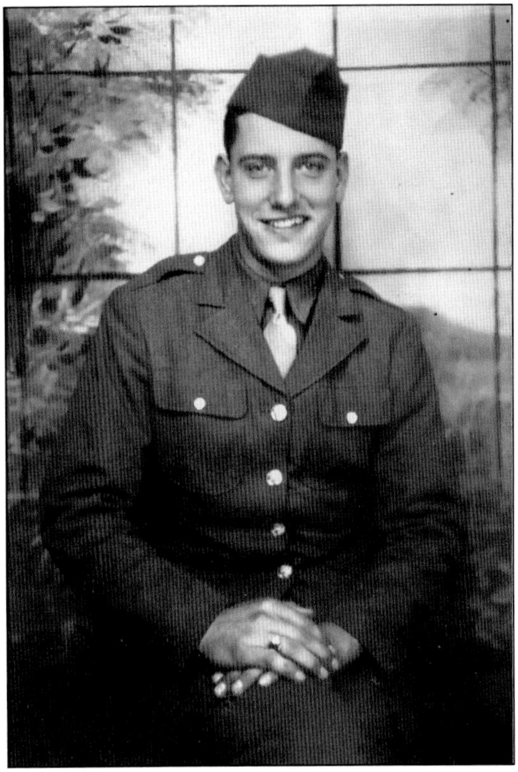

Bill Roberson joined the military at age 19 and served in World War II. (Courtesy of Bill and Mary Nelle Roberson.)

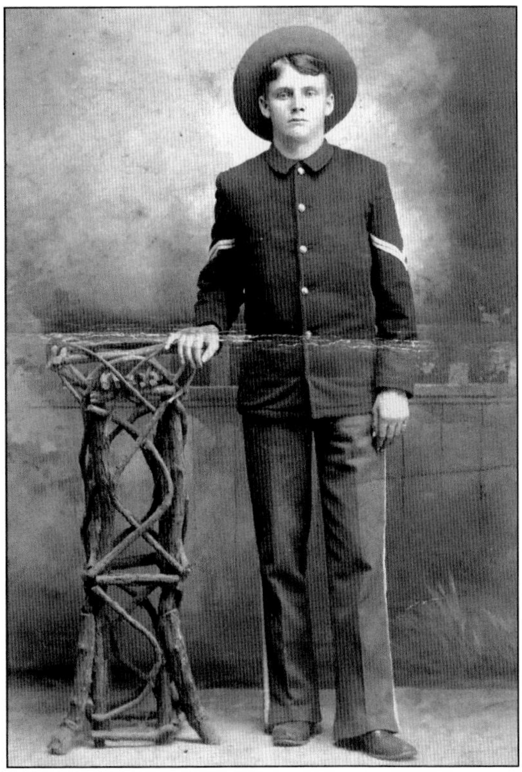

Dr. Joseph Roy McCrary served as a doctor during the Spanish-American War and World War I. He moved his family to this area in the early 1800s and lived in the Wells house in Fall Branch with his wife, Maude, and four children. (Courtesy of Helen Deakins McCrary.)

Nine

COMMUNITY

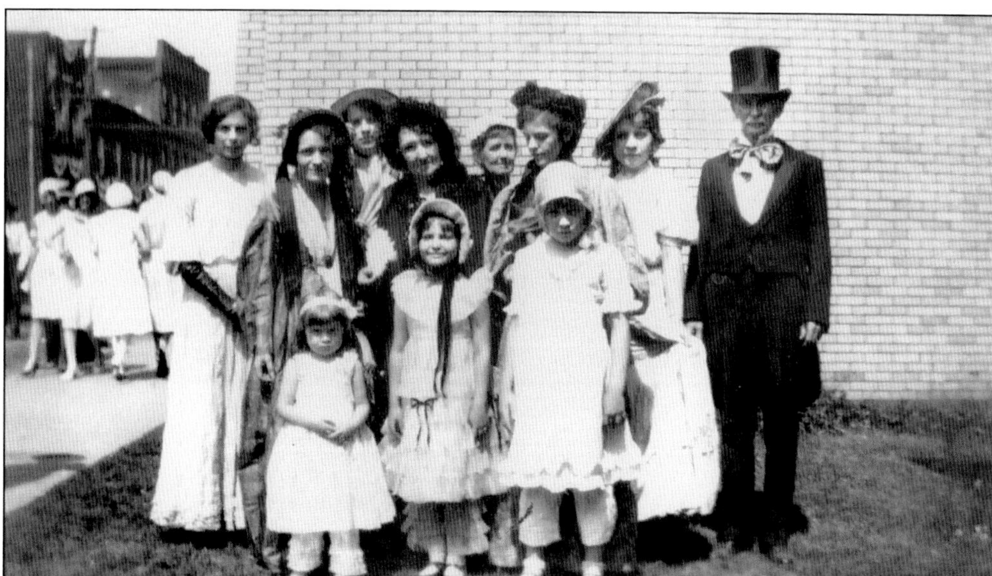

Members of the pageant who performed during the July 4, 1930 sesquicentennial celebration included, from left to right, Mary Nelle Bacon, Nellie Grigsby, and Carolyn Corum, all on the front row. Scott Hickey is on the right, most likely dressed as Andrew Jackson. (Courtesy of Bill and Mary Nelle Roberson.)

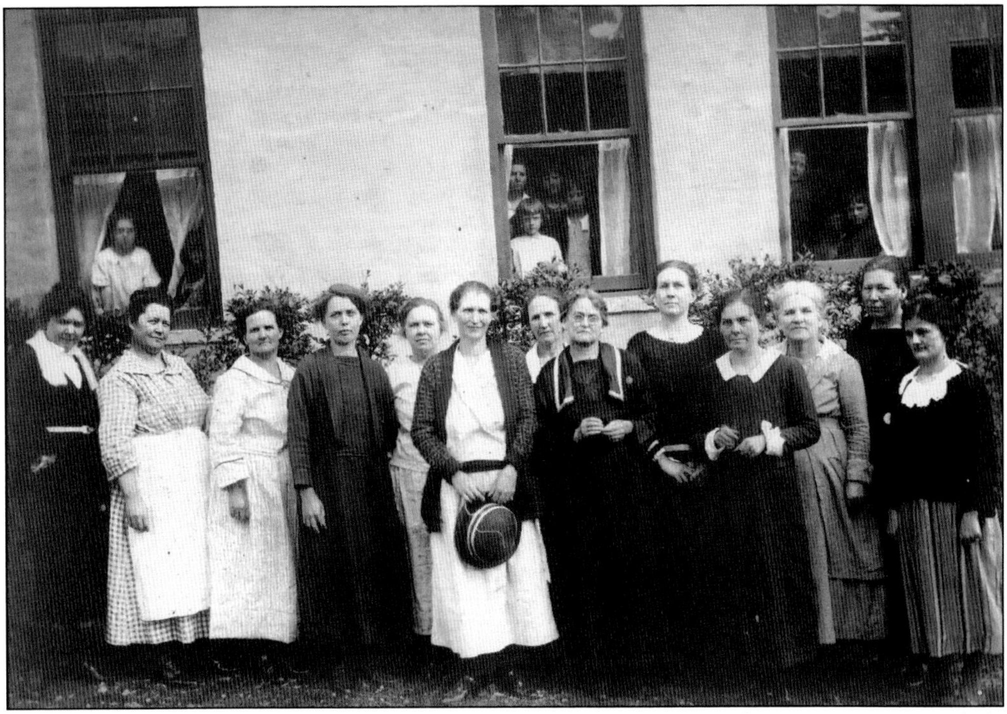

In the late 1800s and early 1900s, the Embreeville community was a thriving area, particularly due to the location of the iron mines nearby. Here, some women pose in front of the Clubhouse as children peek out the windows. (Courtesy of Chip White.)

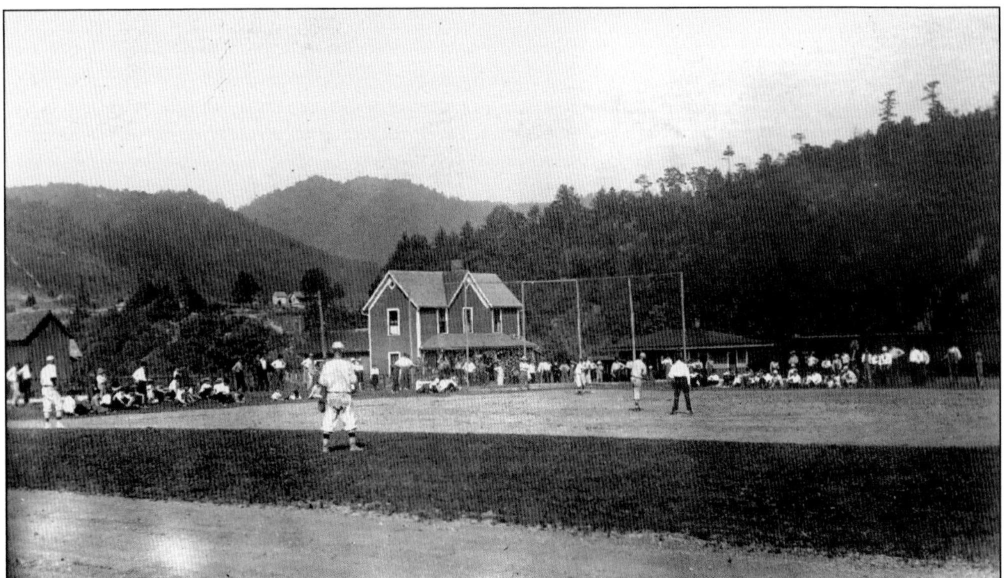

A popular activity in the Embreeville community of Jonesborough was baseball. Notice the Clubhouse, the gathering place for local citizens and visitors, located in the center background of this photograph from the early 1900s. (Courtesy of Chip White.)

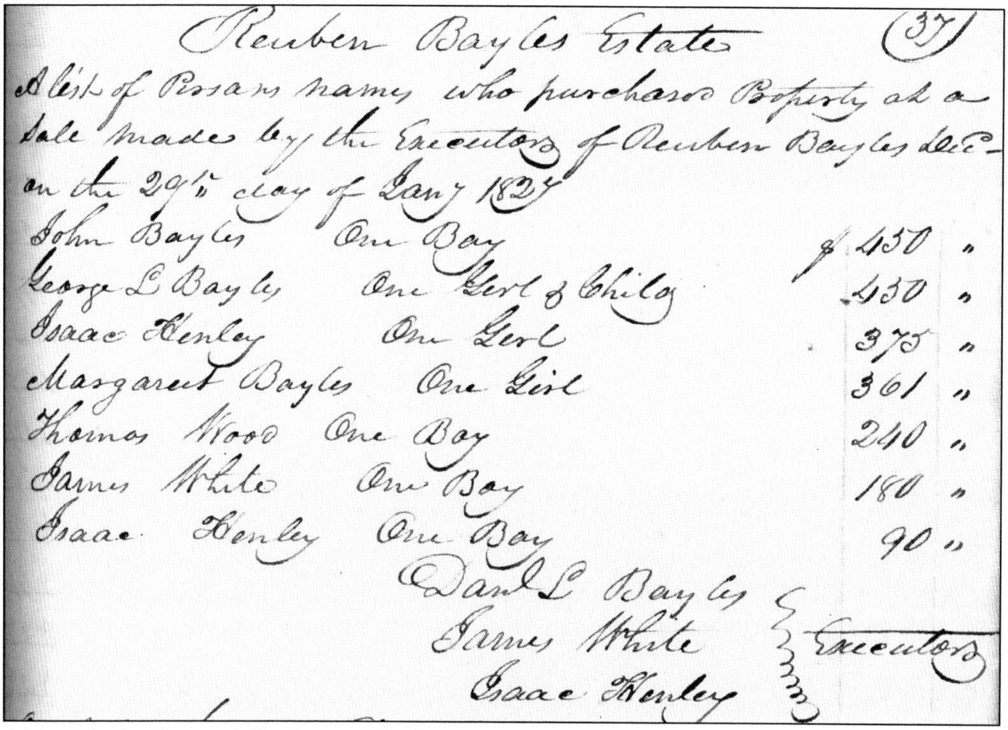

Reuben Bayles Estate (37)

A list of Persons names who purchased Property at a sale made by the Executors of Reuben Bayles Decd on the 29th day of Jany 1827

John Bayles	One Boy	$ 450	"
George L Bayles	One Girl & Child	430	"
Isaac Henley	One Girl	375	"
Margaret Bayles	One Girl	361	"
Thomas Wood	One Boy	240	"
James White	One Boy	180	"
Isaac Henley	One Boy	90	"

Danl L Bayles
James White
Isaac Henley
} Executors

Although the date is difficult to read, this document is from either 1826 or 1827. It is a copy of a portion of the estate sale of Reuben Bayles documenting the sale of boy and girl slaves. Most of the purchasers, listed on the left side of the document, were probably related to Reuben since they have the same last name. (Courtesy of the Washington County Clerk's Office.)

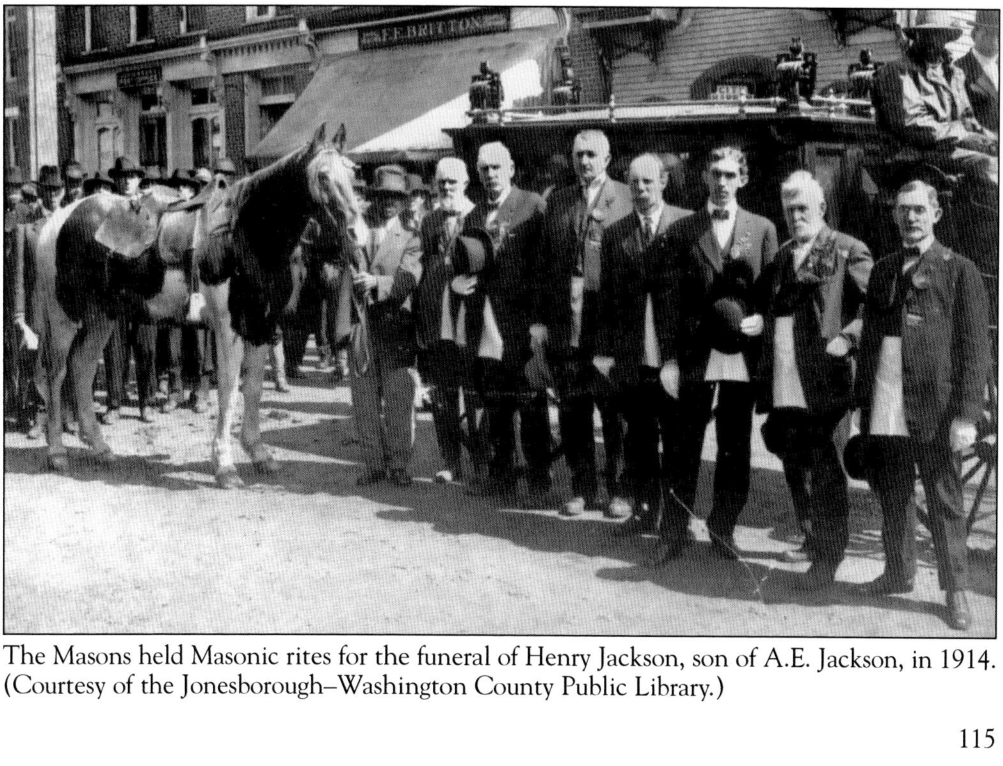

The Masons held Masonic rites for the funeral of Henry Jackson, son of A.E. Jackson, in 1914. (Courtesy of the Jonesborough–Washington County Public Library.)

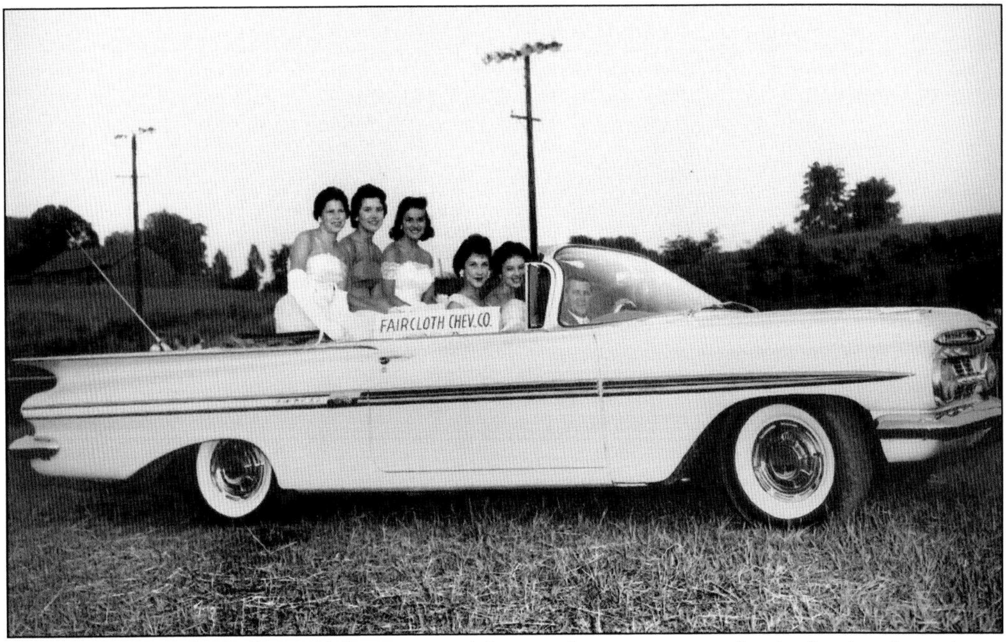

The Jonesborough Riding Club presented horse shows to raise funds for local projects. This money was recently donated to the Crumley House. Pictured here, from left to right, are Barbara G. Smith, Freida Byrd, Sarah Boshears, Linda Rankin, Jill Broyles, and driver F.B. Poteat Jr. Faircloth Chevrolet of Johnson City donated the use of the car. (Courtesy of Barbara G. Smith.)

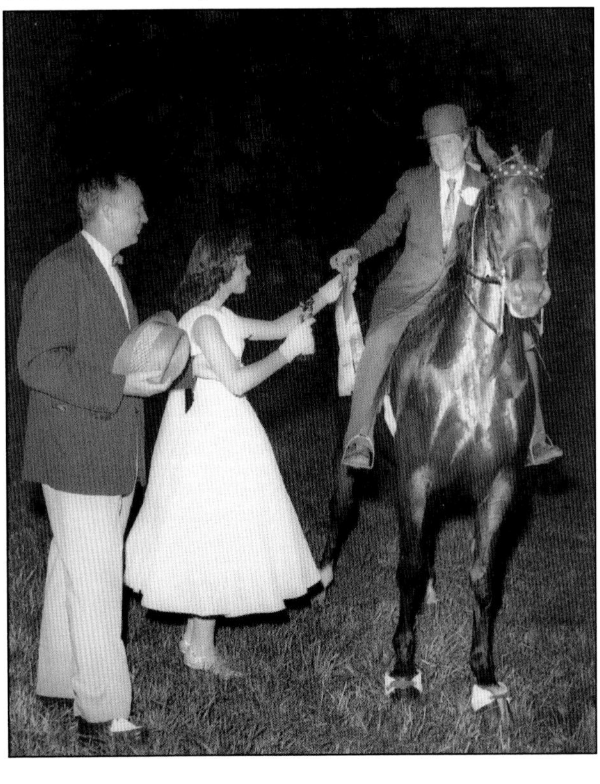

Ringmaster Bill Smith and ribbon girl Jeanne Torbett present a ribbon to a winning rider in a Jonesborough Riding Club horse show c. 1957. (Courtesy of Barbara G. Smith.)

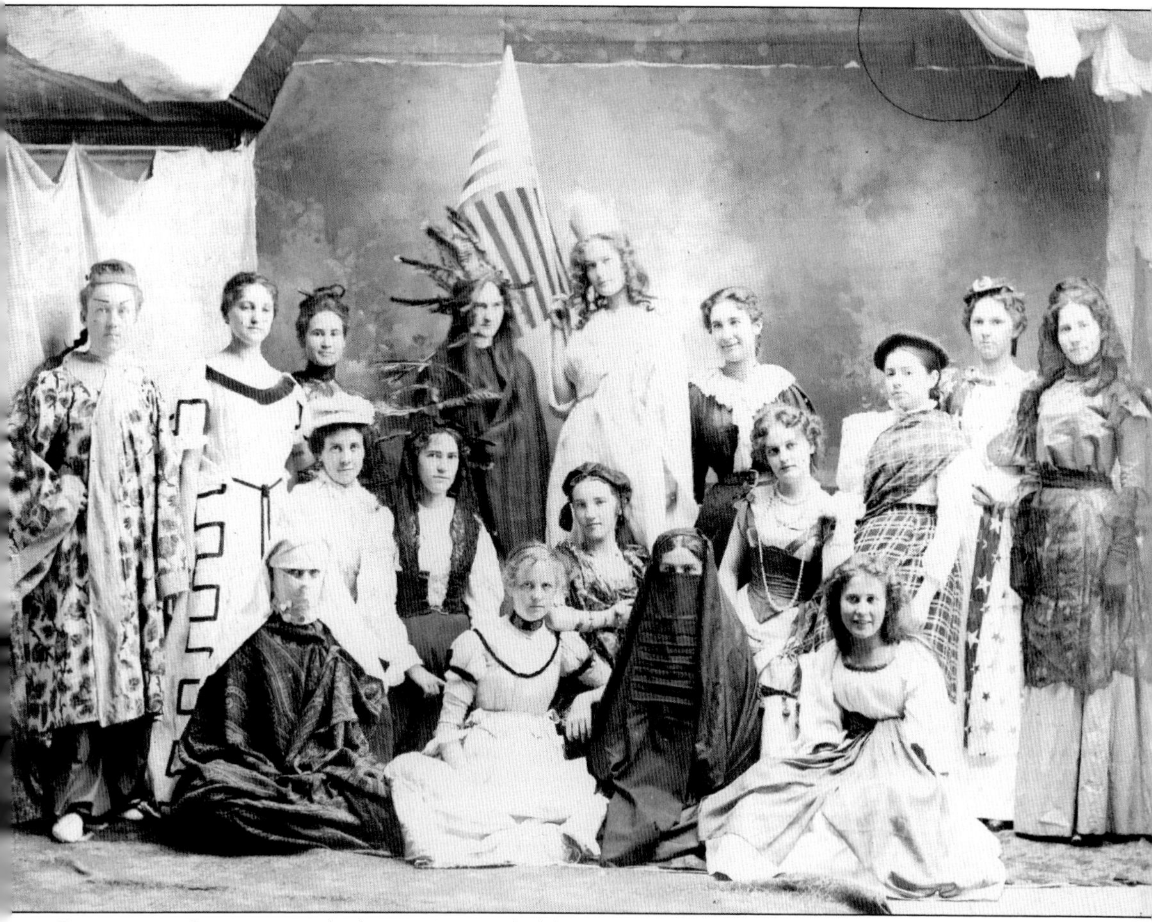

During a performance in the late 1800s, probably c. 1890, young ladies were dressed to represent different countries. The participants pictured include Mattie Pritchett, China; Minnie May, Greece; Lena Thomas, Japan; Ida Seamon, India; Annie Panhorst; Mary Miller, Africa; Pearl Britton, Scotland; ? Smith, United States; Nelle Hoss, Spain; Nelle Printup, Persia; Laura Bruner, Ireland; Nell Mason, Italy; Lilian Dosser, Norway; Bessie Piper, South America; Nita Anderson, Egypt; Daisy Panhorst, Holland; and Buelah Thomas, Germany. (Courtesy of Caroline M. May.)

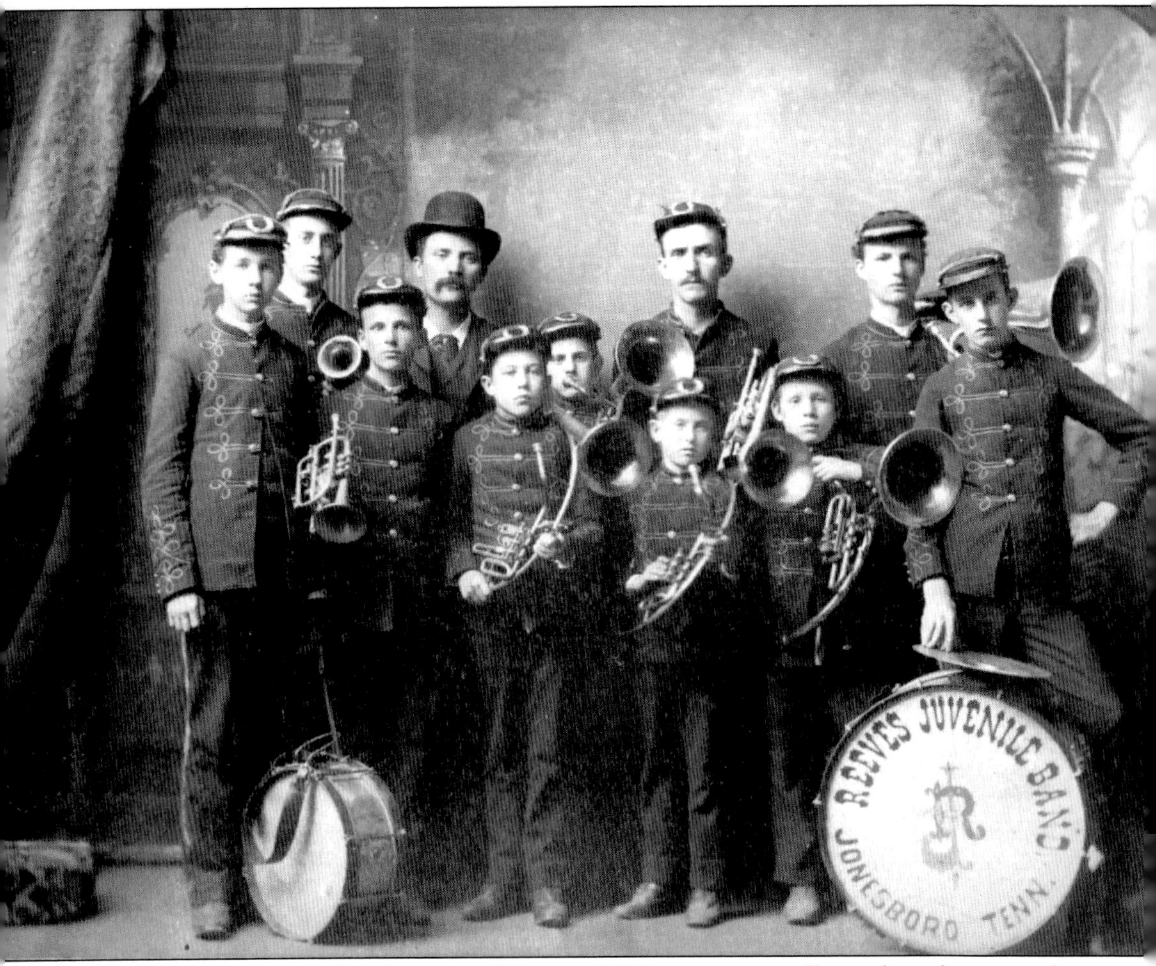

The Reeves Juvenile Band, pictured here c. 1900, was an excellent place for young boys to practice their musical talents and learn to work in a group. Included in this group were Rufus May and Marshall Fink. (Courtesy of Caroline M. May.)

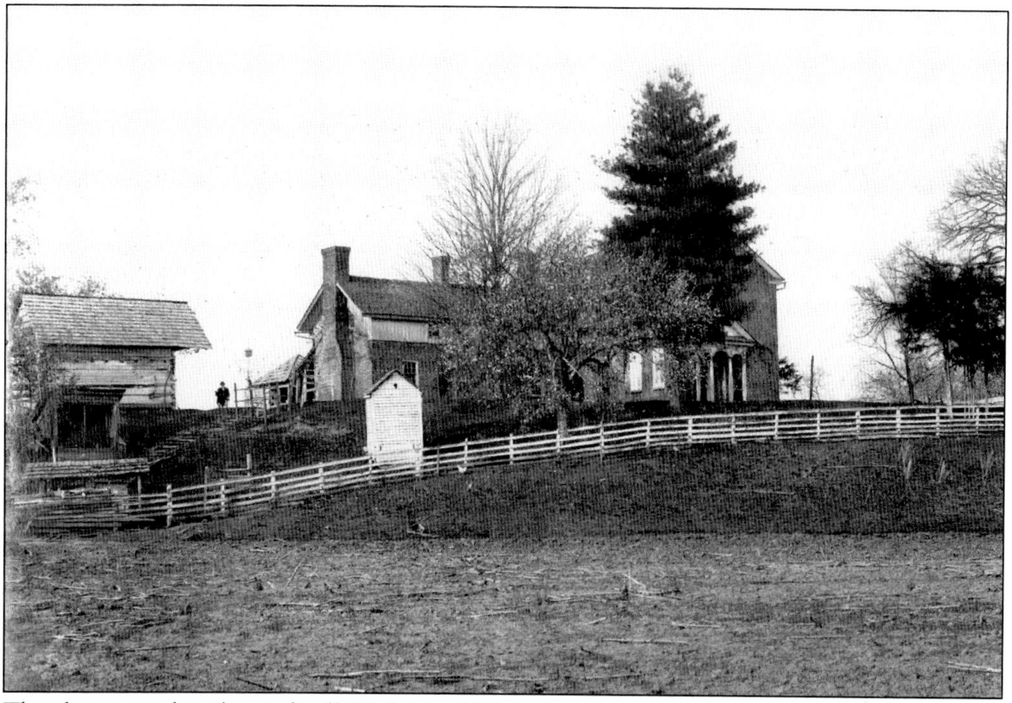

This homestead is located off Highway 11E in northeast Washington County. Valentine DeVault had the home built in the early 1800s, although his father, Heinrich DeVault, had originally purchased the land. A very large, early-era photograph of this homestead is located in at the Washington County Courthouse. (Courtesy of the Washington County Clerk's Office.)

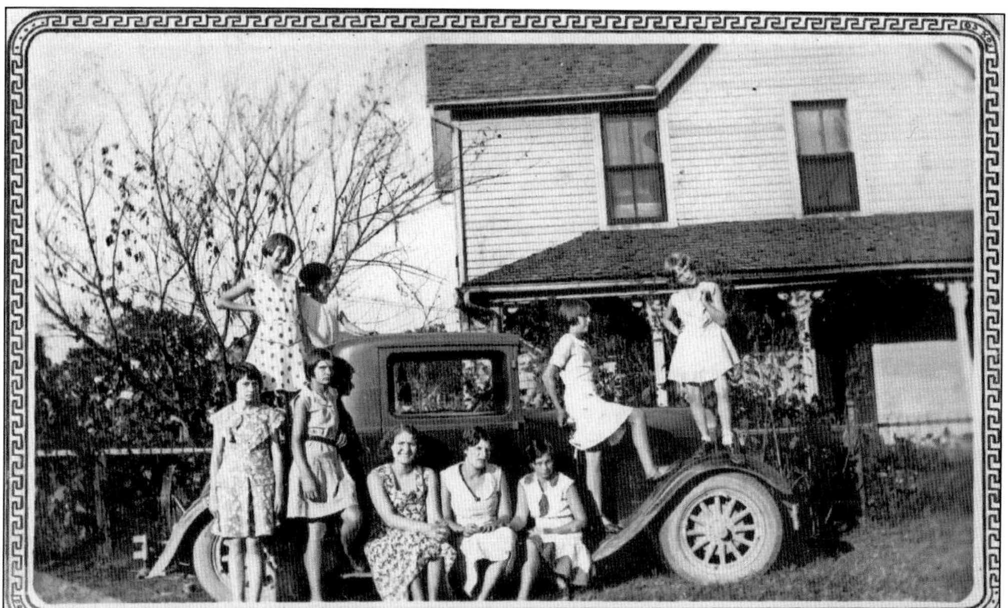

Women and children gather in front of the Embreeville Community Clubhouse c. 1920. (Courtesy of Chip White.)

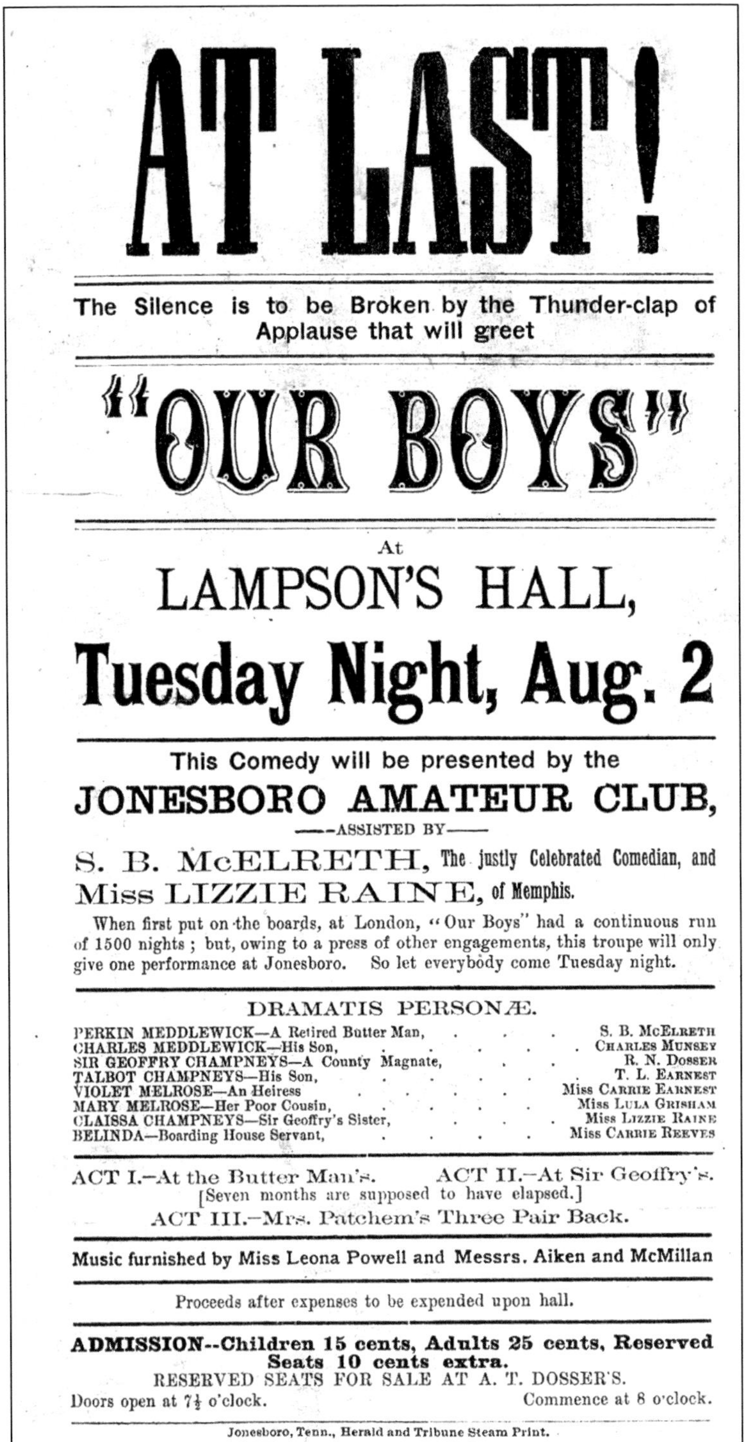

This advertisement for *Our Boys* appeared in *The Herald and Tribune*, probably in the early 1900s. Patrons could purchase tickets at A.T. Dosser's for 15¢ for children or 25¢ for adults and could reserve seats for 10¢ extra. (Courtesy of Lyle Haws.)

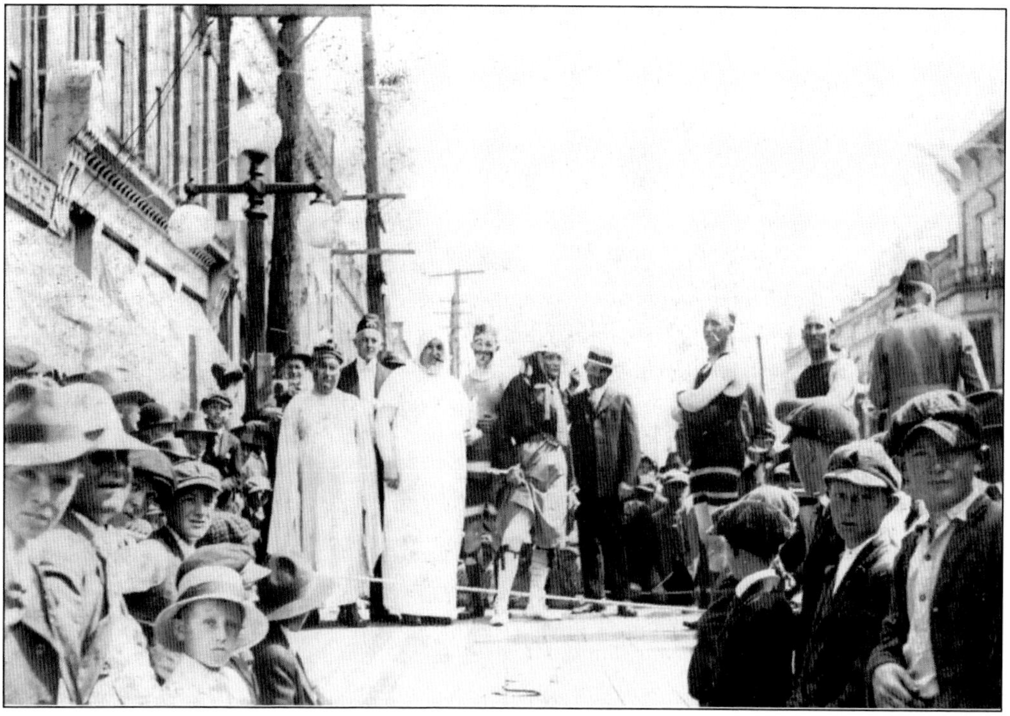

The fabulous sesquicentennial celebrations for Jonesborough that took place on July 4, 1930, included a parade, a pageant, music, and orations from the likes of Alfred Taylor, former governor, and Dr. A.S. Doak, great-grandson of Samuel Doak. This photograph is believed to be of performers in a play. (Courtesy of Caroline M. May.)

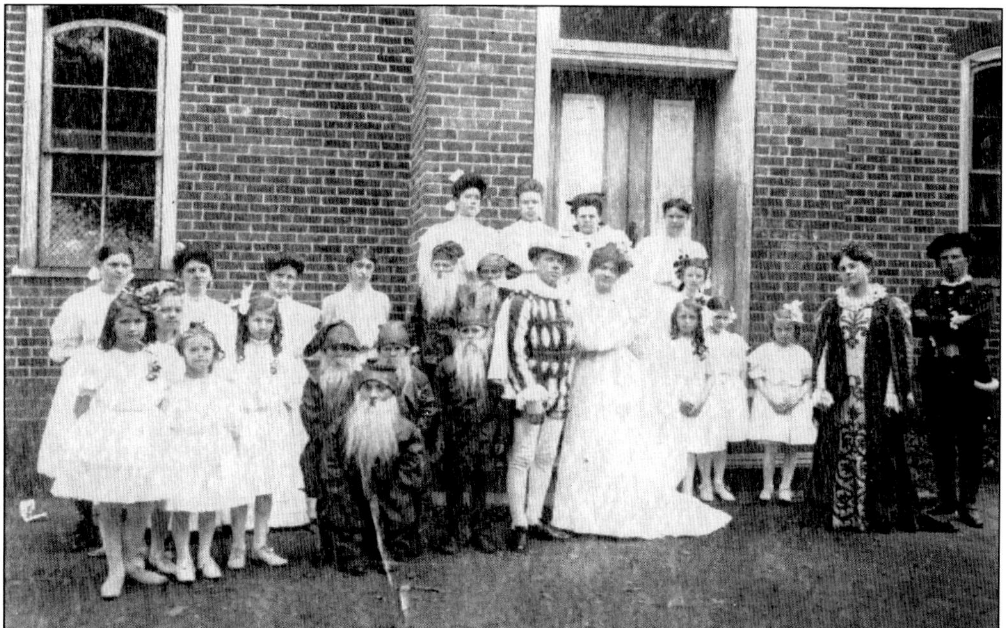

Performers from the Washington College Academy put on a marvelous performance of *Snow White* in 1925. (Courtesy of Washington College Academy.)

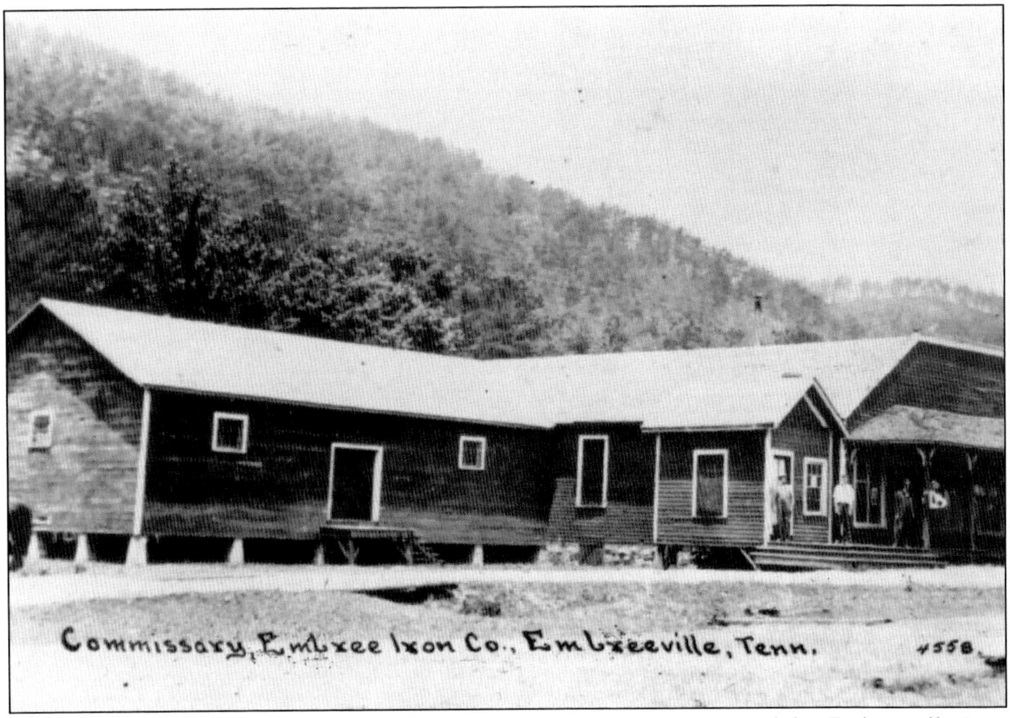

Local citizens and workers could purchase supplies at the commissary of the Embreeville Iron Company. (Courtesy of Chip White.)

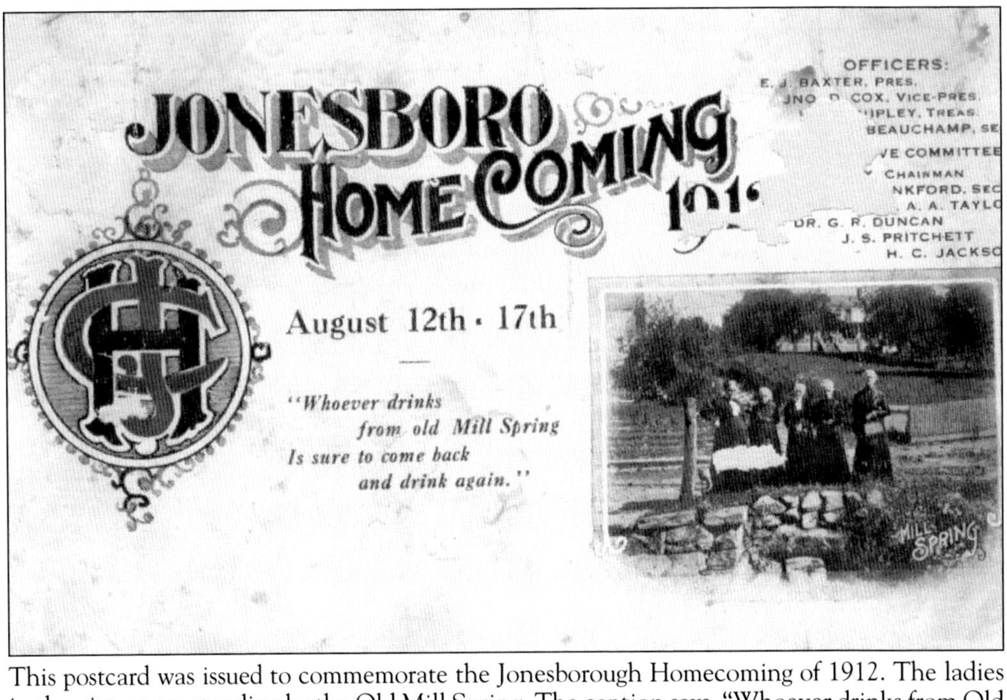

This postcard was issued to commemorate the Jonesborough Homecoming of 1912. The ladies in the picture are standing by the Old Mill Spring. The caption says, "Whoever drinks from Old Mill Spring is sure to come back and drink again." (Courtesy of Betty Jane Hylton.)

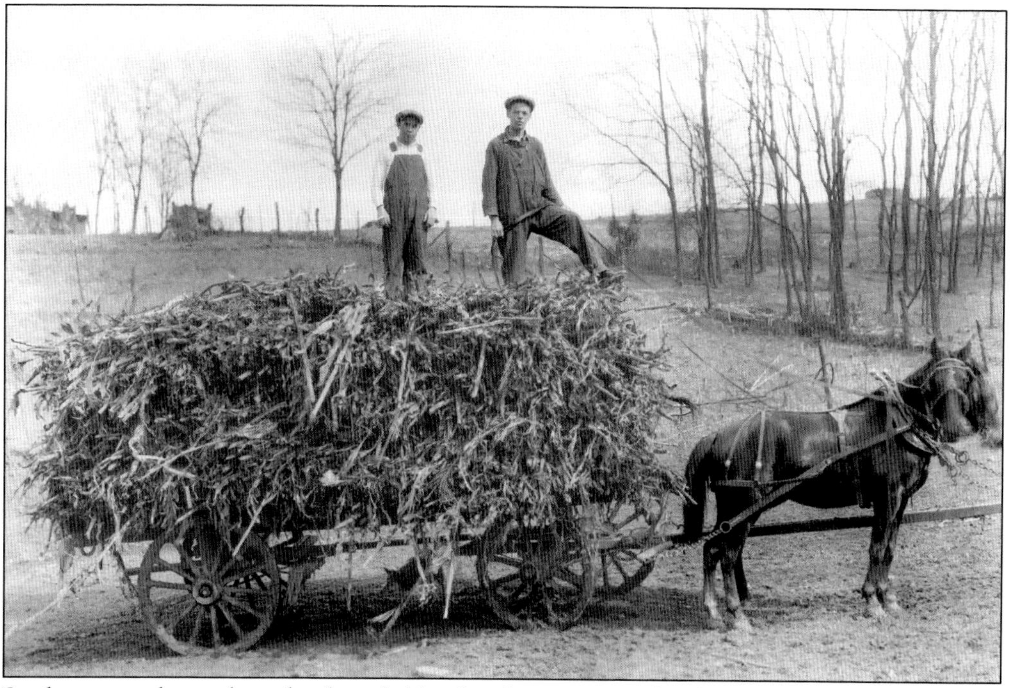

Students are shown here hauling fodder for the cows on the farm of Washington College Academy in the early 1900s. (Courtesy of Washington College Academy.)

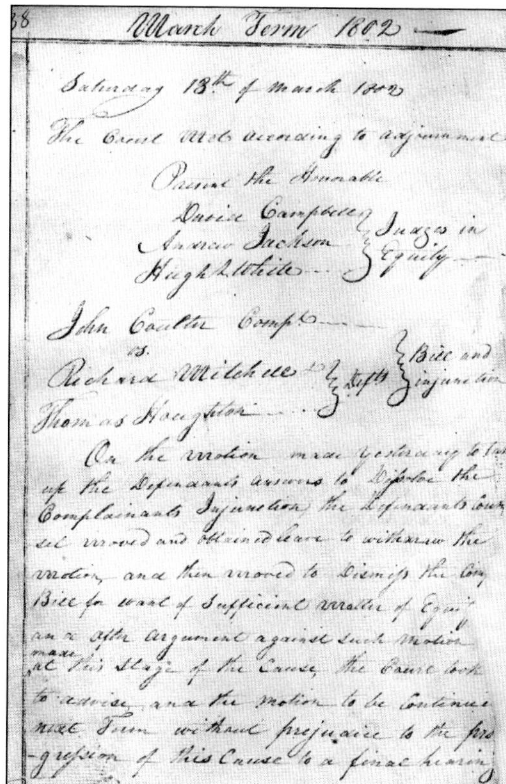

38 March Term 1802

Saturday 13th of March 1802

The Court met according to adjournment

Present the Honorable

David Campbell } Judges in Equity
Andrew Jackson
Hugh L White

John Coulter Compt.
vs. } Bill and injunction
Richard Mitchell & } Defts
Thomas Houghton

On the motion made yesterday to take up the Defendants answers to dissolve the Complainants Injunction the Defendants counsel moved and obtained leave to withdraw the motion, and then moved to Dismiss the Com Bill for want of Sufficient matter of Equity and after Argument against such Motion made at this stage of the Cause, the Court took to advise, and the motion to be Continued next Term without prejudice to the progression of this Cause to a final hearing

In a court document dated March 13, 1802, Andrew Jackson is listed as a judge in equity. At age 11, Jackson was sent to a boarding school where he studied reading, writing, grammar, and geography. Jackson was orphaned at the age of 14 and later moved to Tennessee to practice law. Jackson was the seventh president of the United States. (Courtesy of Washington County Clerk's Office.)

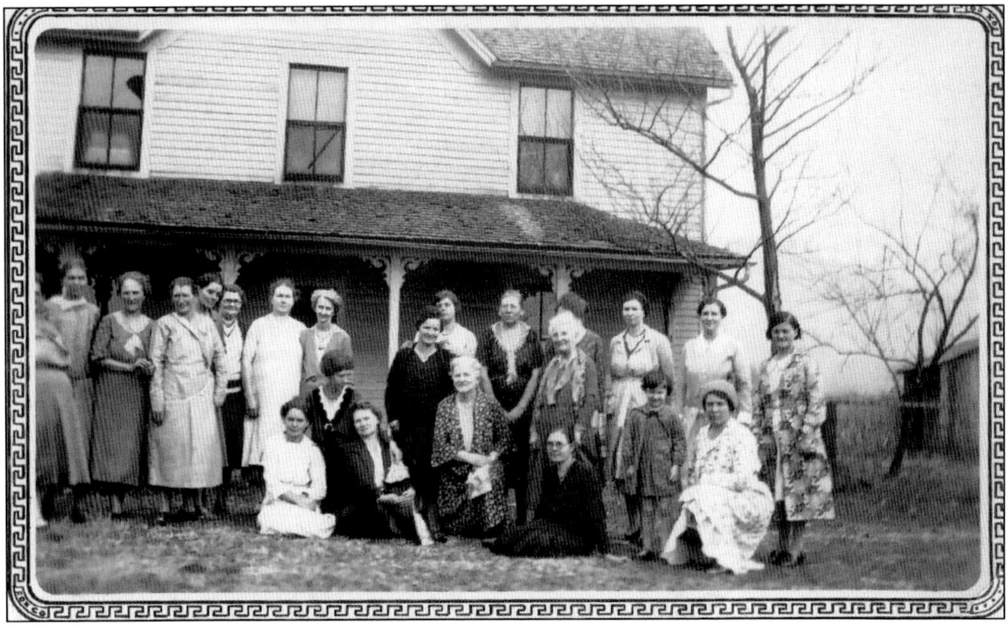

A popular spot to take photographs was in front of the community clubhouse. The communities featured in this book were important to local citizens. Before telephones and television, rural communities relied on local clubhouses, churches, or the local school for news and socialization. (Courtesy of Chip White.)

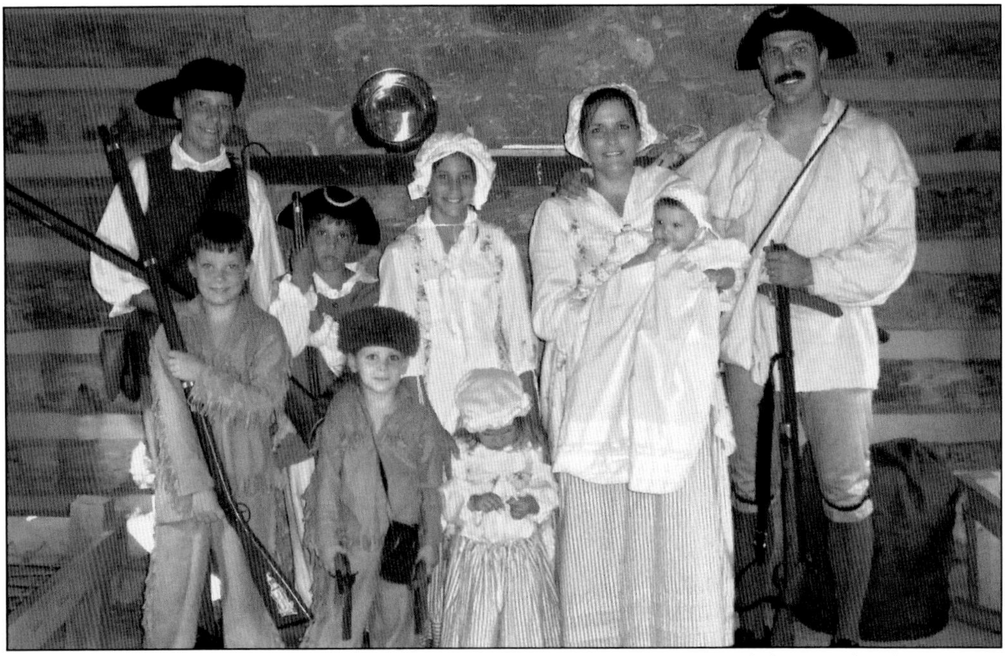

With the rich history of our region, reenactments are popular sources of pleasure for the viewers and the "actors." The Jones family of Jonesborough participates in reenactments of events that occurred at Sycamore Shoals during the 1780s. Dressed in their colonial clothing, from left to right, are (front row) Noah, Jeb, Abby, and Edie (being held); (back row) William, Jonathan, Carrie, Kim, and Terry Jones. (Courtesy of Kim Jones.)

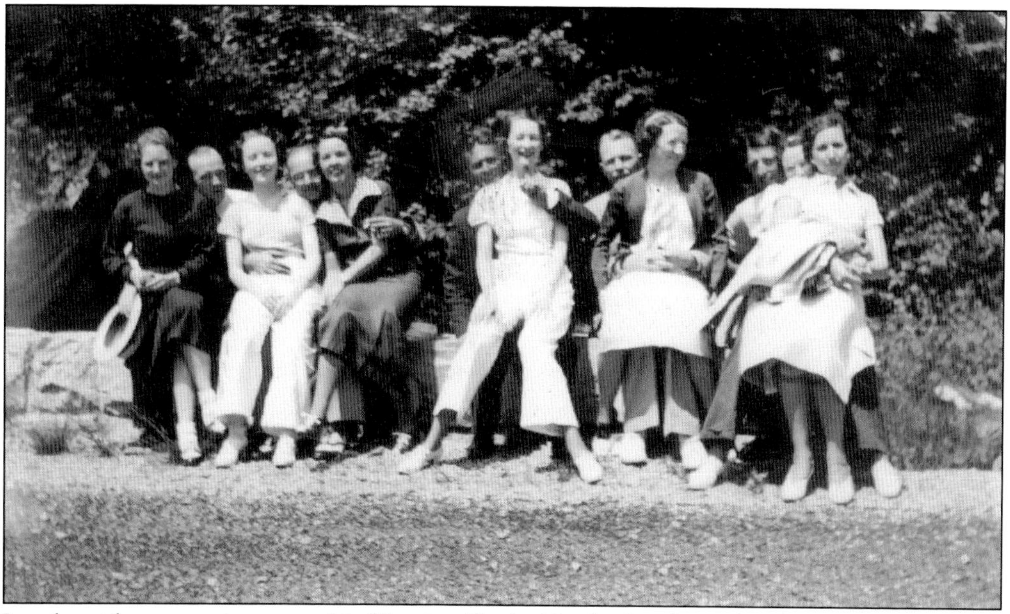

Local residents continue to visit Blowing Rock, North Carolina, for the beautiful scenery. During the 1930s, nurses from the Appalachian Hospital and their boyfriends went to Blowing Rock for a day trip. The young couples were from Jonesborough and Johnson City. (Courtesy of Gladys and Cindy Landreth.)

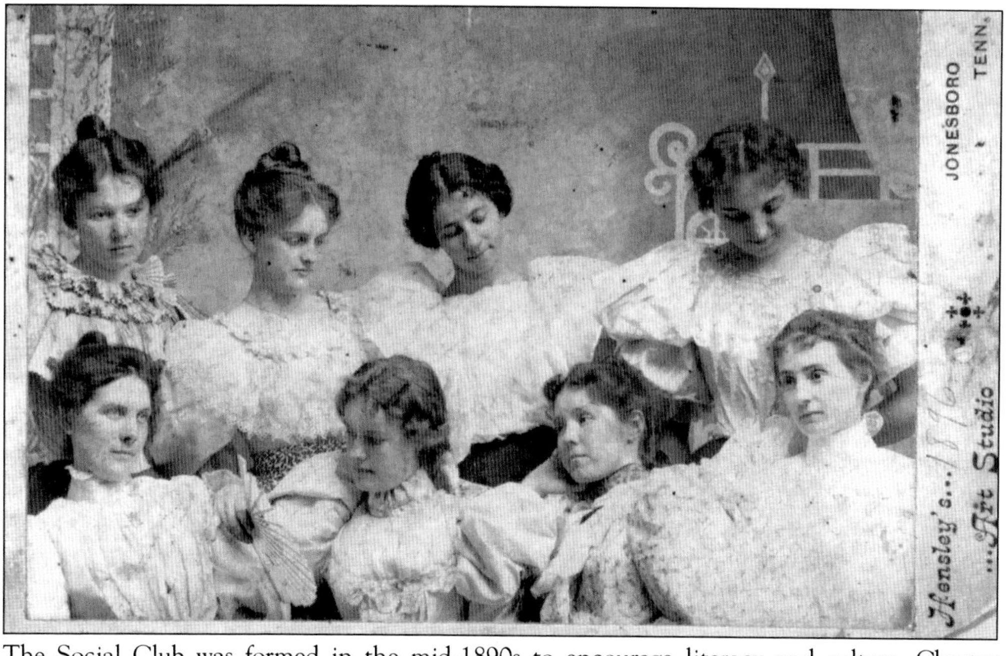

The Social Club was formed in the mid-1890s to encourage literacy and culture. Charter members of the club included Cora Kennedy Whitlock, Nona Pritchet, Lena Anderson, Daisy Panhorst Laird, Anna Panhorst, Kate Deadrick Bartlett, Nelle Hoss, Elizabeth Reeves, and Laura Bruner Dosser. The club was later renamed the Schubert Club and is considered the oldest women's club in Tennessee. (Courtesy of the Schubert Club and the Jonesborough–Washington County Library.)

My dear Son:-

I am well in body but anxious in mind. The people of the Holston are in distress again on account of the savages. I hear that those in the fortications below the hills are very numerous. I think that they will not have a spring harvest: the fate of them will be, they will not be able to live in that section. I sold my farm, and I must move not later than the fifth of June. If the Holston people do not about that time send two wagons for my family, I shall, God willing, conduct them myself------------
I have now no place in which to put my family; I do not despair, but I now think I was too hasty in selling my farm. But nothing in this world is done in vain, nothing accidentally, but all things by the good omnipotent power. I beg you to write me; counsel and care for your brother Matthew. Mother and the others at home are very well. I wrote you by Captain Thompson. This letter goes in the care of Captain Boyer of Virginia and from the home of Chiliaribi McAlister and from the town of that name. May you both live mindful of the future and conduct yourselves in a proper manner(as is becoming). Shun women and wine, you know that these have brought ruin to very many; live soberly, secure the love of all men especially of the leaders. I hope that God will guide me. I have made a mistake in selling my farm too hastily; but I trust that the ruler of the world will bring me to a good end. That God will be with you and be a protection to you is the prayer of your most loving father

Joseph Rhea.

April 19, 1777. 19. April. 1777.

Joseph Rhea died in October 1777
Translated from Latin in which it
was originally written.

This letter was originally written in Latin and was translated into English. One of the most interesting facts is that the author of the letter, Joseph Rhea, mentions a continuation of attacks by "the savages," or Native Americans, which history already documents occurred in this area frequently during 1776 and into 1777. Rhea also seems quite concerned that he sold his farm "too hastily," but he wouldn't have much time to mourn as he penned this letter on April 19, 1777, and died six months later. (Courtesy of Sue Henley.)

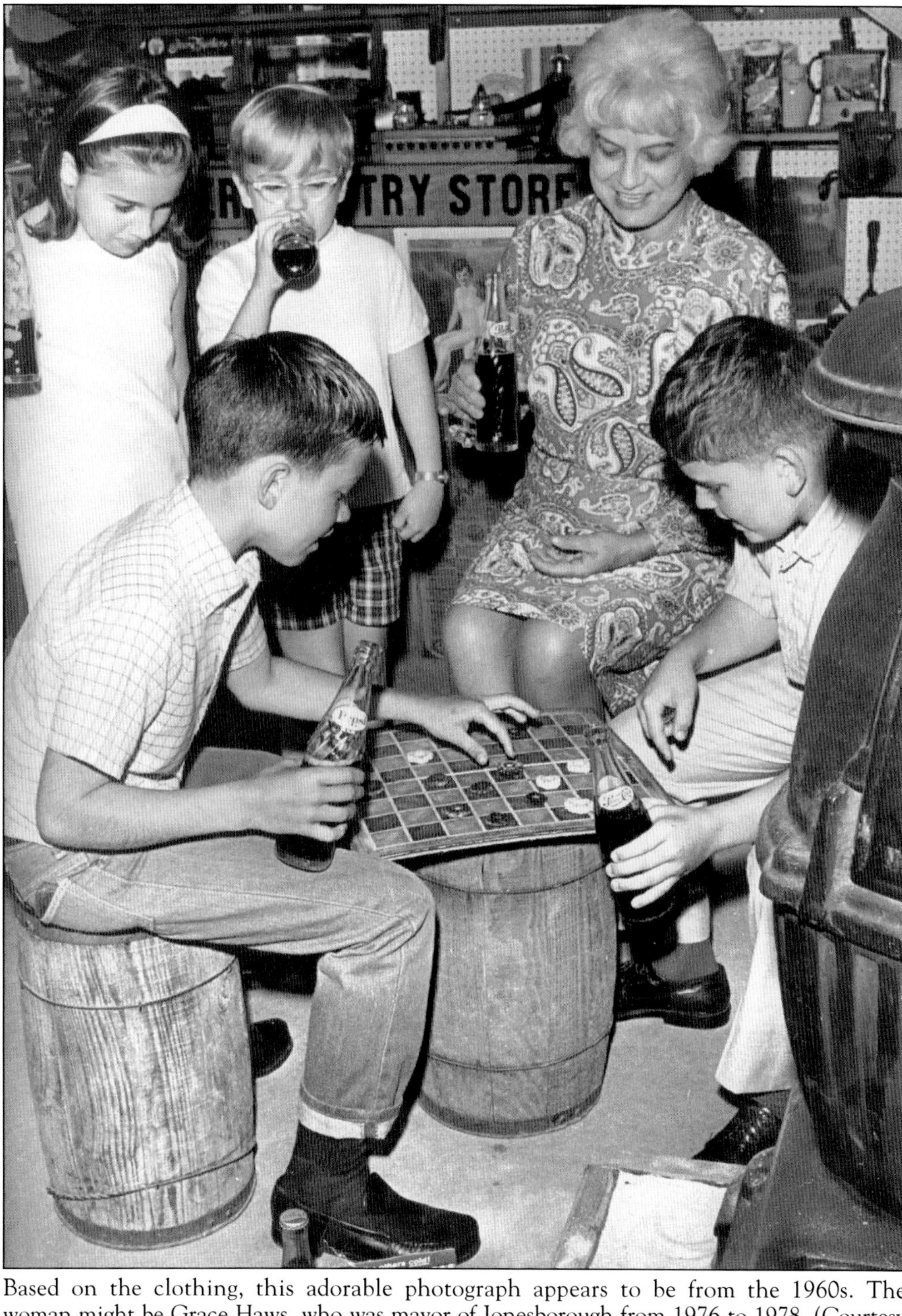

Based on the clothing, this adorable photograph appears to be from the 1960s. The woman might be Grace Haws, who was mayor of Jonesborough from 1976 to 1978. (Courtesy of Lyle Haws.)

BIBLIOGRAPHY

Calloway, Brenda C. *America's First Western Frontier: East Tennessee*. Johnson City: The Overmountain Press, 1989.

Fink, Paul M. *Jonesborough: The First Century of Tennessee's First Town*. Johnson City: The Overmountain Press, 1972.

______. *History of Washington County, Tennesseee, 1988*. Upper East Tennessee: Watauga Association of Genealogists, 1988.

Washington County Historical Association, Inc. *History of Washington County, Tennessee*. Johnson City: The Overmountain Press, 2001.